SCOTTISH SAMURAI
THOMAS BLAKE GLOVER

ALEXANDER McKAY

# SCOTTISH SAMURAI
Thomas Blake Glover 1838-1911

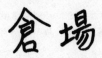

CANONGATE PRESS

First published in Great Britain in 1993 by Canongate Press Ltd,
14 Frederick Street, Edinburgh EH2 2HB

ISBN 0-86241-452-0 HBK
ISBN 0-86241-455-5 PBK

Book Design by Text Effex, Aberdeen, Scotland.
Book Production by Bright Ideas Unlimited, Aberdeen, Scotland.
Printed and Bound in Great Britain by BPCC-AUP, Aberdeen, Scotland.

British Library Cataloguing in Publication Data
A catalogue record for this book is available
on request from the British Library.

*To Sachiko, Emi and Mari*

# ACKNOWLEDGEMENTS

For their patience, encouragement, kindness and help in the writing of this book, I would like to acknowledge the following: in Japan: Brian Burke-Gaffney, Kenji Fujita, Junichi Kusumoto, Hatsuho Naito; in The Netherlands: Jan van Rij; in the UK: David G.O. Carmichael, Dr Hazel Carnegie, Sir Hugh Cortazzi, Robin Denniston, Dr John Edward, Dr John McMaster, Anne Malcolm, Loraine Noble, Dr Sandy Sharp, Commander Brian Wainwright, Billy Watson; in the USA: Mrs Mabel Bennett. I am grateful, also, to Duncan McAra, for his contribution as editorial consultant.

# CONTENTS

A berdeen City Council is delighted to support the publication of *SCOTTISH SAMURAI - THOMAS BLAKE GLOVER 1838-1911* written by Alexander McKay.

During his significant career, Thomas Blake Glover arranged for the building of the first modern Japanese Warships at the Hall Russell yard in Aberdeen. He was also adviser to the fledgling Mitsubishi company, which today, based on 40 years of guidance by Glover, is one of the largest companies in the world. He was the first-ever foreigner to be awarded the prestigious Order of the Rising Sun and is said to have been the inspiration of some elements in Puccini's Madam Butterfly.

It is astonishing that one of the North-east's most illustrious sons, who was born in Fraserburgh, educated in Old Aberdeen and whose father was a coastguard at Bridge of Don, is far better remembered in Japan than North-east Scotland.

His arrival in Nagasaki in the mid-nineteenth century marked the beginning of the rise of Japan from a Third World nation to the economic super-power it is today. There was a meteoric rise in the fortunes of the company he formed and Glover achieved a fearsome reputation for innovation and determination.

I am delighted that Alexander McKay has written the life story of Glover. I am certain that in the future this will lead to closer business links in terms of science and technology along with a greater development of tourism between Japan and North-east Scotland.

The Aberdonian author was based in Fukuoka on a long term offshore drilling contract. He met his wife Sachiko and on their honeymoon visited the Glover House in Nagasaki. He could not understand how a person from his own home area could be so revered and well known in Japan yet so little heard of at home.

The author has now put that right with this splendid publication which I am delighted to say will be readily available in bookshops and libraries throughout our city.

*J Wyness*

Lord Provost James Wyness, M.A., J.P.

5th October 1993

# PREFACE

There is a bridge leading into Nagasaki's once notorious red light district of Maruyama which the Japanese call the *Shian Bashi* or Hesitation Bridge. Further into Maruyama there is a second bridge, *Omoikiri Bashi* or Made-up-your-Mind Bridge. Presumably when potential patrons of Maruyama's pleasures crossed this second bridge any problems of conscience had been overcome.

The bridges of Maruyama were there long before the return of Western traders to Nagasaki in the late 1850s. The fortune hunters then came in droves when Japan's *shogun*-imposed 200-year isolation from the rest of the world ended and the country was forced into dealing once more with the West.

Among those Western traders was a young man from Aberdeen whose one known weakness was perhaps not hesitating enough at the 'Hesitation Bridges' of Japan. Thomas Blake Glover's arrival in Nagasaki marked the beginning of the rise of Japan from its feudal isolation of the nineteenth century to the economic superpower of today.

Glover arrived in Nagasaki late in 1859 and his rise to fame was a rapid one. He formed his own company in 1861 and took over the highly prestigious Jardine, Matheson & Co. agency in the port at the same time.

The rapid expansion of his newly formed company can be compared with the rise of firms such as Sony and Toyota a hundred years later. But it was the complicated political situation in Japan which provided his first opportunities in business.

Glover was intimately involved in the rebellion of dissatisfied samurai which dominated the 1860s. This uprising brought down the *bakufu* - the government, nominally led by the shogun, then ruling Japan. He was involved to the extent that in an interview given shortly before his death he claimed for himself the title of the 'greatest rebel' in the movement which brought down the last shogun and 'restored' the Emperor in 1868.

This rebellion, which ended the Tokugawa family's 200-year grip on the office of shogun, is a watershed in Japanese history. The first Tokugawa shogun had been helped into power by Will Adams, the English pilot of a shipwrecked Dutch vessel and the model for Blackthorne in James Clavell's historical novel, *Shogun*. Two centuries later the last Tokugawa shogun was eased out of power by a young Scottish adventurer.

Glover helped the rebels with money, with arms, and with escape and transport to the West. Supplying arms made Glover rich but there is much more to his story than that.

He helped push Japan into the modern world. His Aberdeen-built slip-dock pioneered the Mitsubishi shipyard complex now sited in Nagasaki, one of the most advanced in the world, containing a dry dock with a capacity of berthing ships of up to 1 million tons. The coal mine he developed with imported British technology at Takashima, near Nagasaki, fuelled the industrialisation of Japan and its exports provided much of the crucial foreign currency necessary to pay for it. His ships formed the nucleus of the Japanese Navy and Merchant Marine.

In 1908, aged seventy, Glover was awarded the Order of the Rising Sun by the man he had helped to power forty years before - Emperor Meiji. The citation for his award lists his achievements for Japan and runs to twenty pages of script.

He died in 1911 at his palatial Tokyo residence. At seventy-three he was a Hero of the New Japan but even to this day he is little known in his own country.

Glover's personal life was as complicated and dramatic as his public one. He had a string of romances with Japanese women and there are at least four recorded instances of children he fathered to different mothers while in Japan. An affair with the completely unknown Maki Kaga early in 1870 led to the birth of a son and almost certainly some elements of the *Madam Butterfly* legend.

No family letters are known to have survived although Glover's business dealings in his decade as Jardine, Matheson & Co.'s agent are well documented. Yet from all the available sources it is possible to track Glover's life with some accuracy.

This is the story of a Scottish samurai.

# Chapter 1

# ThE COASTGUARD'S FAMILy

Thomas Blake Glover's family background was typically that of the Victorian middle class of north-east Scotland - farming and the sea.

His father, Thomas Berry Glover, who had been born in London, was a naval officer whose career with the Coastguard spanned twenty-seven years. As a newly qualified twenty-two-year-old ship's master, he had joined the service in Vauxhall, London, in 1827. The Coastguard was then five years old – formed in 1822 from an amalgamation of the various coastal defence and anti-smuggling organisations then in existence. The officers of the new service were nominated by the Lords of the Admiralty. The Coastguard's main functions were to prevent smuggling and to give aid to ships in distress. Later its duties were widened to include 'searching for mines and torpedoes lost at sea, and performing sundry duties in connection with signals, telegraphs, buoys, lighthouses, wild birds and rare fish washed ashore'.[1]

A string of Coastguard stations ringed the British coastline and Glover took up his first appointment in Aberdeenshire. His base was the station located in Sandend, a small fishing village on the north-facing coast of the Moray Firth.[2]

Isolated as the posting was, it did not take long for the young chief officer to woo and to marry Mary Findlay, the daughter of a local landowner. Mary's family home was in Fordyce, a small farming community a few miles inland from the Sandend station. After their marriage in Fordyce on 3 July 1829, the couple settled in Sandend and their first son, named Charles Thomas, was born in Fordyce the following year; presumably, Mary returned to her parents' home for the birth. Their second child, another boy named William Jacob, was born two years later at the Sandend Coastguard house. Mary went back to Fordyce for the birth of their third son, James Lindley, in 1834.

In November 1835 Glover was appointed chief officer at Fraserburgh's Coastguard station, further to the east of the Moray coastline. At the age of thirty, the posting to the bigger Fraserburgh command was a promotion for him.

The station was situated in the centre of the fishing town's harbour area but the family resided at nearby 15 Commerce Street. This house was apparently rented privately from its wealthy owner, Alexander Malcolm, by Lieutenant Glover.[3] Henry Martin was the next addition to the family, born in their new home in 1836, but he died before his first birthday, in March 1837, and was buried in a local graveyard. Despite this blow, by the end of 1837 Mary was pregnant again.

Their fifth successive son, named Thomas Blake, was born on 6 June 1838, most likely in the house at 15 Commerce Street. He was baptised just over a month later in the local Episcopal church at Mid Street, an easy walk from the station house. The baptismal witnesses were a Mr Fraser and a Mr Gordon, bank agents in the town.[4] A sixth son, Alexander Johnson, was born in 1840, followed two years later by a daughter - at last - called Martha Anne.

The Glovers were sufficiently well off to send their three oldest boys as boarders to Aberdeen Grammar School, the shire's best.[5] The forty-seven miles between Aberdeen and Fraserburgh would have been a very long way indeed in the mid-1840s. During this period of Tom's childhood he would have received some primary education in Fraserburgh, most likely at the local parish school which opened the year he was born. Close to the Coastguard station was the harbour's slip dock on which the boats of the town's fishing fleet were dragged clear of the water for maintenance and repair - a magnet, surely, for the children of the area. The fishing industry brought many northern Europeans to Fraserburgh and the presence of foreigners at the town's weekly market was taken for granted by the thriving community.

As the three Glover boys began to settle at their school in Aberdeen, the rest of the family were on the move. In October 1844 Lieutenant Glover was transferred to the Sutton, then Saltfleet, stations - both situated near Grimbsy. Tom, then aged six, and his little brother and sister would have moved with their parents to the new location. Lieutenant Glover's next career move came almost three years later, in May 1847, and shortly before his ninth birthday young Tom was back in his native north-east Scotland. This time the new posting was the Collieston station, about ten miles north of Aberdeen. Collieston is a picturesque and peaceful fishing village set high on a cliff with dramatic views of the craggy Buchan coastline to the north and the beginning of the sweep of Aberdeen Bay to the south. The Glover family were now reunited. Charles had been attending Marischal College, Aberdeen, since 1844 and William and James were nearing the end of their secondary schooling. Tom, Alex and Martha would most likely have enrolled at the Collieston village primary school.

A big event of this period was the visit of Queen Victoria to Aberdeen in September 1848. She was en route to her newly acquired castle at Balmoral, situated about fifty miles west of the city on the banks of the river Dee. At the time Tom, aged ten, would have gone with his family and the thousands of others from the north-east who flocked to the city for the arrival of the young queen and her consort at Aberdeen's harbour in the royal yacht.

After two and a half years at Collieston, Glover was given what would prove to be his last posting in the Coastguard. According to the records he requested the move to the Bridge of Don station then situated at the mouth of the river Don, north of Aberdeen.[6] There could have been several reasons for his request. Collieston was a little isolated and Tom, Alex and Martha were nearing the age for secondary schooling. There was also the problem of work for the older children. The transfer to the then fast-expanding, affluent Aberdeen area was a good move for the Glovers. The station was a big one, but at the age of forty-five and with a salary of £100 a year, running the Bridge of Don operation with a staff of six or seven was as far as Glover senior would go in the service.

The move from Collieston would have been short and relatively painless. In November 1849 eleven-year-old Tom moved with his family into the substantial, two-storey house which went with the Aberdeen appointment. The house adjoined a terrace of cottages where the Coastguard seamen and their families lived. Fronted by large vegetable gardens, it faced south and overlooked the Don spilling into the North Sea. Wild and open to the elements in winter, the situation of the house in the long summer days was especially pleasant.

From the upstairs windows of his new house Tom could see the prominent landmarks of the village of Old Aberdeen, an easy walk from his home. These were the twin fortified towers of St Machar's Cathedral and, just a little further south, the stone crown on the roof of King's College. These landmarks had dominated the skyline of Old Aberdeen for hundreds of years. The shops of the village would have supplied the Glover household with its everyday needs. For anything more the burgeoning city of Aberdeen was only a short carriage - or horse - ride south along King Street. Indeed, it was possible for Tom to see the mushrooming mill chimneys and church spires of the city from the garden of his house. The harbour and port of Aberdeen had developed round the mouth of the Dee and a second Coastguard station was sited on the north bank. Close by were clustered the city's bustling shipyards. The golden sands of Aberdeen Bay covered the couple of miles between the Dee and the Don.

A schoolmate of Tom later wrote of 'swimming in the Don with the son of the captain of the Coastguard'.[7] Any swimming would have been done a mile or so upriver from the station house, in the less dangerous neuks beneath the Brig o' Balgownie where even in the warmer summer months the water is still icily cold. This was the part of the Don where the young Lord Byron had swum on his half-holidays from Aberdeen Grammar School, fifty years before the young Tom Glover.

Tom, Alex and Martha would have spent many happy days exploring the endless sand-dunes and country and riverside on their doorstep. The three older boys were in their middle to late teens at the time of the move to the Bridge of Don and already in work or training.

The Census returns of 1851 record Charles, then aged twenty, as still living at home and list him as a clerk.[8] He is likely to have been in training with a firm of shipping and insurance brokers in Aberdeen. The second son, William, was eighteen and had already left home to begin a long career at sea in the merchant marine. James, then aged seventeen, is also listed simply as a clerk and, like Charles, is likely to have been involved in shipbroking and insurance in Aberdeen. Both brothers had connections with a firm trading in Marischal Street, close to the city's harbour and shipyards.

The three younger children, Tom, Alex and Martha, were thirteen, eleven and nine respectively at the time of the Census and all are listed as 'scholars'. Since the move from Collieston there had been another addition to the Glover family. Alfred, the seventh surviving and last Glover child, was born in the Bridge of Don station house in November 1850. His mother was forty-three and his father forty-five at the time of Alfred's surely unplanned birth and the baby five months old when the Census was taken. The only other resident at the station house, apart from the Glover parents, was a local girl, Ann Strachan, the domestic servant. With such a large family and a little baby to look after, it is likely that other domestic help came on a daily basis, perhaps daughters or wives of the station seamen.

Tom and Alex were enrolled as day pupils at the Gymnasium, or Chanonry House School, in Old Aberdeen.[9] It was the best school in the area, sited in the village's Chanonry and attended by the sons of the better-off. Old Aberdeen, never more than a large village but for centuries a separate burgh from 'new' Aberdeen, was beginning to be absorbed by its fast-growing neighbour to the south. The school attended by Tom and Alex was about a one-mile walk from their home. On their way to school the Glover boys would have crossed the Don by the 'new' Bridge of Don, within sight of the centuries-old Brig o' Balgownie upriver.

Joining Don Street, they would have continued on into Old Aberdeen by the Seaton Estate, skirting the medieval St Machar's Cathedral round which the burgh of Old Aberdeen had originally developed. The gracious, tree-lined Chanonry, the street where before the Reformation the canons of St Machar's had lived, runs from the Cathedral to Old Aberdeen's Town House. The Gymnasium stood on the west side of the Chanonry, just before this juncture north of the Town House and is the site of present-day Cruickshank Botanic Gardens, part of the Aberdeen University complex.

The school's curriculum emphasised the Classics and Religion and young Tom Glover received the typical Victorian education of a middle- to upper-class schoolboy. There was, though, an Engineering classroom at the school and it was perhaps here that Tom picked up his ability to work on a lathe - a hobby and skill which he kept for the rest of his life.

The Gymnasium was run to a strict routine and for a lively lad such as Tom it must have been restrictive. Yet there were organised games and sports for the boys of the school to burn off any excess energy. There was no St Machar's Drive bisecting Old Aberdeen in those days and the playing fields of the Gymnasium stretched far up Cluny's Wynd. The setting for the school was idyllic.

Perhaps Tom and Alex were a little jealous of their elder brothers having attended the more prestigious Aberdeen Grammar School. But the Gymnasium had its own reputation for excellence and, best of all, it was at most a twenty-minute walk from their home.

Away from the school Tom learned to row and sail. Almost certainly all of the Glover boys were trained in elementary seamanship by their father and his crew. Coastguard boats were tied up on the riverside, only yards from the front of their house. In one surviving photograph, young Alfred is pictured wading in the Don among the boats. It is likely that the Glover lads rowed and sailed with the regular crew of seamen living at the station. The sea dominated the lives of all the Glover family. As well as Glover senior serving as a Coastguard Chief Officer, William was in training as a ship's master and Charles and James were beginning to make their way as shipbrokers in Aberdeen. It was an ideal place for the boys to begin that particular business - the shipyards of Aberdeen then had a reputation for fine ships throughout the maritime world.

Fishing was a popular pastime for the boys. Period photographs of the station house show various sized rods and fishing gear lying against the porch. The countryside around them gave young Tom the opportunity to learn to shoot bird and game. Most likely taught by his father, Tom would continue shooting into his old age.

In 1853, with Tom a fourteen-year-old attending the Gymnasium, the SS *Duke of Sutherland* was wrecked in Aberdeen Bay. Sixteen people were drowned in this tragedy which was witnessed by many hundreds watching from the flat shoreline of the Bay. The ship had foundered when entering Aberdeen harbour on 1 April of that year in an incident long remembered by those who watched. The harbour lifeboat was launched but capsized. Tom's father was based on the Donmouth, a couple of miles north of Aberdeen harbour, but almost certainly would have been involved with his crew in the attempts at rescue. With his home and school within sight of the Bay, it would seem certain that young Tom was one of the many who viewed this drama.

The earliest Glover family photographs date from the mid- to late 1850s. Certainly they were taken before Glover retired from the Coastguard in September 1864, vacating the station house. The photographs, many taken in the garden and around the house, include some of Tom's father in both civilian and Coastguard dress uniform. The background to many of the photographs is the new Bridge of Don. Tom's father is pictured in a stiff Victorian pose - tall, broad and bushy-bearded but, in his middle fifties, beginning to show his age. His mother, Mary, is resplendent in her hooped skirts. Martha, the only Glover girl and surely for that reason alone a little spoiled in a family of six brothers, is seen as a beautiful adolescent with her mother's fresh country looks. The Glovers as depicted in these photographs look like in essence what they were - a large, reasonably well-off Victorian family at a time when the sons of the house were beginning to shake themselves free and seek out lives of their own.

Tom Glover is on record as having attended the Gymnasium as a day pupil until at least 1854. He would then have been sixteen years old and, with no known history of any higher education, he was ready to start work or training of some kind. Although no evidence is known to have survived, it is almost certain that at this time Tom joined Charles and Jim at the Marischal Street shipbroking firm run by James George. There he would have been given a grounding in shipping and clerical work, commuting daily with his brothers the couple of miles from the Bridge of Don station to the office in the town's harbour area. But perhaps the idea of a life in insurance or shipbroking in Aberdeen did not appeal to him. Or more likely the opportunity to go abroad presented itself and he grabbed at it. It was common at this time for the Scots-dominated British merchant houses to seek out and recruit promising young lads for positions, initially as clerks, overseas. Many of these young men, after training, would be posted to the Far East. Most would spend their lives in exotic-sounding places simply as clerks - four or five hours a day routine trading office procedure and evenings in the club. But there was always the chance that opportunities would arise for the brightest to break free and establish themselves as independent merchants and make their fortune - enough of a chance, anyway, to tempt many of the young go-getters of the day. Although exactly how it came about is unclear, almost certainly this was the magnet which drew young Tom into a life of trading and adventure in the Far East.

The would-be merchant was very carefully selected. His passage and kit would cost his employer £300. For this kind of investment - three times his father's annual salary - Tom would have had to be very fit and confident and able to convince his employers that he was potentially capable of taking over and managing a business at short notice.[10]

Tom Glover's exact movements after school are not known. But with the little evidence which has survived, a good guess can be made at the sequence of events which brought him to the Far East. Around this time there were two Glovers resident among the British expatriates in China: George B. Glover, commissioner of Imperial Customs, Canton;

and T.G. Glover of Jardine, Matheson & Co., captain of the firm's ship *Mahamoodie* which was based in Foochow.[11] It seems likely that either or both of these Glovers were in some way related to the Glovers of Aberdeen. It would follow, then, that a recommendation for Tom came from a China-based Glover who may well have been an employee of Jardine, Matheson. In any case it would seem certain that there was some kind of clerical training, most likely with Charles and Jim at the Aberdeen shipbrokers, before Tom left for China in 1857.

A passport was issued by the Foreign Office to Thomas Glover in August 1856.[12] Glover arrived in Shanghai 'aged eighteen or nineteen'.[13] Allowing six months from the issue of the passport until his arrival in China would have him leaving Aberdeen in the early part of 1857 and arriving in Shanghai in May or June of that year, shortly before his nineteenth birthday.

After eight years Tom was leaving the Granite City. In these years he had developed into a well-educated and self- assured young man. He was outgoing and likeable and most probably enjoyed the company of the available young women of the town. But the inner drive which propelled him through his life would not let him settle into a dreary office routine. Would his parents have guessed as they saw him off that it would be ten years before they saw their son again?

If one thing stands out in all the fleeting descriptions of Tom Glover's life which have survived, it is his supreme confidence in himself. So it is not too difficult to imagine the eighteen-year-old brimming over with enthusiasm as he made his farewells to his family, most likely on the Victoria dockside in Aberdeen, from where there were regular sailings south. His brother Alex was seventeen when Tom left, Martha fifteen, and the late arrival, Alfred, a mere seven years old. All of these siblings of Tom would later become involved in their brother's adventures in Japan.

# Chapter 2

# FROM SHANGHAI TO NAGASAKI

The Shanghai where Tom landed in 1857 was far removed from the tranquillity of Aberdeen's Bridge of Don. There were stops on his voyage out to acclimatise him gradually - West Africa, South Africa, India, Singapore, Hong Kong almost certainly - but Shanghai was an entirely new world for him, even if, as is likely, his Glover connections had written to him beforehand. Shanghai, literally 'On the Sea', was a city, a port, and the major commercial centre of China. Lying as it does between the Yangzi river to the north and Yupan Bay to the south, it was base for many of the hundreds of Western traders in the Far East at the time. Tom's employers, Jardine, Matheson & Co., had a major branch of their business there although the head office of the company remained in Hong Kong. Tom's first view of Shanghai was the seven-mile-long stretch of waterfront known as the Bund, behind which clustered the foreign settlement. Most likely Tom was met on his arrival by his Glover connections and shown round the bustling city where he would work and learn for the next couple of years.

Shanghai had been one of the first Chinese ports opened to Western trade and to this day it dominates mainland Chinese commerce. Following the humiliating defeat of the Chinese by the British in the Opium War of 1842, Shanghai had been subjected to unrestricted foreign trade, with the British, French and Americans holding desig-nated areas of the city. Resident in the British sector, Tom would have learned of the then threatening Taiping Rebellion. This peasant revolt against the Manchu rulers of China, in which millions died, was led by a Chinese who believed himself to be the younger brother of Jesus Christ. The fanatical rebel army was in control of much of the country and the Western residents of Shanghai were afraid of an attack on the city.

In Shanghai he picked up the rudiments of Far Eastern trading, gaining experience the hard way - copying letters, making out Bills of Lading and learning the other routine duties of a major trading organisation. Jardine, Matheson's office and warehouse complex occu-pied the prime riverside site of Shanghai, close to the Bund. Major firms - and none was bigger than Jardine, Matheson & Co. - operated in

Shanghai with two or three partners, assisted by about ten European clerks - of whom Tom was one - and fifty or sixty Chinese staff. The Westerners were comfortably housed in a compound but the overpowering smell of sewage and seaweed from the Whangpoo river would be the thing most remembered at that time by many of the foreign residents. Glover's company dealt mainly in silk, tea and opium. The early summer months were the busiest for the firm and during this season the traders worked night and day buying, transporting, packing and shipping tea and silk. At other times the pace was more leisurely, long lunches breaking the few hours spent sweating over paperwork at a desk.

During his first year, Tom would have wakened in the mornings to the sound of sentries patrolling the walls high above the settlement - British and French troops had been stationed in the city to protect the foreign residents. The yelling of their commands would have mixed with the heat, noise, dust and smells of Shanghai - a whirlwind of alien sounds and faces. The most notorious area was Blood Alley, where the price of a seaman's beer included a twelve-year-old prostitute behind a dirty curtain. Shanghai at the time was beginning to earn its later title of the 'Whore of the Orient'.[1]

Tom persevered. He was there almost a year later, in April 1858, when HMS *Furious* anchored in the river. Aboard was the British delegation of Lord Elgin en route to Beijing to negotiate further rights for British traders in China. Elgin's mission found the traders in Shanghai, presumably including Glover, very angry at what they saw as leniency towards the Chinese by the British government. They felt that their wishes - even more liberal trade agreements, including an expansion of the lucrative business in opium - were not being pursued in a vigorous enough fashion. The British delegation was also under orders to secure a trading agreement with the Japanese, whose islands, for so long closed, had recently and reluctantly been opened to the West. Among Lord Elgin's mission was another young Scot - Laurence Oliphant - with whom Glover would become involved over the years.

To the north-east of Shanghai, a week's sail across the Yellow Sea, lay the mysterious islands of Japan. Japan at the time was the last Eastern civilisation untouched by the West and its imminent opening to foreign trade would have been the main topic of conversation in the offices and clubs of the China-based expatriates. The image of Japan held by many of the Europeans of Tom's day was that of a very dangerous place - but there was also a romantic, almost magnetic fascination for the country as well as the assumption in the trading world that fortunes were there to be made once the door was open. The hereditary military ruler of Japan was the shogun, in Glover's time better known as the *tycoon*. The Tokugawa family had held the office of shogun for more than 200 years. The Japanese emperor, or *Mikado*, was little more than a powerless figurehead virtually held in austere custody in Kyoto.

Japan had been all but sealed off from the world since 1638. At that time the then shogun, fearing the spread of Western influence, had expelled all Europeans from Japan and executed all the Japanese he could find who had become Christians. A severe exclusion policy, called *sakoku*, had been strictly enforced for over 200 years and was even then being maintained by the fourteenth Tokugawa shogun. A Japanese fisherman blown by bad weather on to the shores of mainland Asia could not return to Japan - the penalty for breaking the exclusion order was death. Any foreign seamen shipwrecked on Japan were imprisoned or killed. A small Dutch colony had been permitted on the man-made island of Dejima in Nagasaki Bay. Here some limited trade and exchanges of information were allowed but the Dutch contingent were closely guarded and controlled.

Despite the apparently settled state of Japan there was in some quarters deep and serious resentment against the shogun's rule. The *daimyo* were the feudal lords of Japan, each ruling his clan and domain as he saw fit but still under the overall command of the shogun. There were more than 250 of these clans, or *han*, and their domains were spread throughout the Japanese islands. To enforce his authority the shogun made the clan lords in turn spend part of every year in his stronghold of Edo (modern Tokyo). When the lords returned to their domains, their families remained in Edo, virtual hostages of the shogun. The most powerful and resentful of the lords were located in the south-west domains, principally the clans of Satsuma and Choshu. These clans did not have the family ties that bound many of the other daimyo to the shogun. But even in and between these potentially rebellious clans there was distrust.

As the nineteenth century had progressed, the great naval powers had become more than a little restless with the attitude of the Japanese governments of successive shogun. They wanted coaling, watering and trading facilities for their ships and guarantees for shipwrecked seamen. The Japanese found it hard to argue, their country had stagnated technically and militarily during its long seclusion. All of the shoguns had forbidden any ship to be built larger than that required for inshore fishing. Most of the technical advances of the West had completely bypassed Japan.

In the early 1850s, the push by the Great Powers could no longer be resisted by the Japanese. Commodore Matthew Perry of the US Navy and his 'black ship' squadron visited Japan in July 1853 and returned in February 1854. Anchored in Edo Bay, the size and armoury of the American ships quite clearly shocked many of the Japanese. The message from the West was clear - open up the country voluntarily or have it opened by force.

The first reaction of the majority of the Japanese clan lords was that, despite the obvious might of the West, Japan's total exclusion policy had to be maintained at all costs. But as the 1850s progressed the Japanese became more and more aware of the powerful navies beginning to clamour at their doorstep, particularly that of the British, now with a free hand because of the ending of the Crimean War. The majority view now swung in favour generally of the shogun's policy - allowing limited trade with the 'barbarians', though only as a means of preventing war with them - at least until Japan could fight on equal terms. There were active minorities, in about ten clans out of the more than 250 in Japan, who disagreed entirely with this policy. They began to criticise the shogun and his advisers for allowing the foreigners access to Japan at all. Old and deep resentments against the shogunate now had an opportunity to resurface.

The shogun was in a quandary, wanting rid of the foreigners but not knowing quite how to go about it. All the indications were that the Japanese emperor, still powerless in Kyoto, did not want the foreigners either.

The shogun now came under severe pressure and eventually gave way to further foreign demands. Basically, the Japanese were playing for time. Trading treaties with the Western Powers were signed. The Westerners, in general, were unaware of the explosive and complicated political situation in Japan or of the unrest in some of the clans. In the beginning some even thought that the shogun was, in fact, the emperor. To complicate matters even more the shogun did not have the dictatorial powers that many of the Westerners assumed him to have. Over the years the once all-powerful shogun had become in many cases simply a figurehead. The real power in Japan for a long time had been in the hands of the *roju* - a group of four or five leading councillors of the bakufu, the central administration of the shogun. Later the Westerners assumed that, like a European monarch, the Japanese Mikado reigned from Kyoto and that his prime minister or perhaps generalissimo, the shogun, ruled the country from Edo.

In any case, agreement was finally reached on the opening up of, initially, three Japanese ports. There foreign traders could be based and, within certain agreed limits, protected. The ports were Nagasaki, Kanagawa (later to become Yokohama) and Hakodate, and these three ports would come to be known as the Treaty ports.

Lying on the west coast of Japan's southern main island of Kyushu, Nagasaki was the country's nearest port to mainland Asia and had been the centre of Japanese Christianity before the Europeans had been expelled two and a half centuries before.

The deep, natural and protected harbour of Nagasaki with its narrow entrance was the port's main asset. Thick woods of lush greenery pushed down the steep hillsides and surrounded the town which crouched round the harbour's edge. Nagasaki's disadvantages to the West were its size - a population of only around 50,000 - and its distance from the seat of government and the heavily populated areas of Japan far away to the north-east in central Honshu. Many of the incoming Westerners thought that they could establish themselves in Nagasaki until the really rich pickings - in Osaka and Kobe and Edo itself - were available. The treaties signed with the British, Americans, Russians and Dutch in 1858 contained agreements to open several more ports in the coming years.

But the disadvantages of Nagasaki to the traders were seen as major pluses by the shogun - this was a place where the 'barbarians' could be kept at bay, remote from his capital and stronghold of Edo. Of course, Yokohama, too, was opening and this swampy fishing village was close to Edo, but it was hoped that this new settlement could be cut off as effectively as Nagasaki. The third port, Hakodate in the northern island of Hokkaido, was naturally isolated by weather and surroundings. It was then of little importance to the shogun. He was attempting to buy time.

At one time an entirely Christian town where no Buddhist temple was even allowed to be built, Nagasaki had long since been under the direct control of the shogun. A daimyo could not be trusted apparently to hold this still strategic port which was close to the lands of the powerful Satsuma and Hizen clans. It was the natural melting pot for agents of the various factions then beginning to form in Japan, pro- and anti-foreign.

Young Tom Glover had been in China for just over a year when the first Western traders began to leave for Japan, to the Chinese the land of the 'Rising Sun'.

# Chapter 3

# MACKENZIE'S PARTNER

T he official opening date of the Treaty ports of Nagasaki, Hakodate and Yokohama was 1 July 1859. But there were many adventurers among the China-based traders who could not wait until that date and were willing to risk the dangers of working in unknown Japan without any legal protection. Several were operating in Nagasaki by the end of 1858. Kenneth Ross MacKenzie, who had been born in Edinburgh, was one of these. Sent out by Jardine, Matheson's Shanghai office in the autumn of 1858, he was reasonably well established by the end of the year.

MacKenzie was well aware that his presence in Japan was illegal before the beginning of July. It is unlikely this technicality caused him any concern. He had been running a tea business in China at Hankow - 600 miles upriver from Shanghai and an area not scheduled to be opened to foreigners until 1861 - an equally illegal operation.[1] MacKenzie was in his fifties and highly experienced in trade in the Far East, an understandable choice of agent by Jardine, Matheson & Co. to establish their giant trading concern in newly opened Nagasaki. It says much for Mackenzie's courage that by the turn of the year he was arranging his first cargoes to the company's base in Shanghai.[2]

The first arrivals were well rewarded for their efforts. MacKenzie made a small fortune on the export of seaweed to China and silk to Europe, both ventures arranged through Jardine, Matheson & Co., in the spring of 1859; the trading giant traditionally gave its agents a lot of freedom to work on their own account. MacKenzie, exporting 300 bales of Japanese silk in early 1859, took a third interest in these shipments, investing $26,632 of his own, which netted him a profit of $9,536.[3] This amount, earned by MacKenzie in three months, was around twenty times the annual salary of £100 of Glover's father in Aberdeen at that time.[4]

There were very real dangers to contend with in Japan. Anti-foreign fanatics were on the loose and a very nervous British captain carrying a load of 200 tons of Jardine, Matheson's sugar into Nagasaki in February 1859 recalled:

"On my left there was a strong fort bristling with brass guns glittering in the sun; not a soul was to be seen. I was in some doubt to whether they might fire upon me, and send the mast over the side; but no, I was allowed to proceed up the harbour unchallenged."[5]

MacKenzie had found premises to operate from and was well established by the time the first British Consul General to Japan, Rutherford Alcock, stopped off at Nagasaki in June 1859. Alcock was on his way to Edo to establish the British Legation there and noted that weeks still before the official opening date, a dozen Britons were trading in Nagasaki and that fifteen foreign ships were lying at anchor in the harbour.

With Alcock was the first acting British Consul in Nagasaki, C. Pemberton Hodgson. Hodgson was accompanied by his wife and two daughters and his wife's reminiscences of those days, particularly her first trip ashore, show her dislike of the posting in particular and Japan in general. The Japanese were overcome with curiosity at the female 'barbarian' and her children who found themselves surrounded by jostling locals:

"I believe I was the first lady who had been seen in the town ... So the curiosity was excessive and eventually distressing. We got so far that we really did not know what to do, and tried to get into a shop, as I was almost frightened to death ... poor Eva began crying: but the brutes only laughed the more ..."

The lucky few traders in Nagasaki who had struck it rich tried to keep confidential the profits they were making - 100 to 400 per cent was common - but the secret was soon out. Many adventurers decided to move from the China coast to Japan to cash in.

The new arrivals in the main were disappointed. After the official opening date, trade and profits slumped. The rules of the Treaty were now in force. This meant the arrival of new Treasury Guild officials from Edo. The Guild was a shogun-appointed body with power to control trade. Restrictions on the exchange of money were enforced and the highly profitable barter trade of early 1859 stopped.

Yet there was still enough potential in Japan for MacKenzie to be joined by Glover, then aged twenty-one, on 19 September 1859. The most likely explanation for his arrival in Nagasaki is that Jardine, Matheson sent him from Shanghai to assist MacKenzie. It is possible, too, that MacKenzie had come across him while in China, had been impressed and had later sent for him. Whatever the case, Glover would register himself at the newly established British Consulate in Nagasaki the following month as 'Clerk etc' to MacKenzie.

MacKenzie would surely have greeted his young assistant as he disembarked, taking his first steps on the soil of Japan and looking up as so many have done at the lush green hillsides cascading into the ship-filled, bustling harbour. Many of the Westerners arriving in Nagasaki around this time commented on the freshness of the air - especially sweet after the stench of Shanghai. Later Tom would learn that the Japanese collected the town's sewage nightly and brought it to their farms for fertilising their crops. The two Scots would have walked along the waterfront towards MacKenzie's Oura office, past the stalls of the yelling fishmongers on which were displayed conger eels and mackerel and all kinds of shellfish. And on past the warehouses stacked with and smelling of tea and rice and soya sauce - Tom would have noted, like so many others, the near-nakedness of the Japanese labourers. Yet it would be wrong to think of Nagasaki at the time as some kind of primitive community. On the contrary, the Japanese houses and buildings, in general, were perfectly adequate. Inside they were spotlessly clean. The people appeared well fed and there was little or no abject poverty to be seen in what appeared to be a well-ordered society.

Already Western-style buildings could be seen when Glover arrived - one was being used by a Dutch engineer, Hendrik Hardes, who had begun to teach the Japanese the rudiments of the shipbuilding trades some years before. There were, too, the Dutch buildings and houses on Dejima, then still a separate artificial island at the north end of the harbour. The foreign settlement at Oura on the south-eastern side of the harbour was beginning to rise, these buildings alien to those of the surrounding Japanese.

Glover would have had a day or two to look round his new base. Nagasaki's opening had turned the town into a giant market place - a very hot and sticky one, even in mid-September. The port was already known for its pretty girls and their giggling curiosity at the appearance of the tall and fair young Scotsman no doubt attracted Glover.

The streets of the native town were narrow and unpaved and the low-roofed wooden houses unpainted. But like many others, Glover would have been struck by the cleanliness of the people, their houses and their clothing. He would have noticed, too, the complete absence of beggars.

In the back alleys were the stalls of the scissor-grinders and lantern-makers and he would have found umbrellas, ink, incense and spectacles for sale. In the countryside surrounding the town he saw village Japan, where on his approach the children scattered, signalling with their fingers in a circle in front of their eyes. They had been well warned by their mothers to keep clear of the round-eyed *ketojin* - 'barbarian' - who would take them away if they were bad. Late September in Nagasaki is a glorious time of year - the sky is a daily sapphire blue and the breeze blowing in from the bay is cooled by the sea and becomes an almost sensual pleasure as it touches the skin. The land round the town he would have noted was rich in produce. There was rice, maize and millet crowding the small fields and orchards full of apples and oranges and persimmon as well as vineyards heavy with grapes. Among the shrubs there were patches of thistle, recalling for him the countryside surrounding his family home in Scotland.

To escape from the autumn heat he could have climbed the well-worn path to the coolness of the peak of Mount Inasa on the west side of the bay and from there viewed the panorama of Nagasaki below. Far off to the south and west it was just possible to see Takashima among the scattering of other volcanic islands guarding the entrance to the harbour. But before long Glover would have had to get down to work. As MacKenzie's assistant he wrote his first communication to Jardine, Matheson's Shanghai office on 22 September 1859, three days after his arrival in Nagasaki.[6]

Glover moved into a house in the Dutch settlement at Dejima on the northern end of the harbour. This fan-shaped island had been built by the Japanese on the waterfront of Nagasaki as a place where select 'barbarians' could be observed yet kept under tight control during the centuries of exclusion. Dejima had a single street with Dutch houses on one side and a Dutch 'factory' - warehouses - on the other. A sea wall surrounded the island. Glover occupied the second floor of one of the Dutch houses while he looked for a place of his own.

By the time of his arrival, the original bonanza in trade had ended. In the six months following the July opening, MacKenzie could invest only one-third as much of Jardine, Matheson's funds as he did in the previous four months.[7] There were all kinds of problems for the new MacKenzie/Glover team.

The main problems were bakufu inspired - they were doing all they could to hamper trade and discourage foreigners. Within weeks of his arrival Glover could have begun to develop a resentment against the shogun, the recognised leader of the government. The Treasury Guild officials sent from Edo had made it difficult for Westerners to obtain local currency. In the beginning the only money available was a kind of note made from a slab of bamboo with a Japanese figure on one side and an equivalent in Dutch florins on the other. These slabs were withdrawn and replaced regularly. The foreigners could not always get their hands on the bamboo money to buy the silk and other goods they could export profitably. The Japanese traders were not allowed to accept the only international currency of the day in the Far East - Mexican silver dollars. The purity of the Mexican silver dollar was recognised and unquestioned all over the world, but when approached to exchange their bamboo money the Japanese made hand signs to indicate their heads being cut off or of being whipped by a split bamboo - standard and well-used forms of punishment on the China coast.

Another early problem for the Scotsmen was communication with the locals - Dutch was virtually the only foreign language spoken by the Japanese. When the first British Consul in Nagasaki was negotiating with Japanese officials for land in June 1859 he required a Dutch interpreter.

Dispatching the goods they could buy was not easy and they had to push hard to organise shipments. The Nagasaki tides allowed only three hours a day for loading and unloading cargo. The goods were moved in open boats which often overturned or were soaked in rainstorms. Much was lost through stealing. MacKenzie was experienced and shrewd enough to recoup some of these losses by claiming against the Japanese Treasury Guild.

Most serious of all was the problem of the anti-foreign fanatics. Following the murders of two Russian seamen in the same month of Glover's arrival, the safety of foreigners in Japan became a major issue. On 6 November a British national was attacked and killed by samurai outside Jardine, Matheson's office doorway in Yokohama. A lantern had been pushed into the face of the victim while he was run through from behind.

Yokohama's British Consul, F. Howard Vyse, in reaction to this killing notified all British subjects to remain armed. But the Consul-General, Alcock, now based in his Edo Legation, withdrew this notice as being over-reaction. He told Vyse that the Japanese were surprisingly tolerant in the face of foreign provocation.

Alcock's view may well have been true of the vast majority of Japanese - but it was certainly not true of some of the samurai who were not hiding their feelings towards the newcomers.

Perhaps Alcock quickly regretted his own advice. Soon after he was jostled by some samurai while out riding, forcing him to write to London and plead for, among other things, a Royal Navy warship to be assigned to protect the British citizens resident in Japan.

The residents of Yokohama were taking the brunt of the anti-foreign feeling but Nagasaki did not escape entirely. The British Consul, George Morrison, complained in December 1859 of the destruction by fire of two foreign-owned warehouses. The Japanese had offered no help to put out these fires but had saved, it was claimed, the adjacent property owned by a Japanese clan lord. It was the third fire of that year in the foreign quarter.

Yet despite all these difficulties and dangers, more than fifty British cargo ships alone had arrived in Nagasaki in 1859 and Jardine, Matheson, and others, were convinced that Japan would prove profitable in the end. Mackenzie and Glover wanted to develop, in particular, the export of high-quality silk. This was potentially a very big money-spinner but was desperately slow to pick up after MacKenzie's bonanza of the early months. Most of their problems came from the constant interference in trade of an increasingly unhappy bakufu.

Perhaps the Japanese had good reason to be suspicious of the newly arrived ketojin. With the sudden influx of hundreds of foreign seamen in Nagasaki - and these seamen would have been the roughest in the business - trouble was inevitable. They roamed the streets of Maruyama looking for women and in many cases also for an excuse to fight with the locals.

The British and Americans had both established Consulates in Nagasaki in 1859. The British employed a full-time career diplomat, George Morrison, who had taken over when C. Pemberton Hodgson and his acerbic wife moved to Hokkaido in the late summer of that year. The American Consul was a part-time job, filled normally by an American citizen/trader in the port. John G. Walsh was Nagasaki's first US Consul. Incredibly it would seem, Kenneth Ross MacKenzie was temporarily serving as Nagasaki's French Consul at this time. The story behind Mackenzie's appointment is not known. Certainly it was not uncommon for a trader to act as Consul for his own country. But for a major power such as France to appoint a Scot as Consul was not usual, even as a temporary measure. The Consuls of the various nations had to deal with many of the cases of violence involving sailors on leave in the port as well as normal diplomatic business.

Very early in 1860 the American Consul, Walsh, was writing to his Secretary of State in Washington regarding compensation for an injury done to a Japanese by a petty officer from the US steamer *Mississippi*. Walsh was aware that it was not normal for the Consulate to pay such expenses but that he had examined the case and felt it proper for the Consulate to compensate the victim in this particular instance. The result of the attack on the Japanese was horrific - the loss of both eyes.[8]

Incidents like this would not have helped in developing trust in those very early days and would have been played on by the fanatics. And, of course, the rules of the Treaty did not allow the 'uncivilised' Japanese to administer Japanese law on the foreigners. There was some justification for this. Japanese law allowed summary executions and quite horrific tortures - so the agreement was that Consular Courts would handle foreigners charged with an offence in Japan. This became a particularly sore point with the fiercely proud Japanese and these extra-territoriality laws would remain a festering grievance for many years.

William Keswick was Jardine, Matheson's agent in Yokohama and was having a lot more luck than MacKenzie and Glover in Nagasaki at this time. Keswick had apparently picked up a little Japanese and could communicate directly to a certain extent with the locals. Educated in Edinburgh, Keswick in later years would become the Jardine, Matheson & Co. *aipan*. MacKenzie did not hesitate to use his position as French Consul to help company communications. He wrote to Jardine, Matheson in Shanghai offering to use his right as a Consul to send an overland messenger to Yokohama to pass on to Keswick any company business 'of importance'.[9]

But they were a good team, the older and highly experienced MacKenzie balancing the enthusiasm and optimism of the younger man from Aberdeen. MacKenzie was about the same age as Glover's father and clearly served as his mentor. By early January 1860, Glover was confident enough to be signing his own name to the regular letters sent by them to Jardine, Matheson in Shanghai.[10]

The foreign settlement was nearing completion in 1860 and the two Scots had to settle for a less than prominent allotment at Oura 21. Oura was a prime waterfront area on the eastern side of the harbour and a cluster of foreign buildings now began to straddle the Oura river. The complicated rules for application for land by partnerships meant that Glover and MacKenzie's plot was at the rear, two streets back from the harbour front.

Their building would have been sparsely furnished, at least initially, as was the Japanese way. It is likely to have been built in the style of Westerners' houses in China, with offices and perhaps a warehouse on the ground floor and living quarters above. They would have engaged local servants.

Many of the foreign arrivals in Japan at this time were struck by the differences between China and Japan. The discipline and eagerness to learn of the Japanese was startling. Everything in Japanese society was ordered. Every 5 May, for example, the population en masse began wearing their summer kimono. On 9 September winter clothing was put back on - again by everyone. Every action of the people was supervised and the shogun's spies were everywhere and knew everything. Instant and utter obedience to Authority was expected.[11]

Glover's first year in Japan was spent looking for and arranging export of cargoes to the China coast. Seaweed, a delicacy in both China and Japan, and silk dominated this export trade. Imports were a problem with Jardine, Matheson feeling strongly that their expensively chartered ships should carry a full load both ways. It was essential for Glover to find Japanese markets for the goods they had to import, mainly Chinese medicines, cotton and sugar.

Until he became fluent in the language, it would have been necessary for Glover, like Keswick in Yokohama, to pick up a smattering of Japanese and use an interpreter only when required. But it is certain Glover realised even this early the importance of direct communication with the Japanese; he made up his mind to master the language.

Trading in those early days meant trudging through the mud or dust of Nagasaki to deal directly with the Japanese selling the products he could export profitably. It meant following MacKenzie and becoming familiar with the older man's methods and with his contacts. It meant haggling with the Japanese and in the early days, at least, dealing with shopkeepers rather than merchants.

In China Glover would perhaps have been accustomed to inspect a sample of merchandise for his company before ordering a shipload for Europe. But in Japan in the beginning only frustratingly small amounts of goods could be ordered. And the Japanese merchants he did deal with in many cases had to borrow from him before they could purchase the goods they were able to sell. But clearly Glover felt there was a future for him in Japan.

It is clear, too, that during his first year he began to grasp the complicated political situation in Japan. Alone among the foreigners Glover appears to have quickly had his finger on the Japanese political pulse.

Tom Glover in 1860 was a normal, fit and healthy young man. He was tall and fair skinned, hair long and waved. His very appearance would have made him an object of curiosity to the available girls of Nagasaki most of whom had never seen a European. Another attraction would have been his generosity which is mentioned in most surviving descriptions of the man. He was reportedly 'endowed of a fine physique and a courtly manner that captivated Japanese and foreigners - men and women alike'.[12] It is no surprise then to find him at the end of his first year in Japan seeking and finding some feminine company.

In September 1860 he went through a form of marriage with a Japanese girl, Sono Hiranaga. It is said that Sono was the daughter of a poor samurai.[13] This was almost certainly not the first time Tom had some kind of relationship with a Japanese girl. And it was certainly not the last, but it is the first recorded.

Little is known in detail of the marriage, but temporary marriages of convenience between lonely Western bachelors and Japanese women were then becoming common in all the newly opened Treaty ports. Quite simply there were no available Western women in these ports which were considered dangerous places in which to live.

Nagasaki, in particular, was famed for its local girls, said to be not only the prettiest in Japan, but also the easiest to live with. Glover was a resident and a gentleman and his arrangement with Sono bears no comparison with the rough-and-ready red-light trade indulged in by visiting seamen.

The usual routine for the respectable foreigner in these cases was to be taken to a certain tea house by a go-between. These go-betweens were often Customs officials, people with whom Tom would have been in constant contact. The suggestion for taking a 'wife' may well have come from one of these officials. The tea house was probably a two-storey, balconied building in Maruyama and Tom most likely crossed the 'Hesitation' and 'Made-up-your-Mind' bridges to reach it.

Inside the tea house, Tom would have been seated on a tatami mat in the twinkling light of a paper lantern. Drinking sake from thimble-sized cups, he would have listened to the melancholy strumming of the samisen and the swish of silken kimono. These tastes, sounds and atmosphere are uniquely Japanese.

He would have viewed various pretty girls and after a while selected the one most pleasing to him. He would have promised 'marriage' and

Coastguard station, Bridge of Don, Aberdeen, the Glover family home 1850 - 1864.
*(Courtesy: Aberdeen Maritime Museum)*

Lieutenant and Mrs Mary Glover, in the garden of the Coastguard station, Bridge of Don, late 1850s.
*(Courtesy: Dr G. Sharp, Bishops Stortford)*

Possibly 18 year old Thomas Glover, early 1857, posing in a Coastguard seaman's uniform. Uncaptioned photograph taken in the field above the station, now part of Balgownie Golf Club. *From the collection of Alexander Glover's wife Ann (Finlay)*

A kilted Alfred Glover, aged around 12, Bridge of Don, c. 1862. *(Courtesy: Dr Sharp)*

William, left, and Charles glover, Bridge of Don, late 1850s. *(Courtesy: Dr Sharp)*

Charles T. Glover, Aberdeen studio portrait, mid 1860s. *(Courtesy: Dr Sharp)*

Martha (George) Glover, aged around 20, Aberdeen, early 1860s. *(Courtesy: Dr Sharp)*

Young Tom Glover, aged around 21, Nagasaki. *(Courtesy: Yomigaeru Bakumatsu (The Pre-Meiji Years Revisited), Asahi Shimbun Company, Tokyo, 1987)*

Jim and Jane Glover, Aberdeen, mid 1860s. *(Courtesy: Nagasaki City Hall)*

Lieutenant Thomas Berry Glover, late 1850s, Aberdeen. *(Courtesy: Dr. Sharp)*

ROUGH SKETCH OF BUILDINGS AND GROUNDS.
*From " The Gym."*

1. Main House.
2. "Govie's" Room.
3. Wing.
4. Dining Hall.
5. Big Hall.
6. Play Room.
7. Tutor's Room.
8. Little Hall.
9. Wooden Class Room.
10. Engineering Class Room.
11. Large Class Room and Vestibule.
12. South Class Room.

The Aberdeen Gymnasium school in Tom Glover's day, (1849-54)

The Aberdeen Gymnasium school today; on the left as you look down the Chanonry.
The Main House is still there, part of Aberdeen University's complex housing the
Cruickshank Botanical Gardens.

Nagasaki harbour, early 1860s. From the collection of Charles Glover.
*(Courtesy: DGO Carmichael, Boxted)*

This was captioned High Japanese Officers. Nagasaki c. 1863.
*(Courtesy: Dr Sharp)*

View of newly built Glover House, Nagasaki, c. 1863.
*(Courtesy: Dr Sharp)*

Sketch of Glover House, Nagasaki, drawn around 1863. The Glovers called it 'The Bungalow' - to th
Japanese it was known as *Ipponmatsu* (Single Pine Tree). The house was built round a pine tree, cu
down in the early 1900s. *(Courtesy: Dr Sharp)*

This *ronin,* named Hayashida, paid the ultimate price for a suicidal attack on [fo]reigners. He was beheaded in the 1860s [a]s a common criminal, deprived of the [sa]murai's traditional and face saving *hara kiri. (Courtesy: Yomigaeru Bakumatsu)*

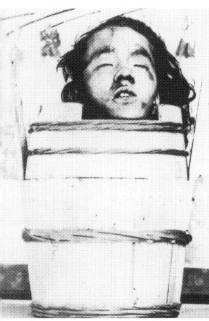

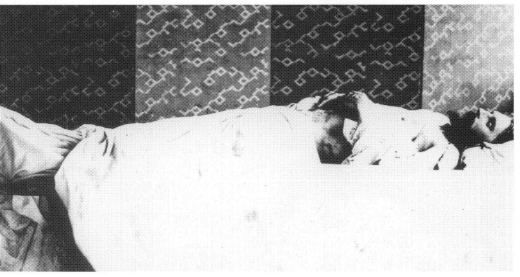

The mutilated body of Charles Lennox Richardson, lying in the US Legation at Yokohama, September, 1862.
*(Courtesy: Yomigaeru Bakumatsu)*

Japanese Samurai, Nagasaki mid 1860s.
*(Courtesy: DGOC)*

it was the go-between's job to arrange this, an accepted union in Japan. A house to rent for the couple would often be part of the deal. It was normal for the girl to live with the foreigner as long as he stayed in Japan, or in some cases until he got bored or a baby was on the way. When he did decide to leave, for whatever reason, the marriage dissolved itself. There was a poignancy about these inevitably sad affairs which would in time grow into the *Madam Butterfly* syndrome - the faithful Japanese woman betrayed by the golden-haired scoundrel.

It was normal for the new wife, in many cases the daughter of a respectable but poor family, to stay in the house her husband provided, as was the case anyway with most Japanese wives. Glover's wife, Sono, would not normally have taken part in the social life of the foreign community in Nagasaki. She would have remained in the company of her family or with other Japanese wives in similar circumstances when not with her husband.

Tom and Sono had a son whom they named Umekichi. He died as a baby of four months in the following year. The marriage did not last - Glover and Sono 'divorced', amicably it would seem, for Tom is said to have provided the finance for her to travel abroad to study some years later.

This early affair of Glover is worth looking into even with the scanty facts which have survived. For the period he appears to have conducted this affair with unusual sensitivity and respect. In later years another liaison of his would much more closely follow the *Madam Butterfly* theme.

Glover was only one of many Westerners who took a Japanese wife at this time. George Smith, the Anglican Bishop of Hong Kong, on a ten-week visit to Japan in 1860 was outraged at the number of foreign bachelors with native wives. He thought it tantamount to government approval that Customs officials could be involved in such scandalous matters. The Bishop failed to mention that no Western women were available.

The Bishop wrote a book on what he had observed on his Japanese visit. He reckoned that it was 'sad indeed the temptations to which young Englishmen are exposed who take up their residence in Nagasaki ... after 9 p.m. nearly half the population [of Nagasaki] are inebriated'.

Nagasaki's newspaper, a four-page sheet which began publishing in the summer of the following year, 1861, called the Bishop's remarks a 'libel'. In its review of the Bishop's book the writer thought that 'the mother, the sisters and friends of young bachelors would be led by these [the Bishop's] expressions to believe that these were as the cities of old, peculiar for their vice, and, horrors, we deny it.'[14]

It is not known what Tom's mother, sister or friends in the Bridge of Don would have thought of these remarks if they had read them. Aberdeen was a world away.

# Chapter 4

# tbe PbanCom ano tbe FanaCics

In an otherwise mundane business report to Shanghai from MacKenzie and Glover in January 1861, a very significant change in Japanese trade was noted. At the end of an account of a cotton-marine product barter, MacKenzie mentions that the Japanese Satsuma clan had bought the British steamer *England*. This fast, screw-driven ship of 1,500 tons had been purchased in defiance of the shogun's ban on such imports. Ostensibly it had been bought for carrying the clan's products from the remote Satsuma capital of Kagoshima in the far south of Japan to the markets of the heavily populated north of the country. The *England* was not new but it was modern - at the time most transatlantic crossings were still being made by smaller paddle-steamers - and it was important because an example had been set for other potentially rebellious clans. There were some in the Satsuma clan who were not at all happy with the shogun's impotence to prevent the foreign presence on the sacred soil of Japan. Others felt that much could be learned from the Westerners and wanted to encourage and promote trade with them - but they, too, resented the shogun. The divisions in the Satsuma clan were beginning to appear in the other powerful clans of south-west Japan. The general situation was one of confusion with the hotheaded anti-foreign fanatics the most dangerous faction of all.

Ships such as the *England* would be vital in the event of civil war breaking out among the rival factions in Japan. In a country with virtually no system of roads, transport of troops by sea would be crucial in a conflict. There was the chance, too, that guns could be mounted on the ship at a later date. Another major point to be taken from the purchase of the *England* by Satsuma was that the shogun's monopoly of steamships then in Japan was over, another sign of the underlying weakness of the bakufu.

Glover shrewdly noted the price paid by Satsuma for the *England* - $128,000 - which included $8,000 worth of bribes, presumably for the Nagasaki-based government or Customs officials not noticing that the shogun's ban was being broken. This was potentially very big business indeed - equivalent to multi-million pound deals in the late twentieth century - and would have raised the hopes of the traders who were then ready to quit what they saw as a shogun-restricted, declining Nagasaki. Glover had strong shipping connections - his father a Coastguard commander, two brothers shipbrokers, a third now a ship's captain. His interest was most certainly aroused.

Glover's partnership with MacKenzie broke up in the early part of 1861. By May of that year the older Scot had decided to return to China after his stint of almost two years in Japan. MacKenzie was well regarded in Nagasaki. The announcement of his going had the British Consul, George Morrison, writing:

"It is with much regret that I learn the hour of departure has arrived whereby I lose the valuable aid of your experienced Council and, in common with the rest of the community, an esteemed friend."[1]

MacKenzie's reasons for leaving are not clear - he may well have thought his prospects better in Hankow, where he had been operating before his move to Nagasaki. In any case his going gave Glover an opportunity the twenty-two-year-old quickly snatched. Before Mackenzie had even left Nagasaki, in May 1861, Glover officially declared himself as a general commission agent.[2] He was now an independent merchant trading under the name of Thomas Blake Glover and was the sole agent in Nagasaki for Jardine, Matheson.

MacKenzie left for China on 18 June 1861, leaving $2,300 of Jardine, Matheson's money with Tom. Part of his last communication to the company, written on the day of his departure, reads:

"... after great delay and much trouble I obtained a large and beautifully situated hill lot held upon very easy terms as to annual rent which Mr Glover will cause to be planted and will hereafter build a bungalow upon it at a cost of $800."[3]

The day after MacKenzie's departure, Glover was writing to Jardine, Matheson's Shanghai office complaining of the depressed state of the market but optimistically reporting that the building of the company's own premises were 'all but completed'.[4] These premises were a warehouse on the best Oura allotment of all - No.2 on the waterfront. Glover had supervised the building and even lived for a while in the house above the warehouse. He was taking good care of his prestigious agency for Jardine, Matheson. The 'bungalow' on the 'beautifully situated hill lot' referred to by MacKenzie is the famous Glover House which was completed in 1863.

Glover had entered the tea business. By June 1861 he had already sent samples to the company in Shanghai who showed interest and offered to put up cash for more.

In the early summer of 1861 prospects were looking good for young Glover. Established as Jardine, Matheson's agent, he was elected to Nagasaki's first Chamber of Commerce as one of its three British representatives - the others being William Alt and Robert Arnold. At twenty-seven, Arnold was the oldest of the three and he and Alt were the best-known British merchants in the port. Not yet twenty-three and still requiring to prove himself in business, Glover's election was most probably a reflection of his position as agent of the mighty Jardine, Matheson. Politically, things were quiet and there was money to be made in tea and silk if he could get things going properly and the shogun did not interfere too much. The foreign community in Nagasaki was settling well and becoming more organised.

According to the Consul, Morrison, there were around twenty-five British residents in the port in early 1861, 'a very well-ordered community ... giving no occasion for complaint on the part of the Japanese'.

By June that year a British Club had been founded and its members were looking for more land for a recreation ground.[5] The site of the club, Lot 31, was at the extreme rear of the Oura concession and backed on to the native part of the town. The establishment of a Club was another sign to the Japanese hotheads that the foreigners were here to stay.

Tom Glover was not the only Aberdeen man busy in Nagasaki that summer of 1861. James Mitchell, formerly of the city's Alexander Hall & Co. shipyard, had also established himself in the port. Mitchell was an associate of Glover, a master shipbuilder, and had arrived in Nagasaki at about the same time.[6] He had founded a small shipyard at Lot 1 on the waterfront of the Sagarimatsu concession on the other side of the Oura river from Glover's office. He called his establishment the 'Aberdeen Yard' and was off to a flying start.

Mitchell is credited with building the first European ship ever constructed in Japan. The launch of the *Phantom* attracted wide attention, with the newly started and short-lived local English-language newspaper reporting:

"The fact of it being the *first* appears to have led others beside ourselves to attach an importance to it which would otherwise have not been the case of the launching of a small schooner yacht, for on winding our way to the Aberdeen Yard, the premises of Mr J. Mitchell, the energetic builder, we found we were far from being alone, although it was barely six o' clock, indeed it was evident that a considerable number must have risen with the sun that morning ... we hope ... Mr Mitchell, the builder, may bring his skill and energy to bear among us."[7]

At 38 tons and with an overall length of 60 feet, the *Phantom* was launched into the waters of the harbour where, a little over a century later, tankers of several hundred thousand tons would be launched and serviced regularly.

The yacht was built for William Alt, a friend and fellow member with Glover on the Chamber of Commerce. The wife of Captain Pederson named the ship. The Aberdeen Yard was bedecked with scores of flags and pennants for the occasion and the guests at the launch adjourned to a breakfast laid on by Alt. Glover certainly was present at this launch and at the celebrations after it and it would seem likely that the two Aberdeen men

- Glover and Mitchell - would have discussed Nagasaki's future as a shipbuilding centre. There are indications, too, that Glover provided financial help for Mitchell's shipyard project.

Yet there were other, more ominous, matters to concern all the foreigners resident in Japan that summer. Violence had erupted in the capital and the launch of the *Phantom* soon would have been out of the news.

Forty armed fanatics had attacked the British Legation in Edo (Tokyo) and 'several of the English party had received wounds'.[8] George Morrison, Nagasaki's British Consul then on a visit to the Legation, was in the building at the time of the attack and shot and killed one of the assassins. Laurence Oliphant, secretary at the Legation, was one of the wounded British.

The news of the attack was greeted with disbelief. It was simply not thought possible that in the mid-nineteenth century fanatical samurai would attempt to murder British diplomats in Japan. The Legation had been housed in part of a temple in the Edo suburb of Shinagawa. It was separated from the sea by a road on one side and protected by a large gateway and a 300-yard-long avenue on the other. Behind this, a second gateway and a force of 150 samurai, many of these mounted, guarded the building and its occupants. The shogun was well aware of the need to protect the British representatives, and the potential consequences from the then most powerful nation in the world if he did not.

On the night of the attack in July 1861, Oliphant was wakened by a noise coming from the corridor outside his room in the Legation.[9] He grabbed the only weapon he could find - a leather hunting whip - and made his way out of the room to investigate. In the narrow and dimly lit passageway he came across a Japanese advancing on him with sword raised above his head, held two handed in the classical Japanese style. Trying to defend himself with the riding whip, Oliphant was aware of the Japanese slashing at him, time after time bringing his sword crashing over his head but somehow, miraculously in the dark, missing his target. He then felt a blast from a handgun at the side of his face and he was more than relieved when Morrison briskly leaned over him and shot the intruder. The attacker was chainmailed and masked and had managed to badly wound the British secretary on the wrist during their struggle.

Later Oliphant discovered that it was the low beam in the unlit temple passageway the Japanese had struck as he repeatedly swung his razor-sharp *katana* over his head. He realised the beam had saved his life when he examined it the following morning and found it covered in hacks. Morrison shot and killed another of the attackers in the continuing fracas.

At last organised, the samurai guarding the British Legation established control of the situation, killing one more of the attackers. The rest apparently escaped.

In a gory finish to his account of the night, Oliphant tells of returning to his darkened room exhausted and feeling in the blood beneath his feet a human eye. A body lay in the centre of his room, headless. Oliphant later discovered the missing head beneath his sideboard.

The attack on the British Legation was sensational and the news spread quickly through the Treaty ports, sending a shock wave through Nagasaki's foreign settlement. The British residents in particular were now casting nervous glances over their shoulders. If not even the heavily guarded British Legation was safe from attack, what chance had the traders in far-off Nagasaki?

Nagasaki's newspaper had the standard answer of the day to the problems. Gunboat diplomacy was required to bring the Japanese into line: 'quick, sharp, decisive measures can no longer be abstained from'.[10] This may well have been true but it was also perhaps the reaction the hotheads were hoping to provoke.

The British Consul in Yokohama tried to cool things down. F. Howard Vyse, in an official notification to British subjects in Japan the day following the attack, wrote:

"The undersigned requests that British subjects will be careful, how they walk about during the next week, ... and to endeavour to remain at home during the evening."[11]

Vyse in his note went on to plead for calm and added that a Royal Navy warship, HMS *Ringdove*, was on its way.

The upheavals and dangers in the north did not appear to unduly upset Glover. The majority of the British traders in Nagasaki were young - seven out of the ten registered at the Consulate were under twenty-five in mid-1861 - and they seem to have carried on with their businesses regardless.[12]

A real community was forming in the Japanese port. Japan's first municipal council was elected in Nagasaki that year and two Britons, William Alt and John Major, served on it with the American, Franklin Field. A sailing regatta was scheduled for the late summer and there were organised picnics and amateur dramatics as well as the inevitable British Club. A church and hospital were also planned for the foreigners now numbering around one hundred.[13] Their enclave clinging to the eastern edge of Nagasaki harbour was as near a Western village as could be managed in the circumstances.

Yet perhaps the tensions of living in Nagasaki did surface at times - import returns indicated that plenty of drinking went on.[14] There was the mandatory four or five hours' daily slog in the heat of the office for Glover, trying to keep his employers in Shanghai happy and at the same time keep up the perpetual search for the big breakthrough of his own. Politics in Japan were a powder keg, ready to blow up at any time, and if civil war erupted the foreigners were unwillingly in the front line. It would have been easy to unwind with a couple of drinks in the Club on the way home, perhaps attend a dinner party at a friend's where a few more could be sunk and, occasionally, finish the evening by crossing the bridges into a certain house in Maruyama.

# Chapter 5

# CONTACT WITH RENEGADES

G lover's first independent business venture had been in the export of Japanese tea. Tea, silk and, later, coal would be Japan's major money-earners in its early years after opening. Tom became involved in all three.

Using experienced Chinese supervisors he had established his own tea business by August 1861. Japan exported almost 4,500 tons of tea in the 1861 season and although half of this amount went through Nagasaki, it was not quite the lucrative trade Glover had imagined.

Tea was planted on the hillsides of Japan's interior on land unsuitable for rice and the work of planting and picking was done mostly by the women and children of the farms.[1] It was a part-time occupation and the tea was dried after picking by the farm women over home-made fires. Drying was necessary for the long voyages to Europe or the United States, as too much moisture left in the tea would cause mould and ruin the cargo. The Japanese drying method was simply not good enough and the foreigners were banned from leaving the Treaty ports to supervise and organise the operation themselves. The tea could be bought only through Japanese agents.

Glover got round this by establishing a tea refiring plant in Nagasaki in August 1861 - a building where the tea could be properly dried and prepared for a long voyage - this solved the problem but added expense. A long and not very successful struggle with the tea business had begun for Glover.[2]

A second Glover brother reached Nagasaki that same month. Tom had gone to Shanghai and returned to Nagasaki with his older brother, James, arriving off the Japanese port on the night of 7 August 1861. They arrived on the *Gharra* and high winds kept their ship from getting into Nagasaki harbour that night. James Glover's photographs show him to be tall, slim and dark, thick hair stiffly parted, physically a complete contrast to his younger brother.

Accompanying the two Glover brothers on the *Gharra* was Edward Harrison, another young China-based trader being sent to Nagasaki as an agent for a British firm, Blain, Tate & Co. The trio waited until the following day for the winds to abate enough for their ship to drop anchor and for them to be rowed ashore.[3] Despite all the problems confronting his tea business, Tom Glover must have had some hopes for success in bringing over his brother to join him.

Jardine, Matheson were still a little cautious of their young agent. In an earlier letter they had told him that they were interested only in establishing a sound trade - not in speculative adventures.[4] How much heed to this warning Tom took is not known but the company rapped his knuckles in a letter of 10 September, saying:

"Your draft for $2,000 has been presented & honored - we should, however, beg you to note that we wish to be advised beforehand when you are in want of funds, for we make it a rule not to accept drafts unless permission to draw on us has been granted."[5]

Clearly the headstrong Glover, presumably still resident in the lower half of the company's warehouse/office complex on the Nagasaki waterfront during the building of his bungalow on the hill, would have to be held on a tight rein.[6]

The planned regatta went ahead on schedule at the end of September. The winners of the various races were not published on that occasion but over the years the Glover brothers did well in what became an annual event at the port. Their training in their father's Coastguard boats in the rough of the North Sea was evident.

Early in October Glover sent off a muster of tea samples to Shanghai - 'tea pressed and fired in our own establishment'.[7] His 'establishment' at Oura employed several hundred Japanese women heating, packing and sorting teas. They would have been supervised by a Chinese who separated and graded and generally ran the show. The sound of crying babies strapped to their mothers' backs, the singing women, the shouting Chinese and the clattering of hundreds of iron heating pans were joined with the aroma of roasting tea and a mixture of all of this wafted out on to the streets of Oura - an unforgettable memory for visitors to the Treaty ports at that time.[8]

Despite the industry and employment Glover's tea business had brought to Nagasaki, costs remained high and profits low and by the beginning of 1862 he was forced to look at other possibilities of making money. He was not short of ideas.

It was now necessary for him to bring in like-minded people to his organisation. With Francis A. Groom, he founded Glover & Co. on 1 February 1862.[9] Groom had been a partner in Robert Arnold's firm in the port and his move to Glover would indicate that he was impressed by the ambitions of the young Scot.

Jim Glover and Edward Harrison, who would specialise in property management, became the third and fourth partners in Glover & Co. later that year.[10] Harrison had arrived in Nagasaki with Jim the previous August and, like the Glover boys and Frank Groom, was young and bright and prepared to have a go.

Even with the new talent to help, Glover's tea business stubbornly refused to pick up. The company were not happy with his product or with the price he was charging. But with his usual optimism he was sure he could reduce production costs once his plant was fully utilised and a temporary shortage of tea pickers and inspectors was over.[11] Tom's enthusiasm seems to have won over the hardheads in Shanghai - the company agreed to go on backing his project.[12]

Other avenues of business were also beginning to open up. Harrison's property expertise now began to show dividends and they were also dabbling in foreign exchange, moving currency between Yokohama and Nagasaki to gain from the considerable swings in the rate between the two ports. This particular enterprise would have been only just within the law. They were young and eager and into many things. Even with the backing of Jardine, Matheson and their regular supply of market prices in Europe and the United States, trading in those days was at times not much more than a form of gambling. Three months or more could pass between shipment in Japan and arrival in the West and wild changes in the price of goods were common.

Life in the port was improving for the foreigners. For example, 1862 saw the opening of an Episcopal church, a Dutch-supervised hospital, a bowling saloon and hotel and a two-monthly overland postal service to Yokohama.[13]

Glover by this time appears to have become a leading member of the community and well settled in Nagasaki. On 12 May Dr William Willis, described as a gentle giant of an Irishman, stopped off at the port en route to take up his post as medical officer at the British Legation in Edo. He stayed at Glover's home while in Nagasaki and found his host kind and courteous - descriptions of the Scot which consistently recur. Willis wrote of his stay at Glover's home:

"It is surprising the affluence of all good things here ... the real comforts that are to be found in Nagasaki. It is the custom here to have some eggs and tea early in the morning and a late breakfast at 12 p.m., where all good things of the season and a number of European delicacies are met with, such as can be preserved. Dinner is at 7 p.m. equally good."[14]

Willis became a well-known figure in Japanese and foreign circles during the following years, both as a doctor and a diplomat. Another new arrival at the British Legation in September that year - a student interpreter, Ernest Satow - would have a profound effect on the destiny of Japan. But despite the apparent comforts of Nagasaki in 1862, that year also saw a worsening in the political situation.

The adolescent shogun, Iemochi Tokugawa, had married a sister of the emperor in an attempt by his advisers to placate what was growing into a powerful alliance of discontented samurai of various clans. Some of these samurai were beginning to use the Japanese emperor as a rallying point. But the marriage had little effect. Part of the Tokugawa shoguns' strengths over the previous centuries had been distrust between rival clans. Now younger and more radical samurai in many of the clans were developing a common cause, a cause which would demand that inter-clan rivalries be put aside.

Two incidents that summer of 1862 brought an already uneasy situation to the boil. In June a marine corporal was killed in another attack on the British Legation in Edo. A second incident in September was even more serious and brought Japan and Britain close to war.

A British party from Yokohama left that Treaty port on a riding trip. Their journey took them through the nearby village of Namamugi. On a road near there they failed to give way to a Satsuma clan procession which was on its way from Edo to Kyoto. Leading the procession was the Satsuma daimyo's uncle, Hisamitsu Shimazu - the regent and effectively the ruler of the powerful clan. His escorting samurai attacked the Britons, killing one - Charles Lennox Richardson, a merchant based in China - and wounding two others.

The murdered Richardson was no innocent. Earlier a Consular Court in China had fined him for a brutal and unprovoked beating of a Chinese servant. And prior to the attack by the Satsuma samurai he was advised by his friends to respect Japanese custom and turn back or leave the road to the daimyo's procession. He chose not to. His body was brought to the nearby US Consulate where it lay as the news spread.

The British residents, including the recent arrival, Dr Willis, were furious. They wanted British troops landed to avenge the attack and demanded that the Satsuma give up the guilty samurai for punishment. The clan refused, their argument being that their actions had been traditional and customary, that the punishment for not giving way to the procession of a daimyo was death. They blamed the shogun and his administration, the bakufu, for the whole sorry business, for signing treaties which allowed foreigners into Japan in the first place. The shogun could not placate the British or the most powerful clan in Japan which ironically wanted trade and contact with the West expanded.

The Satsuma withdrew to their stronghold of Kagoshima in the deep south of Japan, leaving the shogun to handle the British fury. Satsuma could not be controlled and the British were making ever more threatening noises. Other potentially rebellious clans watched the developing situation with interest.

By this time various clan lords, including Satsuma, had stationed agents in Nagasaki to make contacts with the foreigners who alone could provide modern arms and ships if civil war broke out.

Tom Glover had been drawn into this twilight world of intrigue and political manoeuvring. Still only twenty-four years old, he was about the same age as many of the idealistic young Japanese rebels with whom he was now in contact. In clandestine meetings in inns and teahouses, and speaking in faltering Japanese, he listened to their arguments and grew to sympathise with them. Perhaps for the first time he realised that there were many in the clans who resented the restrictions on trade as much as the foreigners did. Some argued that their fight was with the shogun, who monopolised trade, not the foreigners with whom they wished to develop contact. What is certain is that about this time Glover made up his mind to help those samurai opposed to the shogun.

Glover's motives at this stage are not known. Like the other foreign merchants in Japan he resented the shogun's stifling of trade in one form or another. It is possible he saw a big future for his own company in a more liberal Japan with the bakufu's powers lessened and the rebels in positions to make decisions on trade. More than most he must have realised the possible repercussions if he did become involved. Whatever was the case, he now felt strongly enough to risk his own life in the coming struggle to bring down the shogun.

It was a very dangerous game Glover had begun to play. The clan agents would compete for his favour and he would find it difficult to know whom to trust. Efforts were made to kill him - no details have survived but Glover attributed several of these assassination attempts to Gunhei Aoki, a Choshu clan samurai and one of the first of that clan with whom he came in contact. He said of Aoki, 'He was a bad man, he tried to kill me, more than once.'[15] Certainly Glover survived these attempts on his life, perhaps saved by his bodyguard. Foreigners were now accompanied wherever they went by an armed guard of samurai - clearly the shogun did not want another incident to embarrass the bakufu and push the foreigners into a war which Japan was not ready or able to fight. Some fanatics were executed but there was no protection from a terrorist who was himself prepared to die in the attack. Glover's contacts with the clan agents continued.

The shogun's quandary in 1862 had no solution. He was forced into officially lifting his ban that year on the import of ships - but as well as allowing the clans loyal to him to buy, it also gave the potentially rebellious clans of the south the same opportunity. It was a recipe for disaster and brought civil war even closer - a war in which Glover would be prominently involved.

# Chapter 6

# IPPONMATSU

Much of the action behind the scenes in the frenetic mid-1860s took place in Tom Glover's house, the 'Bungalow' as he called it, in Nagasaki. Construction of the building by a master carpenter, Hidenoshin Koyama of Amakusa Island near Nagasaki, was completed in 1863. The site chosen was on the most prominent and beautifully situated part of the *Minami Yamate,* or southern hillside, foreign concession. The waterfronts of Oura and Sagarimatsu were directly below the house, Dejima a little further north and in the panoramic view across the bay Glover could see the western side of the harbour and the mountains beyond. The house was built round a pine tree and became known to the Japanese as Ipponmatsu, or single pine tree.

It was a fitting place for an up-and-coming young businessman, a place to relax and a place where he could work when required. It was the venue for the talks between Glover and the clan agents where momentous decisions regarding the entire future of Japan would be taken. It was the house where British Ministers and admirals would stay while in Nagasaki and where renegades and rebel samurai would hide and plot the downfall of the shogun. The comings and goings at Glover House would be noted by spies and passed on to the shogun.

The house was built as a Japanese thought a Western house should be and is a curious mixture of East and West.[1] The rooms are large, high ceilinged and airy and Tom and Jim Glover would have lived there comfortably, even in the hottest days of summer cooled by the breeze skimming the water of the harbour below. They could have entertained their friends there with some style. This was a decided improvement on the early clapboard, Wild West style of building in Oura which was house, warehouse and office combined - a style the highly skilled Japanese carpenters had copied from outdated pictures of Western architecture.[2]

There are photographs, some captioned as early as 'Nagasaki 1863', showing the now familiar honeycomb shape of Glover House shortly after it was built.[3] In one of these Tom and Jim are posing on the steps of the porch in a group containing their partner Edward Harrison with some others. The distinctive 'rising sun' windows are visible above the door behind them. Significantly these early photographs also show some of the Westerners carrying rifles. In those days the brothers were still 'Tom' and 'Jim' - only later would Glover acquire the more stately 'Thomas' or 'TB'.

A croquet green had been laid on the level above the house and the level below overlooked the masts and sails of the many ships lying at anchor. In another of the photographs two Western women are pictured on the croquet green with their partners and it is most likely that Glover House was a favourite gathering place for Nagasaki's foreign residents.

Much of the social life at this time would have gone on at the homes of the residents. Western women were still at a premium but there was apparently no shortage of local girls. In a Japanese directory of foreign residents in Yokohama, dated 1861-2, thirty of the seventy-nine registered households had a resident *musume* (literally daughter or girl, at the time the word was taken to mean a mistress).[4] The register lists no musume resident at the homes of married men whose wives were with them in Japan, or at the homes of clergymen, doctors and certain others. In houses shared by two bachelors there were two resident musume. It is safe to presume the same arrangements were in force in Nagasaki.

The four partners in Glover & Co. had plenty to keep them occupied - letters for dispatch by mail steamer to keep Jardine, Matheson happy, bargaining with the tea and silk dealers in an effort to keep up with changing prices, running the tea refiring plant which now employed hundreds - as well as run-of-the-mill problems of thieving by native labourers, crooked Customs officials and belligerent ships' captains. On top of this, Glover in early 1863 was continuing to keep close and clandestine contact with agents of the Satsuma clan.

Shogun-induced problems with foreign exchange the previous year had eventually been referred to London. Francis Groom was in Britain on Glover & Co. business at this time and gave his version of affairs in Japan to British Treasury officials - perhaps contradicting the views of the British Minister in Edo, Rutherford Alcock.[5]

But currency problems were not the only problems Glover had to face in the early part of that year. He was in trouble with his own Consul for apparently taking the law into his own hands.

Okoobo Bungonokami, Nagasaki's governor, wrote his letter of complaint to Morrison, the Consul, on 21 February 1863. In it he accuses Glover of 'having seized a number of coolies' whom he suspected of stealing silk he was shipping and of binding them with cords 'besides painting the faces of seven of them with tar' before handing them over to the Japanese police.[6] The Consul in reply said that it was not Glover but Edward Harrison who had been involved and that he was at present absent from Nagasaki but would be punished on return. The governor would not accept this, insisting that Glover was also involved and that both Britons should be punished for breaking the Treaty rules. He went on to say that the 'coolies have since been examined' and that only one had stolen the silk while another had attempted to do so - both of these had been punished according to Japanese law and the remainder set free.

According to the Consular records, Glover and Harrison were 'severely reprimanded' by the Consul and Harrison fined ten dollars.[7]

But as the cherry blossom season approached and the cool of Nagasaki's early spring was replaced with the warmer air of April, much more serious events events were occupying the Consul's mind.

**Chapter 7**

# ESCAPE OF THE 'CHOSHU FIVE'

T he late spring and summer of 1863 in Nagasaki was long and hot. For the British community in particular it was also a very dangerous time and Glover's letters to Jardine, Matheson during the period chart the drama.

The background was the impending British retaliation against the Satsuma clan for the murder of Charles Richardson the previous September. Early in the year the British had demanded £100,000 from the shogunate in reparation. As well as this the Satsuma clan were ordered by the British to execute the samurai involved and to hand over £25,000 as their own reparation for the crime. Rear-Admiral Kuper of the Royal Navy's China squadron was standing by with nine ships to discipline the hotheaded Japanese clan if they failed to comply. They were well aware that the shogun could not control the Satsuma clan, particularly in its distant stronghold of Kagoshima.

The anti-foreign faction urged the shogun not to give way to the British. A decree was finally issued by the shogun in Edo. The Japanese language is notoriously imprecise and the decree was read by moderates as a start to new negotiations with the West over the Treaty port arrangements. But to some fanatics in the Choshu clan it was read as approval for attacking and finally ridding Japan of all 'barbarians'. This they quickly prepared themselves to do.

On 6 April 1863, Edwin St John Neale, the acting British Minister during Alcock's absence on home leave, presented the shogun with an ultimatum. The Japanese had twenty days to respond to the British demands or face the consequences.

Tension mounted in Nagasaki, much closer to Satsuma country than Edo or Yokohama, where a squadron of the Royal Navy were standing by to protect the British residents there if need be. Morrison's report from Nagasaki to the British Legation in Edo on 14 April sets the tone.[1] He reported that he had pleaded for calm with the residents, but went on to point out the proximity of Nagasaki to Satsuma should hostilities break out. He continued:

"The Prince [of Satsuma] has had agents in this port making earnest enquiry as to the measures which will be anticipated on the part of the

British government, and some of his high officers are in constant association with foreigners, especially with Mr Glover of Glover & Co.

This gentleman has informed me that the Commander-in-Chief of Prince Satsuma's forces has himself been in Nagasaki to gain information; and that another high agent wished him to be the medium of offering any sum of money that might be desired."

When Glover had pressed the Satsuma men regarding punishment for the murderer he was told that it 'was out of the question'. He was now the only Briton with direct access to the Satsuma.

He kept Jardine, Matheson well informed, writing, for example, on 29 April:

"... the community has been told to hold themselves in readiness to leave ... considerable bodies of Japanese troops are ... moving down into the forts at the entrance to the Bay."

On 6 May:

"... we hear from native sources that Satzuma is most indignant at the British demands and declines altogether to listen to them. In such case we fear there is no alternative but hostilities."

Jardine, Matheson had replied asking him to 'use his best endeavours' for the protection of their property in Nagasaki. Glover wrote again on 16 May:

"War now appears inevitable and the communities are leaving the port with their valuables. The Governor states that a distinction will be made between the different nationalities but the Americans, Dutch and other foreigners do not put much faith in this ... Full particulars are forwarded for publication in the *North China Herald & Recorder.*"[2]

Morrison's dispatches to Edo were on the same lines as those of Glover to Shanghai and almost certainly he was the Consul's source of information. He wrote on 10 May, 'The train is laid for civil war and the foreign question is the match to light it,' and nine days later, 'By night the settlement forms a tempting bait to the hosts of thieves and bad characters who always abound in periods of trouble.'[3]

In the middle of May Glover, at twenty-four the leader of the community, called a meeting of the foreign residents. The British ultimatum had been extended until nearer the end of the month at the request of the shogun and this breathing space was very welcome to those trapped in Nagasaki. They discussed whether or not they should abandon their properties and take refuge on the two warships now in the harbour - at least until the crisis was over. It was finally decided that they stay put. They decided to gather each evening at the home of William Alt, presumably the residence most easy to defend, and to keep an armed watch from there.

These nights at Alt's house must have been nerve-racking. The guards on duty would have been chosen, probably by some kind of rota system, to watch while the others slept. Peering through the blackness in the stillness and humidity of a summer night, they would have watched for a sudden movement or the glint from a sword or knife which would betray an assassin. They would have listened for the breaking of a twig above the chorus of the cicada. In the morning they returned to their homes and places of business and tried to continue with their lives as normally as they could.

Continuing normally in Glover's case was writing a letter to Jardine, Matheson on 26 May in which he reported that the traders had been forced into taking their books and papers out to ships lying at anchor in the harbour and from there had attempted to carry on a semblance of trade. He went on:

"... owing to the political troubles Trade is almost completely stopped ...

... The extra time allowed the Japanese expires tomorrow and we shall probably learn the result on 31st.

... All reports agree ... a civil war was almost inevitable ... there is every appearance of hostile intentions on the part of the Japanese and large bodies of men are working day and night in constructing sandbags, battery and carrying guns.

... We have made an inventory of all our property and duly attested it at the British Consulate."[4]

June came to Nagasaki with the penetrating heat of its bright sun and its intervals of torrential rain and still they waited for news from Edo. Morrison wrote on the first of the month commenting on the weather - 'the beautiful foliage sparkling in the summer sun' - producing a false sense of security; in the same letter he mentions also the well-constructed gun batteries which 'could sink every vessel in the port including H.M. Ships *Rattler* and *Ringdove*'.[5]

Just when a fresh batch of wild rumours began to circulate in Nagasaki, the news broke - the shogun had agreed to pay a deposit on his indemnity for the murder of the marine and Richardson. Suddenly the pressure was off. The chances of war between Britain and Japan had faded although the Satsuma problem remained - they had still not surrendered their guilty men or paid their indemnity.

By mid-June the agents of Satsuma and Choshu were back in Nagasaki and business showed signs of picking up again. The Glover brothers and the others no longer spent every night at Alt's home. Glover could write to Shanghai on 17 June:

"... panic among the native inhabitants here has quite subsided and they are daily returning to their homes. The shops in town have opened and the merchants are resuming their business with foreigners."[6]

But this peaceful interlude was the passing of the eye of the storm.

During the crisis month of May Glover had been approached by members of the Choshu clan. He had been asked to help in the escape of five young Choshu samurai to the West. He had agreed and with the help of Jardine, Matheson - both their Yokohama agent, Keswick, and the Shanghai and London offices became involved in this great escape - it was arranged. As it turned out Glover's own family in Aberdeen would also become involved. Glover was central to the plot although few details have survived - this clear breaking of the shogun's strictly enforced law on foreign travel was not the kind of thing to discuss in company correspondence.[7] What is clear is that Glover was the mainspring for the escape of the 'Choshu Five' - this is verified by the lifelong respect and regard he was held in by two of the 'Five'.

The 'Five' wanted to study the West at first hand. Two of them, Hirobumi Ito and Kaoru Inoue, were to become very famous figures in post-shogun Japan. Ito would become the country's first Prime Minister in 1885 and Inoue would serve in many high offices, including that of Foreign Minister. The remaining three would also become leaders of the New Japan.

But in the summer of 1863 Ito and Inoue were both, like Glover, in their early twenties and all three were perhaps a little apprehensive but brave and determined and ready to take a chance. It was later said that Ito had been involved in the attack on the British Legation two years before - and certainly in his old age he did not deny this.[8] If indeed Ito or any of the others had belonged to the anti-foreign fanatics they were now convinced that much could be learned from the foreigners - blind hatred was no longer an option.

Late in June Keswick arranged passage for the fugitives on a Jardine, Matheson ship leaving Yokohama for Shanghai. They were smuggled on board at Yokohama after arriving there on a Glover ship from Nagasaki. Perhaps the more obvious starting point of Nagasaki for the trip to China was avoided because of the seemingly imminent outbreak there of violence. In any case they reached Shanghai and early in July Ito and Inoue - split from the other three - left on the 300-ton sailing ship *Pegasus* for London. Their voyage would be a horrendous one and never forgotten by the two - because of language difficulties the warrior-gentlemen were thought to be seamen apprentices on the *Pegasus* and treated accordingly. Ten days later the remaining three of the 'Five' - Kinzuke Endo, Yakichi Nomura and Yozo Yamao - left for the same destination on the tea clipper, *White Adder*. The escape of these five young men to the West would have profound effects on the future of Japan.

# Chapter 8

# in the Land of the 'Barbarians'

No sooner had the 'Five' left than the country was once more plunged into violence and confusion. Anti-foreign elements in the Choshu clan had snatched the balance of power and on 25 June attacks on foreign shipping by that clan's forces began in the Straits of Shimonoseki.

The Straits - a stragetically important stretch of sea between the main Japanese islands controlled by the clan - were the main sea route between Yokohama and China and much used by foreign shipping. Glover had not forecast these events and appears to have been as surprised by the attacks as everyone else. An extremist faction in Choshu had taken over and decided that it was now their turn to act decisively and eject the 'barbarians'. They knew that their attacks on the foreigners would embarrass the shogun and, they hoped, cause an all-out war with the West.

The American steamer *Pembroke* arrived in Nagasaki on 8 July. It had been fired on while passing Shimonoseki on its way to Shanghai from Yokohama and other reports of violence were coming in almost daily - Glover had even been told that Morrison was in danger of assassination. A second confirmed attack on a French ship caused fatalities. Glover had written to Shanghai on 4 July, telling the company that everything in Nagasaki was 'remarkably quiet'.[1] Six days later his tone was entirely different:

The treacherous attack on the *Vienchang* is attributed (as in the case of the *Pembroke*) to the Prince of Cho-siu who has command of the forts at Shimonoseki. This Prince is said to belong to the Oshima Mikado party and is bitterly opposed to foreigners. It is not yet known whether he was carrying out the Mikado's orders or simply acting on his own responsibility.[2]

By the end of the month the Straits were closed. The situation was fast getting out of control. Glover wrote on 25 July: 'The country appears to be in a very unsettled state, & a civil war among the Princes *certain...*'[3]

These Choshu attacks quickened British determination to act - the Japanese would have to be taught a lesson. Kagoshima, capital and base of the Satsuma clan, was to pay the price. The shogun had paid his indemnity for the murder of Richardson but the Satsuma still had not paid theirs - or given up the murderer. Rear-Admiral Kuper, accompanied by the acting British Minister, Neale, and his staff, anchored his squadron off Kagoshima on 13 August 1863. A young member of Neale's staff that day was the student interpreter, Ernest Satow. At this stage Satow was not sympathetic to the rebel cause but his later views were very much in line with those of Glover. The British presented their demands again. The Satsuma reply was evasive and the next day the British opened fire.

In the course of the Royal Navy's shelling, Satsuma lost three British-built ships which were at anchor in the harbour - two of these ships almost certainly bought through Glover. Satsuma pride was saved by several hits on the British warships, notably on the British flagship *Euryalis* which strayed on to the firing range used by the Satsuma gunners for practice. Two officers and eleven men on the British ships died in the action and several were wounded. Neale estimated Satsuma dead and wounded at 1,500 - and the property loss at £1 million. Many considered these claims an exaggeration, but essentially it was an attack by the strongest and most powerful Navy afloat on a town of wooden houses, defended by a force little more than medieval by European standards.

This lesson in gunboat diplomacy was well learned by Satsuma, none more so than than by Heihachiro Togo. Togo is another illustrious figure in Japanese history who would become close to Tom Glover. But in August 1863 he was the sixteen-year-old son of a prominent Satsuma samurai family. He had helped man the defences of Kagoshima, such as they were, that day. Dressed in his samurai regalia, two sword handles protuding from his wide belt, Togo loaded shot into the Satsuma cannons in an attempt to hit back at the mighty Royal Navy. But rather than holding a grudge against the British, Togo had been impressed. He would go on to be trained by the Royal Navy and in time become Japan's Nelson. His path and that of Tom Glover would cross many times.

Glover informed Jardine, Matheson on 27 August:

"... 3 Japanese strs *Contact, England* and *Geo. B. Gray* sunk! ... It is stated that the Prince [of Satsuma] & many of his friends were anxious to meet the [British] demands but the war party proved too strong for them."

In the same letter Tom complained:

"... scarcely any produce is arriving in consequence of the Prince of Cho-siu having stopped all junks coming to Nagasaki by the Shimonoseki route."[4]

The British bombardment convinced any lingering doubters in the Satsuma camp - the 'war party' as Glover called them - that they had no choice but to absorb the military and industrial technology of the West - and do it quickly. To do this it would be necessary to develop the existing relationship with Glover. Within weeks of the incident, representatives of Satsuma in Yokohama agreed to pay an indemnity to the family of Richardson and 'to do their best' to seek out his murderers.[5] They promised to execute the guilty samurai, when found, in the presence of British officers. Further north the belligerents in the Choshu clan, still controlling the Straits and attacking foreign shipping, learned of the British attack on Satsuma and wondered if they would be next to feel the wrath of the West.

The Kagoshima incident reflected the political uneasiness of Japan as a whole in 1863. The Choshu attacks only increased the tension. Anti-foreign feeling again intensified and reached the point that trade at Nagasaki was completely halted.

The news from Yokohama would not have helped. A Japanese merchant dealing in silk with the foreigners had been beheaded near there and his severed head mounted on a pole under a placard warning of the same treatment for all who dealt with the Westerners. Six similar killings occurred in Osaka during September 1863 and another beheading was accompanied by a sign saying that the execution had been carried out in punishment for 'trading with the foreigners who are lower than brute beasts' and promising the same for a named list of twenty-three Yokohama merchants and agents - all Japanese - at least ten of whom promptly packed their bags and left the town.[6]

Glover's business was undoubtedly disturbed by the unrest of 1863 but as autumn approached and Nagasaki's shades of green turned to pale gold, things began to pick up. Throughout the year mundane business had gone on as cicumstances allowed. In mid-1863 Glover was employing more than one thousand pickers in his tea project which remained his main concern - even if it was still failing to make money.[7] Silk and marine products were also exported and woollen and cloth manufactured goods were imported. Some of the clothing he imported may well have originated from Aberdeen. Crombie's Mill, situated very close to his family's Bridge of Don home, used Jardine, Matheson & Co. as their selling agents in the Far East. He also started importing British coal in 1863. At this time none of the primitively produced but, in part, high-quality Japanese coal was considered good enough to export unmixed. But this fact, and the knowledge of the need to fuel the ever-growing number of steamers visiting Nagasaki, had certainly registered with Glover. His company's land holdings had increased in this period, too, under Harrison's guidance. But shipping was beginning to dominate Japanese trade.

Demand for ships had been high and only during the midsummer events prior to the bombardment of Kagoshima did it let up. The Nagasaki people had remained friendly even with the Choshu hotheads terrorising foreigners further north.[8] Satsuma began negotiating with Glover for the purchase of a second-hand steamer, the *Sarah*, within weeks of the shelling of the clan's capital - presumably with much of the town still in ruins. It is clear that the clan wished to rebuild its small fleet as soon as possible. Glover wrote to Shanghai on 27 October:

"We sold a few days since to Satzuma the SS *Sarah* for $75,000 - the affair was hurriedly managed the str leaving the same day she was purchased for Kagoshima."

There is no mention in his correspondence of another ship being built in Aberdeen at about the same time. Work began on that first Aberdeen-built ship for the Japanese in mid-1863. Not surprisingly, it too was destined for the Satsuma clan. It was necessary for Tom to have written to his brother Charles in Aberdeen with the order by at least the first half of the year. Certainly it must have been on order before the British attack on Kagoshima on 14 August. The ship, the 282-ton, three-masted barque *Satsuma* was completed and launched at William Duthie Jnr's shipyard in Aberdeen early the following year, 1864.[9]

The commander of the *Satsuma* for the maiden voyage to Japan was Tom's older brother, William. The ship was built for Charles Glover - now a registered shipbroker in Aberdeen.[10] This was Charles' first recorded involvement in his younger brother's adventures.

The year ended with Tom and Jim Glover settled as partners in Glover & Co. in Nagasaki. They had been joined by their brother, Alexander Johnson, in the latter part of that year. Charles was running the show from the Aberdeen end, and with William shuttling between there and Nagasaki, five of the six Glover brothers were employed on the *Satsuma* project. Alfred, the youngest Glover boy, was thirteen years old in 1863 and still attending the Gymnasium school in Old Aberdeen. It would be four more years before he too would sail for Japan and become embroiled in the affairs of Glover & Co.

The Glover family were visited by two of the fugitive 'Choshu Five' during this period.[11] It is not known if the two - Ito and Inoue - stayed at the Coastguard station house or at nearby Braehead House which became the Glover family home when Tom's father retired from the service in August 1864.[12] Certainly for a period at this time the Glovers were listed as occupying both houses.[13]

It would seem certain that Ito and Inoue were shown round the shipyards of Aberdeen by Charles Glover during their stay in the Bridge of Don. Perhaps they viewed the *Satsuma* in the stocks at William Duthie's yard. The two Japanese were enjoying their stay in Victorian Britain. After their extremely rough trip to London from Japan they had arrived in England in mid-October. There they had been met by Hugh Matheson, of Jardine, Matheson's London office, and from then on treated as VIPs. Alexander William Williamson, Professor of Chemistry at University College London, became their guardian and friend - the company could clearly pull strings at the highest level.

They lived at Williamson's home and, later, joined by the remaining three of the 'Five', tried to take in as much of Western life as possible. There were visits to factories and shipyards and to universities, galleries and museums as well as simply making friends with many of the University students they met.

It was during this period they would have made their trip to Aberdeen.

How much practical knowledge was absorbed by Ito and Inoue is not known. But a third member of Glover's 'Five' - Yozo Yamao - was much more technically inclined than the politically motivated Ito and Inoue and he would later study shipbuilding practice and theory in Glasgow. Yamao's stay in Scotland would prove to be the best investment of all in Japan's future - and perhaps the first step in Japan's emergence as a world leader in technology.

These impressions of Victorian Britain would remain with Glover's 'Five' for the rest of their lives - they now had a model to which Japan must aim. Britain was also a small group of islands off the coast of a large continent - if they could do it, why not the Japanese?

# Chapter 9

# SHOWDOWN AT SHIMONOSEKI

The Satsuma were not Glover's only customers for ships at this time. Certainly he had formed very strong links with that clan and a Satsuma trading station was set up in Nagasaki early in 1864. Toamatsu Godai, a progressive young Satsuma samurai, was assigned by his superiors to run this station.

But Glover sold ships to others. His company began to sell ships on commission for Jardine, Matheson, and others, or they would buy and use ships themselves and then sell them. In the beginning the trade in ships was mostly in second-hand, Chinese river boats and coasters. Some had boilers and hulls which were dangerously thin and some were bad enough to have had wooden plugs jamming the holes. A few even exploded before they could be used at all.[1] And yet there was no shortage of buyers. The Japanese, though, were quick to learn. Glover would write to Jardine, Matheson that year informing them that the Japanese ship buyers were insisting on Dutch engineers checking the ships' boilers during the customary trial run before buying.[2] And as far back as 1862 the Japanese had specified new boiler tubes in some contracts.[3] No checks would have been required on the modern, Aberdeen-built *Satsuma*, which in early 1864 was heading for Nagasaki skippered by William Glover.

Two of Glover's 'Choshu Five' were also speeding back to Japan that spring of 1864. Ito and Inoue had read in *The Times* of their own Choshu clan's attacks on foreign shipping. The attacks had started around the time the 'Five' had left the year before - but the report also told of the plans of the Western navies now to settle that score, much as the British had settled the Satsuma business at Kagoshima. The two Choshu samurai had now seen the might of the West for themselves. They wanted to pass on to their clan leaders what they had observed in Britain and at all costs prevent a confrontation with the West - at least until the Japanese were ready. Abandoning their studies, they left London for Japan on the first available ship.

Glover meanwhile was moving into the arms business in a big way. In April Satsuma requested 3,000 Minié-style rifles from him - a huge order, doubtless noted by the shogun's spies.[4]

If Glover was worried by this commitment to the rebellious and increasingly anti-shogun Satsuma clan it did not show. His company was now the biggest foreign concern in Nagasaki with ten European employees running its various enterprises - and this number did not include Alex Glover who had joined Jim and Tom earlier that year. A fourth brother, William, had arrived in Nagasaki on the *Satsuma* in the late spring of 1864. All four were involved in the Nagasaki regatta held in May of that year.[5]

In that contest Tom and Alex Glover won a silver tankard, the 'Sakkicup', for clipper gigs. Ryle Holme, a Glover & Co. employee, won the 'Nagasaki Cup' - all the indications are that despite the underlying political tensions things were quiet and reasonably settled in Nagasaki at that time.[6]

The *Satsuma* was Glover & Co.'s first venture into shipbuilding. Unfortunately, this ship had a very short life. William Glover had remained skipper and was captain when the *Satsuma* was reported lost off the Japanese coast in June 1864.[7] It went down in a storm in the Sea of Japan. This disaster to their glittering new vessel did not put the Glovers off the shipping business. William survived the sinking and returned to Aberdeen.

By midsummer the Choshu blockade of the Straits of Shimonoseki had been going on for over a year. A strong force of British, French, Dutch and American warships were being assembled to discipline the Choshu extremists. The shogun, under pressure from the foreigners to act against the belligerent Choshu, had ordered a land-based attack on the clan by Satsuma. Although no blows had been struck this move caused resentment and some age-old enmity between these rival clans resurfaced.

Around the middle of July Ito and Inoue were back in Japan. The British Minister, Alcock, newly returned after home leave, saw an opportunity of using the two in a last-ditch attempt to prevent hostilities over the Choshu blockade. Alcock 'delivered to them a long memorandum for presentation to their prince' - it was nothing less than the immediate and unconditional reopening of the Straits as well as an indemnity. Only these actions would now get the Choshu off the hook.[8] Accompanied by Ernest Satow of the British Legation, and several other officials, the two set off from Yokohama on 21 July 1864.

Two British warships - HMS *Cormorant* and HMS *Barrosa* - carried the group up the Bungo Channel towards Shimonoseki where they anchored off Himeshima island on the night of 26 July. Early the next morning they landed the Japanese on the island of Kasato, off the coast of Suwo.

Satow had translated Alcock's ultimatum into Japanese for delivery to their lord. After a year in Britain these two young men needed all the courage they could muster to offer to go on their own and deliver the demands of the 'barbarians' to the Choshu extremists - one observer with Satow remarked that their chances of getting their heads removed 'were six or seven out of ten'.[9] The British promised to return and pick them up on 7 August.

Arriving back in the dark of the evening of 6 August, they found Ito and Inoue already waiting. They had survived their mission but the reply they brought from the Choshu was verbal and evasive although the clan agreed they could not fight the West. Ito and Inoue went further. Privately they admitted to Satow that war was the only way to settle the matter. They suggested that the foreigners should throw the shogun 'overboard'; that they should go straight to Osaka, where the Emperor's ministers were based; that through these ministers they should conclude a treaty with the Emperor. They claimed the shogun's policy was not to limit trade with the foreigners - it was to keep all the lucrative foreign trade to himself. Finally they claimed that 'these feelings were shared by most of the people of the country'.[10] Satow now became convinced - as had Glover the year before - that the future of Japan lay in the hands of young men such as Ito and Inoue.

But there was no way this kind of answer could satsisfy the foreign powers waiting in Yokohama - now with an assembled naval force of seventeen warships and 1,500 Royal Marines.

With the shogun apparently at a loss, the foreigners took action. On 5 September 1864 the multinational force of warships, more than half of them British, entered the Straits. The Choshu shore batteries were shelled heavily and troops landed to dismantle them. The shogun's dread of a united and powerful Western alliance confronting a divided Japan was now a fact. The Choshu quickly capitulated and agreed to reopen the Straits and pay the indemnity. Their protest in the end had been useless and the lesson was there for all to see - Japan could not fight these 'barbarians' until they had the ships and arms to match them. More humiliation came for the shogun when his government finally agreed to pay the $3 million cost of the Western expedition against the Choshu. Like the bombardment of Kagoshima the year before, the attack on Shimonoseki had a chastening effect on the Choshu clan. Younger, more progressive, members of the clan - men such as Ito, Inoue, others of Glover's 'Five' as well as the home-based Takayoshi Kido and Shinsaku Takasugi - began to take over. As with Satsuma, blind fanaticism was no longer an option.

The Choshu crisis had an adverse effect on trade but Glover's company appears to have been immune to this downturn. In fact, 1864 was the first of Glover & Co.'s boom years. Even in September, the month the Choshu crisis came to a climax, Glover had been asked by Jardine, Matheson to sell their steamer *Carthage* in Nagasaki. He could write back encouragingly to their Hong Kong office on 3 October:[11]

"Re *Carthage*

Yesterday the Japanese visited the steamer and expressed themselves quite satisfied ...

... Tomorrow Dutch engineers from the Factory are to examine her thoroughly [boiler tubes had given trouble on the trip from Shanghai to Nagasaki]

... Have done my best to overcome this by seeing the engineers who are to examine the *Carthage* who fortunately are very great friends of mine ...

... I have obtained from the *Fusiyama* ... some new tubes and I am in hope that all may yet go well."

But this letter contained in its final paragraphs details of a potential moneyspinner that would make even the commission on the sale of the *Carthage* look small - the supply of gold to the Japanese. Earlier he had asked Jardine, Matheson to ship 100 gold bars. Now he could reply:

"... the 100 Bars sent per *Pembroke* I have sold at $220 per Bar, this I have done more as an experiment in order to get into some arrangement for larger transactions. I have received an order for a monthly supply of 1,000 Bars but I think if you sent me one lot of 1,000 pieces I shall be better able to advise you as to future shipments...

... In sending over gold please have it packed as Mexican dollars as I find some of my American neighbours are very anxious to find out my friends ..."

The Chinese had enjoyed the gold supply monopoly to the Japanese and would not have been pleased by these developments. Glover went further in a letter dated only two days later, 5 October - an indication perhaps of his anxiety on this - asking if Keswick would consider a loan of $200,000 to the shogun's government. This loan, he felt, was a good investment as well as the possible means of securing the contract to be the sole suppliers of gold to the Japanese.[12]

Business continued to boom for Tom. Apparently the inspection of the *Carthage* by his Dutch engineer 'friends' had gone well. A 'present' of £100 each to the engineers presumably helped. He wrote to Hong Kong on 24 October:[13]

"We are enabled by this opportunity to advise the sale of the st. *Carthage* for $120,000, a figure which we trust will be considered to be very satisfactory by your Shanghai House...

... *Carthage* today will be formally transferred to the Japanese government."

The capitulation of the Choshu did not entirely stop the terrorism which persisted throughout 1864. In one night that year alone ten Japanese who dealt with foreigners were killed or wounded in what must have been planned attacks.[14] It was still a very dangerous place in which to live and work. Two British soldiers - Major Baldwin and Lieutenant Bird of the 20th Regiment - were assassinated at Kamakura on 20 November 1864 by two samurai. These two brought the number of foreigners murdered in Japan since July 1859 to thirteen. But things were changing. For the first time the murder of foreigners was publicly declared to be a crime - up to that point the shogun's fear of an anti-foreign fanatic backlash had prevented this - and the murderers of Baldwin and Bird were to suffer the ultimate shame for a samurai and his family. They were publicly decapitated - purposely not allowed the warriors' death of ritual suicide, *hara-kiri* - and their heads displayed under placards stating their crime.

The year 1864 saw the beginning of the rise of Glover's company to heights he could only have dreamed of. It had not been all success - the high purchase cost of tea had forced the closure of his expensive refiring plant - but there were compensations.[15] There was the gold, the ships and, more ominously, the arms to take up the slack.

The samurai now beginning to exert influence in the formation of Choshu policy, like those of the Satsuma, were joining the queue for ships and arms at Glover's Nagasaki base. These emerging leaders wanted nothing less than the ending of the shogun's rule in one form or another. Ito and Inoue's connections with Glover were well known by the Choshu decision-makers. These connections would be used to the full to win favour for the clan from the Scotsman. Only he could bypass the shogun's ban on the import of ships and arms to their clan. To add to the confusion the shogunate itself wanted to use Glover's expertise in gaining the same commodities - ships and arms - as well as gold. He had begun a rather precarious tightrope walk.

The shogun's laws were now being disregarded entirely by Glover. There was a total ban on the export of rice but he had been approached by 'many of the smaller princes' who were anxious to buy ships but had only rice with which to pay for them. He wrote to Shanghai at the end of October:

"I am sending you over musters of Japanese Rice for which please give us quotations by an early opportunity and keep as secret as possible this Rice business as I hope if I can once break the Ice by obtaining one cargo a large trade and many steamer sales can be arranged."[16]

Jardine, Matheson's reply was positive but warned Glover to make allowance for the loss of weight in the rice while in transit.[17] Neither Glover nor Keswick mentioned the shogun's ban on the export of rice.

The British Minister, Sir Rutherford Alcock, left Japan on 24 December 1864 en route to London before being appointed Minister in China in April of the following year. Alcock had not been popular with the resident traders in Japan whom he had once called 'the scum of the earth'.[18] The correspondent of the *Japan Times* judged him as being not up to dealing with the 'young, ardent, active spirits' of the merchant adventurers.[19] Whatever the case, his post was temporarily filled by Charles Winchester, the Yokohama Consul, until the arrival of a new Minister.

On 31 December 1864 James Glover resigned from Glover & Co. and headed back to Aberdeen. He had been with Tom in Japan for just over three years.[20] His departure split up the three Glover brothers in Nagasaki but appears to have been well planned. Tom, Alex and the eight others running Glover & Co. continued to expand the business.

At the end of August that year Glover senior, still chief officer of the Bridge of Don Coastguard, had retired on an annual pension of £70 - after a career of twenty-seven years in the service.[21] The family were relatively well off and Braehead House, or Cottage as it was then called, became their only residence. Young Tom's profits on the *Satsuma* and *Carthage* deals alone were many times more than his father's annual income. He was well on his way to becoming very rich.

## Chapter 10

# ARMING THE REBELS

Tom Glover emerged in the 1860s as the greatest rebel of them all in the movement to bring down the shogun. The dealing in tea and silk went on but now more and more of his time was spent looking for and supplying ships and arms. His gold business had run into trouble - the Japanese had compared his metal, supplied by Jardine, Matheson, with that of the Chinese. They claimed Glover's gold was nine per cent alloy and wanted the price dropped accordingly. Glover believed that the company's gold was not at all inferior and was sure the Chinese were obstructing the deal.[1] He carried on with the gold dealing but the general impression at this time is that his attention was centred on arms and ships.

Glover was no arms expert. He had started from scratch, not knowing how or what to import. Jardine, Matheson kept clear - at least at the start - of this Glover venture, so little documented evidence has survived.[2] What is clear is that Glover was in at the beginning of this very lucrative enterprise and that he did not take long to establish contacts with arms suppliers - mostly of rifles - in Britain and in the Far East.

But Glover did more than simply supply arms to the rebels at this time - he became involved in dispatching a second group of young renegade samurai to Europe. Assisting bright and progressive young Japanese overseas to see the West for themselves would do more to bring down the shogun than any amount of arms.

His second group - the 'Satsuma Nineteen' - left for Europe in the spring of 1865. The idea had apparently been raised earlier that year by Toamatsu Godai, Satsuma's agent in Nagasaki, while a guest at Glover House. Godai wanted the best and brightest of his clan's young samurai to follow in the wake of the 'Choshu Five' who had gone two years before. Glover considered the idea and took it up enthusiastically. The Satsuma clan now unreservedly wanted to absorb Western technology. Glover was prepared to back up the plan with his own cash and more importantly he agreed to try to persuade Jardine, Matheson to help. With the company's world-wide connections, the Satsuma men would be well looked after.[3]

It is easy to imagine Glover and Godai - at twenty-six, the Scot was four years younger than the Japanese - perhaps sitting out on the verandah of Glover House in the cool of the evening and enjoying a drink as they worked out their plans. Nagasaki harbour below them would have been lit by the reflections of the ships at anchor there as well as by the blazing lights of the surrounding hills.

Glover soon after left for Shanghai and further discussed the matter there with William Keswick. Arrangements were finalised and in April 1865 the nineteen young Satsuma students left for Europe on a Jardine, Matheson ship. They were under the care of Ryle Holme of Glover & Co. and the group included Godai himself as well as a second sprinkling of young men who would become influential in post-shogun Japan. The Satsuma clan agreed to deliver cargoes on order to Glover & Co. for Jardine, Matheson's credit until their debts were cleared.[4]

The Choshu clan did not want to be outdone by the Satsuma. Now much more so than their rivals, they were on a collision course with the Japanese government. The shogun had announced an expedition to discipline the clan - now controlled by rebels - on 6 March.[5] Choshu desperately needed to arm and train their army and navy before they could fight. The access to rifles and ships was through Glover and by early 1865 he was in close contact with their agents in Nagasaki.

In other moves behind the scenes at this time, Satsuma and Choshu were putting out feelers towards an alliance of sorts - the idea of these two powerful clans united would have indeed frightened the shogun.

The acting Minister, Winchester, was well aware of what was going on. The shogun had protested in January 1865 about the secret arming of the 'rebellious Prince' by foreigners from ports outside those recognised by the Treaty.

Winchester, in answer to the protest, sent a circular to all British Consuls in Japan reminding them of the Treaty requirement that trade could be carried out only in recognised ports - and that even in these Treaty ports the sale of arms to all but the Japanese government was prohibited. The sting was in the tail of the circular - the Consuls had to tell the traders that 'British ... subjects engaging in any illegitimate traffic would forfeit ... any claim to protection and should be dealt with as the consul saw fit'.[6]

The message was clear: be caught running guns to Choshu and the British and the shogun would be on your back. Glover would have to convince the British that the rebels' cause was the right one but he must have understood, too, that the shogunate was the recognised government of Japan and that his Minister had to follow international rules of law. He chose to ignore the warning. In the meantime the shogun's preparations for war against the Choshu went ahead.

Two Choshu men arrived in Nagasaki in the spring of 1865 hoping to get abroad with Glover's help. The new British Consul in the port, John Frederick Lowder, and Glover convinced them that it would be better for them to stay in Japan and instead attempt to have the Choshu port of Shimonoseki opened to foreign trade.[7]

All the Japanese were aware at this time of the imminent arrival of Rutherford Alcock's replacement as British Minister in Japan - the formidable Sir Harry Parkes. Parkes had been assigned to the hot seat of Japan to straighten out the British side of the complicated diplomatic mess of shogun, Emperor and clan lords. Britain's power and influence at this time was paramount. The factions vying for power in Japan would clearly try to make their point of view the most compelling one to the new Minister.

Parkes came to Japan at the age of thirty-eight, leaving his post in China where for many years he had represented Britain and gained a reputation as a very brave and uncompromising diplomat.[8]

Glover's two Choshu visitors gave him a letter to pass on to Parkes whom they knew would be stopping off at Nagasaki on his way to take up his new post in Edo. Choshu knew also that the shogun would give Parkes a one-sided view of the rebel clans as being anti-foreign and they wanted to correct this. The letter suggested that the new British Minister send his own representatives to the individual clans and he would then find out that the daimyo of Japan were not anti-foreign.

New information now reached the shogun about more guns being delivered to Choshu. He ordered his Navy, such as it was, to stop these violations.[9] At this time Tom was buying some of the arms himself on the open markets of Hong Kong and Shanghai and travelling back to Japan with the contraband - now he had the shogun's Navy to avoid as well as the pirates who plagued the China coast.[10] Certainly he was back in Nagasaki by the last week in June. At the beginning of that month the shogun had left Edo to take charge of his armies which were assembling near Kyoto for the assault on Choshu.[11]

Nearing the end of the month, the arrival of Harry Parkes was expected daily but the acting Minister, Winchester, was still handing out warnings to the gunrunners. On 22 June he issued an official notification to 'all British merchants, traders and shipmasters resident in or frequenting Japan' that Her Majesty's warships would support the officers of the shogun in their measures for its [gunrunning] suppression.[12] Glover would presumably now be dodging the Royal Navy too.

Sir Harry Parkes arrived in Nagasaki on 27 June 1865. He took the opportunity of spending a few days there to acclimatise himself with Japan before heading on to Edo - a week's sail to the north-east. He arrived in Nagasaki on the British Far Eastern squadron's flagship, HMS *Princess Royal.* Vice-Admiral George King was the squadron commander and he and Sir Harry entertained the prominent British citizens resident in the port on the night of their arrival.

Glover's own description of that first meeting is revealing. He describes how Vice-Admiral King[13]

"... then took Parkes and myself and some others out for supper. At about one o' clock, when supper was finished, everyone left except Parkes and I.

'Somehow I've got to help the shogun for the sake of Japan's future,' Parkes said.

I answered, 'You don't know it, but the future of Japan is in the hands of the southern daimyo. Japan's future depends on them.'

Parkes didn't agree with me. We talked on till dawn. Parkes couldn't decide whether he should support the shogun or the Satsuma and Choshu clans."

Glover had lost no time in putting forward the case for the rebel clans. The new British Minister appeared to need more convincing - presumably all he had heard of the Satsuma and Choshu clans up to this point was of anti-foreign belligerence. Glover needed more time to convince him that the situation was not quite that simple. The Scot saw things in black and white - Parkes the diplomat was perhaps taking the broader view. Still, it had been a promising start.

Parkes was described as a 'small, wiry, fair-haired man with a great head and broad brow, almost out of proportion to his body; he was absolutely fearless, very excitable and quick to anger'.[14] Clearly he impressed the residents of Nagasaki at that first meeting after what was considered to be the negative approach to trading of his predecessor.

The day after Parkes' arrival a presumably tired and hungover Glover was writing to Armstrong & Co. at their Elswick Works in Newcastle. He ordered 'thro' Matheson & Co. London' a total of thirty-five Armstrong guns and ammunition - a shopping list of arms costing $183,847 - for 'the Japanese governement'. His letter to Armstrong's went on:

"We urge you to hasten the order as the Japanese government is extremely anxious to have the guns with as little delay as possible.

... We shall be obliged by your adding anything that you may consider necessary to make the guns more complete. As this is the first shipment we have ordered we are unacquainted with minor details."[15]

This order for the shogun - with a profit of $40,000 - seems quite incredible at a time when Glover was risking his life to supply the rebels.[16] It stretches belief further when, as will be seen, Tom passed on his Armstrong guns profit, and more, to the Satsuma. And that same month of June the clan had asked for and received from him a further hundred Minié rifles.[17]

Nagasaki was still a very dangerous place to be that summer of 1865. Three days after landing there Parkes wrote to the Foreign Secretary, Earl Russell, in London. He mentions in his letter the latest outrage in the port - a Japanese fanatic rushing through Nagasaki's foreign settlement with drawn sword - on 11 June. Apparently the would-be assassin had wounded one European and five Chinese before escaping 'under the eye of a Japanese guard'.[18]

But Glover was now involved in a much more dangerous business. Ito and Inoue of Choshu arrived undercover in Nagasaki at this time to complete negotiations for arms and ships started in secret earlier that year. The two were now dealing directly again with their mentor Glover and surely would have discussed in detail their trip to Britain and their stay in the Glover family home in Aberdeen. They presented him with a photograph of the 'Five', taken in Maule & Co.'s London studio in 1863. But soon it was down to business. They bargained for 7,300 Minié rifles and the ammunition to go with those arms.[19] They discussed the purchase of vitally important ships. When they had arrived in Nagasaki the two knew they were marked men and so disguised themselves as Satsuma samurai and put up at the Satsuma trading station in the port. These arrangements needed the assistance of Ryoma Sakamoto - a Tosa clan rebel based in Nagasaki who was trying to bring together the rebel clans - and Takamori Saigo, Satsuma's military commander-in-chief. Every move was now crucial as Choshu and Satsuma edged towards an anti-shogun alliance. Glover later recalled that dangerous summer of 1865:[20]

"They [Ito and Inoue] wrote to me before they came to Nagasaki. Originally they hid out at the Satsuma residence. They came to me a number of times, always at night. They came not only to buy small arms but a steamship as well. They always came disguised as Satsuma samurai. When I sold them the guns and the ship they gave me a deposit, the arrangement was that the balance was to be paid in yearly instalments."

Ito and Inoue's visits were made while Glover was sheltering other Choshu renegades. Risking the wrath of the British as well as that of the shogun, Glover was now orchestrating the beginnings of the rebellion proper:

"It was like this. I hid many renegade Choshu at my place. Aoki, Kido [a prominent Choshu rebel leader] too was there. The authorities found out and made attempts to capture them. They were carrying guns, in my garden at night, but pretended to look as though they were trying to shoot birds. They came at night and often went away in the middle of the night.

That same year someone from the authorities complained to the British Consul that I had been hiding Choshu rebels and this caused a lot of problems for me. The Consul told me that if I was protecting such people he would have to expel me from Nagasaki ...

But I liked what Kido had been doing. He wanted to open ports and lead Japan towards Western civilisation. I agreed with him and I didn't care what happened to me, I wanted to help him escape. That night [Kido was being pursued by pro-shogun samurai and had asked Glover for help] I put him on board a ship of mine which then sailed.

Next morning when I was asked why I let the ship sail, I said it had to go for repairs."

Glover was not exaggerating British displeasure. The shogunate was still the recognised government of Japan and Sir Harry Parkes quickly left no reason for doubt. The shogun had announced the dispatch of two warships to seize any vessel they found proven to be gun-running and asked Parkes to pass this intelligence on to all British ships in the areas concerned. Early in August Parkes issued a 'Notification' to all British subjects on the shogun's move and went further by adding that Vice-Admiral King's squadron would be assisting the government's ships in surpressing this 'illegal trade'.[21] Yet despite numerous warnings and threats during these years no evidence has survived of any effort on the part of the British to apprehend or penalise any of the smugglers.

Glover had calculated a profit of $40,000 on the sale of the Armstrong guns to the shogun - the deal clinched apparently when he sent the order to Newcastle at the end of June. The profit, of course, was supposed to be split with Jardine, Matheson. But Glover at this time was beginning to act independently. On his own authority he advanced $30,000 to Satsuma - apparently for the purchase of silk in the interior - his own Armstrong guns profit as well as half of Jardine, Matheson's to a clan he knew was on the brink of joining Choshu in open rebellion against the shogun.[22]

In mid-October the 'Japanese government' had paid Glover the first instalment of the Armstrong guns money - $40,000.[23] One crucial move now followed another and the stakes were rising. Through Jardine, Matheson Glover had arranged for £70,000 to £100,000 to be made available for purchases for his 'Satsuma Nineteen' then in Britain. The only stipulation to the Satsuma use of Jardine, Matheson's money was that any articles bought were forwarded by the multinational.[24] In an attempt to boost imports into Japan, the company had earlier sent Glover $100,000 to invest in Japanese currency.[25] These figures would suggest that at this stage Glover was implicitly trusted by Jardine, Matheson and that his business was booming - his confidence and self-assurance is evident in his correspondence.

Near the end of 1865 Glover was able to keep his promise to Choshu's Ito and Inoue when the steamship *Union* was delivered to their clan. Not only had he begun to bring together the Satsuma and the British - he was also becoming deeply involved in settling the differences between Satsuma and Choshu. Ryoma Sakamoto, the Nagasaki-based Tosa clan renegade, was the main architect of this vital reconciliation. Inoue had gone to Kagoshima in September to offer Satsuma the Choshu clan's formal thanks for their help in rearming the clan through Glover.

Only one year before a Satsuma army led by Saigo had marched against Choshu, under orders of the shogun. But the progressive elements in both clans now held power. The close links now forming between these formerly hostile clans were further blows to the shogun - as was Glover's strengthening of Choshu's forces. The clan's modern weaponry would prove to be of crucial importance in the coming conflict. The trade in arms was big business for Glover. British Consular Reports on Trade put the number of rifles imported during the years 1865-8, in Nagasaki alone, at more than 170,000. These were valued at $2.4 million, more than £500,000.[26]

Open warfare had so far been avoided but it could not be held off very much longer.

# Chapter 11

# SAMURAI IN ABERDEEN

With his seemingly endless efforts for the rebels in 1865 it is difficult to imagine Glover finding time to concentrate his attentions on anything else - but he was doing things in this period which would make him famous and his name long remembered.

He managed to import the first steam locomotive into Japan from Shanghai. Railway tracks, a couple of hundred metres long, were set up beneath his house on the waterfront of the Oura coast road on which to run it. This was a sensational new development and the Japanese were mesmerised by this latest example of Western technology - at one point apparently driven by Glover himself. Visitors came from all over to gaze open-mouthed at this new wonder. Glover's vision appeared to have no limits and he acted quickly and decisively. This was a strength but it would prove to be a weakness, too, as events would show. His locomotive, the British-built *Iron Duke*, ran on a 2 ft 6in. narrow gauge rail, burned Japanese coal, and pre-empted Japan's first steam-driven train service using locomotives by seven years. Eventually his *Iron Duke* was moved to Osaka for more demonstrations. The Nagasaki runs of his steam train in 1865 could have been little more than a publicity stunt - his isolated port and home was too far away from the heavily populated central belt of Honshu to have any practical hopes of a permanent railway at that time.[1]

Aberdeen was the destination of at least one of the 'Satsuma Nineteen' sent to Britain by Glover in April 1865.[2] In the Granite City Charles Glover was then thirty-five and the newly returned Jim thirty-one. Neither was yet married and both were still living with their parents at Braehead House. There had been little disruption to the lives of the family with the move from the Coastguard station the year before. Braehead is situated about a mile upriver from where the Coastguard house stood and enjoys a magnificent setting overlooking the famous Brig o' Balgownie.

Martha Anne, the only Glover girl, had married her sweetheart James George of Old Aberdeen. At the wedding ceremony held in the Coastguard house four years before, Martha had been a very beautiful nineteen-year-old. Charles Glover was James George's best man and had been closely associated with his new brother-in-law's shipbroking and insurance business for some years.

The Georges were now living at No.11, Chanonry, close to St Machar's Cathedral and the Gymnasium school. Early in 1864 Martha's first child, a daughter Mary, had died before reaching her second birthday. A few months later Martha gave birth to her only son Charles at her home in the Chanonry. She would have been nursing this baby boy when her brother Jim returned to Aberdeen from Japan early in 1865.

On his return Jim had joined with Charles in forming Glover Brothers (Aberdeen) Shipbrokers Ltd. Their company's first office was located at No.19 Marischal Street, the steeply banked road between the harbour and the east end of the city's central thoroughfare of Union Street.[3] Their office overlooked the shipyards as well as the harbour of Aberdeen and Martha's husband James continued to run his business from the same address. It would seem certain that the move of Jim to Aberdeen and the setting up there of Glover Brothers would have been discussed and agreed to by Tom before his brother had left Japan.

Alfred, the late arrival of the Glover family, was fourteen in 1865 and still attending the Gymnasium, the third Glover brother to do so. No doubt he spent the long evenings of the spring and early summer of that year listening enraptured by the fireside of Braehead House to brother Jim's tales of mysterious Japan. Two years before, Alfred had met Ito and Inoue, the Choshu rebels on the run from the shogun, when they had stayed for a spell at the Glover home in Aberdeen. Now, he had learned, a third fugitive was on his way to Braehead, this time for an indefinite stay. The Glovers were becoming entwined with the power struggle in Japan and with the development of the country - and this at a time when Japan was unknown to the vast majority of Aberdonians.

In the midsummer of that year Kanae Nagasawa - one of the 'Satsuma Nineteen' - arrived in Aberdeen and moved into Braehead House. Clearly this move had been arranged by Tom Glover. The Satsuma youngster was about the same age as Alfred and was soon enrolled at the Gymnasium. As day pupils at the school, Alfred and Nagasawa would have walked there together daily over the Brig o' Balgownie and on by the Seaton Estate into the Chanonry and Old Aberdeen - much as Tom and Alex had done ten years before. For lunch the boys could have walked the short tree-lined route to Martha's house. Alfred Glover was young Nagasawa's first native English-language teacher and the Japanese boy would prove to be a brilliant pupil.

Some of the finest ships then being built anywhere in the world were beginning to come to Japan through the Glover brothers and Aberdeen's shipyards. These yards were at the peak of their fame and this reputation for excellence clearly rubbed off on the Japanese. In August 1865 the

*Owari* was launched at John 'Yankee Jack' Smith's yard in Aberdeen. The *Aberdeen Journal* report of the launching of this 'beautiful clipper' says in part:

"This vessel has been built to order of our enterprising townsmen Messrs Glover and is intended for the Japan trade, for which ... these gentlemen do a large business ... As the vessel slowly moved into the water, she was gracefully named *Owari* by Mrs Glover. Among those present were four Japanese officers of distinction, who are in this country on a visit."[4]

Owari was the name of a then pro-shogun clan in the Japanese power struggle and the 'four officers of distinction' at the Aberdeen launch were samurai loyal to the shogun. A group of eleven high-powered Japanese government officials - which included a Commissioner for Foreign Affairs - were then on a visit to Britain and presumably the 'four' were part of this delegation.[5]

Kanae Nagasawa of Satsuma was living at Braehead House at the time of the launch. Also living in the mansion were the two Glover brothers who had arranged the building of this fine ship. Yet Nagasawa's very presence in Aberdeen was illegal as far as the shogunate was concerned and the punishment for illegally leaving Japan was death.

It is fascinating to wonder if the four samurai knew of Nagasawa. Presumably they did not, but if they had been told would they have attempted to assassinate the young Satsuma rebel? And what would have been the reaction of Victorian Aberdeen to a clash of samurai in the city? In any case it is most likely that Nagasawa was kept well hidden in Braehead House during the launch of the *Owari* and the stay of the shogun's samurai in Aberdeen.

Another mystery in the *Aberdeen Journal* report is the 'Mrs Glover' who launched the ship. Charles or Jim had not yet married and the only woman who could have fitted the bill was their mother Mary. Tom received $30,000 for his ship.

On 7 September 1865, Jim Glover married Jane Donnell of Manchester and the ceremony was held in her home parish church of Staleybridge.[6]

The year 1865 had been a boom year for Nagasaki and for the Glover brothers there and in Aberdeen. More than 200 ships had docked in the Japanese port. Twelve ships had been sold for almost $700,000 - five of them by Glover & Co.[7] The report for the year by the British Consul in Nagasaki reflected the boom:

"Notwithstanding the continued unsettled state of internal affairs in Japan, that trade in Nagasaki is prospering, and continues to improve. ... Many visitors from China remain here during the summer months to recruit their health ... and bungalows for their reception are rapidly being built in the beautiful hills surrounding our charming lake like harbour."

There were now around 150 foreigners in Nagasaki, half of them

British. At twenty-seven, Glover was not only the leading member of the group, he was also by far the best-known Westerner to the Japanese. He had reached the point in his career where he could have retired to Scotland a very wealthy young man. He decided to stay.

# Chapter 12

# the gReatest rebeL

J im Glover moved with his now pregnant wife Jane into a house in Old Aberdeen's Chanonry - possibly No.11 which was occupied by his sister Martha and her family - early in 1866.[1] He would have commuted the couple of miles daily from his new home to the Glover Brothers' office in Marischal Street. There was plenty to keep the Aberdeen-based Glovers busy. Charles and Jim were keeping their eyes on the stocks of John Humphrey & Co.'s yard - visible from their office windows - where the *Kagoshima* was nearing completion. This was their next Japan-bound ship. Built this time for the Satsuma clan, with Tom as intermediary, it was a 'beautiful and graceful white ship' crafted with the bow for which Aberdeen-built ships were now becoming famous.[2] A fifth Glover brother became involved at this stage - William was the designated captain of the *Kagoshima* and its destined maiden voyage was to Japan.

Tom Glover was meanwhile directing operations in Japan as the inevitable civil war drew ever nearer. He continued to push the Satsuma cause, convinced of the sincerity of the clan's daimyo and of the justness of their case. In business he had found that the Satsuma daimyo had been 'most honourable in all his dealings and without a single instance of attempt at fraud'. The dealings Glover referred to were major ones - fifteen steamers, one sailing ship and two more of each on order. Satsuma was indeed a 'potentially great source of business'. He considered himself the only foreigner 'personally known' to the daimyo.[3] Tom was clearly encouraging co-operation between Satsuma and Jardine, Matheson and pushing for his own company to be their intermediary. He was not pleased with Jardine, Matheson's high interest rate - the rival Netherlands Trading Society was charging a good deal less - and claimed that it was only his belief in the future of Japan which made him continue.[4] There is no reason to believe that Glover was not entirely sincere in his claim.

Early in 1866 Glover finally arranged the crucial visit of Sir Harry Parkes to Kagoshima. He had first met the British Minister at the end of June when Sir Harry had stopped at Nagasaki on his way to take up his post in Edo. He had then apparently put forward the justness of the rebels' cause. Now, with Parkes resident in the British Legation in Edo, he felt the time had come to press his case further. He had received a request from the Satsuma daimyo asking that he pass on to the new Minister and to the commander of the British squadron the following message: 'We were once at war with each other but now we want friendship with you. Please come at once to Kagoshima.'

Glover claimed he did go to Edo and passed on the Satsuma request. The reaction of Parkes at this stage is not known but Glover left Edo for China shortly after as a passenger on the British commander's ship.[5]

Back in Nagasaki after his China trip, Glover was himself invited to Kagoshima by Tatewaki Komatsu, a leading Satsuma rebel. He was, of course, well known to the Satsuma leaders, having stuck by the clan after the bombardment of Kagoshima two years before. His company was continuing to deal heavily with the clan - to the point of standing as guarantors for them at this time in a bank loan.

He took up the Satsuma invitation and set off for the clan's stronghold of Kagoshima in the ship *Otento Sama*.[6] The Satsuma leaders were aware of Glover's mansion in Nagasaki and of his retinue of servants 'which would befit a daimyo of 300,000 *koku* income'.[7] He was given full honours on his arrival in Kagoshima. A four-gun salute was fired and he was presented with a gift of cycad trees which he later planted in his garden and which remain there to this day.

Glover and the Satsuma daimyo Shimazu got on well - they went out riding together alone, an honour usually reserved by a daimyo only for fellow daimyo.[8] They talked of trade and politics. Tom was again asked to use his influence and attempt to talk the British Minister into visiting Kagoshima. They felt sure that if only Sir Harry could be persuaded to listen to their case, he would be convinced. Takamori Saigo was one of the clan leaders involved in these crucial talks.

But it wasn't all politics. Glover took time off from the discussions to make the short sea trip to the Ryukyu chain of islands. These islands stretch from the south of Japan to Taiwan and included Okinawa. They were under the control of Satsuma but China had long disputed ownership. Glover was interested particularly in the sugar factory the clan had established there. He was very much interested too in handling the clan's silk trade and urged them to deal directly with his company, rather than through silk brokers.

The results of the talks were that Glover agreed to attempt, again, to persuade Sir Harry Parkes to visit Kagoshima.

From Kagoshima the seemingly tireless Scot travelled back to Edo. He repeated his case to Parkes for Satsuma recognition and asked him to go to Kagoshima to see for himself. According to Glover, Parkes heard him out then laughed and pointed to one of his aides and said, 'I often intended to visit the Satsuma resident in Edo, but this man stopped me from going.'[9] He goes on to say that the next morning he rose early and woke up Parkes' aide. Foreigners at the time were not allowed out without a personal bodyguard but Glover and the aide left the Legation on their own. A Japanese guard spotted them and warned them of the danger of being out unprotected. Glover ignored the warning.

They went into the Satsuma *yashiki* (residency) and were welcomed by the clan's representative and given tea and cakes. The result of the visit was that the Satsuma resident promised to call on Parkes the following day. When Glover reported to Parkes on the intended visit to him by the Satsuma man, the Minister was surprised. He warned a hovering shogunate official not to interfere. Clearly the shogun would not have been pleased by these developments.

Next morning the Satsuma representative called as planned and talked with Parkes. The meeting was a success. Before he left for Nagasaki Glover was given what he had struggled for months to achieve - an assurance from Parkes that if a proper invitation was sent to him by Satsuma, he would visit Kagoshima.

Reinstalled in Nagasaki, Glover passed on the news of his Edo trip to Satsuma's agent Komatsu. Preparation for a formal invitation for Parkes to visit Kagoshima was the result.

As Glover fought the Satsuma case with Jardine, Matheson and the British diplomats in Japan, the two main rebel clans were drawing ever closer. It is inconceivable that Glover - with his almost blood-brother connections in both rebel camps - was not aware of the negotiations then going on between the two regarding an anti-shogun alliance. Kido of Choshu, saved from capture by Glover the year before, led his clan's delegation at the secret talks held in Kyoto early in 1866. Takamori Saigo represented Satsuma and, pushed by Ryoma Sakamoto, eventual agreement was reached.[10]

The alliance was signed on 7 March 1866. The main clause was that if the shogun attacked Choshu - and this was looking more and more likely - Satsuma troops would assemble in Kyoto and Osaka. This action would restrain the shogun. Now, armed and backed by Glover and Satsuma, the Choshu felt strong enough to take on the man whose family had provided Japan's military rulers for the previous two centuries - the fourteenth Tokugawa shogun.

A week after the secret alliance was signed Ernest Satow - the translator and aide to Parkes at the British Legation whose views were now identical to those of Glover - published an article in the *Japan Times*. He was openly critical of the shogun: 'and to arrogate to himself the title of ruler ... was a piece of extraordinary presumption on his part'.[11] The article was translated into Japanese and widely circulated as official British policy, despite Parkes' apparent lack of knowledge of it.[12] Glover agreed entirely with the sentiments in the article - in fact, could have written it himself. Yet despite the apparent personal nature of the attack on the shogun in the article, it is clear that Satow - and Glover -

were targeting the entire bakufu for removal. They were well aware that the young shogun was merely the figurehead for the oligarchy within the government making the real decisions. But the article added to the pressure on the shogun to be seen to be acting quickly and decisively.

The pressure was not only being applied in Japan. In Britain some of Glover's 'Satsuma Nineteen' were playing their part. In the last week of March one of them, Koan Matsuki, had several interviews with the Foreign Secretary, Lord Clarendon, in London. The interviews had been arranged by the Foreign Office official, Laurence Oliphant, hero of the attack on the British Legation four years before and a friend of Matsuki and Glover.[13] The Japanese restated the arguments of Glover and Satow - that the great daimyo felt no hostility towards foreigners and that their resentment was against the shogun's monopoly of trade. And that if a new government, more broadly based and centred on the Emperor, was set up then Japan would accept its international commitments and live up to them. Clarendon was impressed. A dispatch to Sir Harry Parkes followed, suggesting that he might try to interest the shogun in broadening the Japanese political process. Glover and Ernest Satow were already pressing the British Minister in Japan and a Glover protege was now applying pressure in London.

As Matsuki argued his case in London, 500 miles north in Aberdeen the *Kagoshima* had been launched. Nagasawa was still living at Braehead House but was not in hiding for the launch of this ship, his own clan's finest. With the Glover brothers he is certain to have attended the ceremony.

The leader of Glover's 'Satsuma Nineteen' - Godai - in his letters home was full of praise for Western law, science and technology. In England Godai negotiated the purchase of equipment for Japan's first modern spinning plant. He even went as far as to arrange for his clan's products to be shown at the Paris Exhibition planned for the following year of 1867, at which for the first time in Europe the Japanese had a major display. Godai had learned much from his mentor Glover and like the Scot was thinking on the grand scale.

A second *Japan Times* article by Satow, published in May, stoked the flames of civil war as another long hot summer approached. This time he wrote of the shogun's 'assumption of a dignity which did not belong to him' and of 'the proved treachery of the shogoon in the affair of Shimonoseki'.[14]

Glover's Nagasaki was meanwhile retaining its reputation as the main centre for dealing in clandestine arms. The captain of the US steamer *Anna Kimball* was fined $1,000 at his Consul's court there on 30 May for gun-running. But the stakes were too high and the profits too great for fines to be a deterrent. Glover continued to be the main source of arms for the rebel clans.

The foreign community in Nagasaki appear to have been well

insulated from the excitement of the impending war. Glover was chairing meetings of the British Club and even found time to contribute $100 towards the stipend of a new chaplain. The port's annual regatta went ahead in May as normal with several Glover & Co. men winning prizes. The Westerners gathered for a photograph on a picnic outing to Nezumishima off the Nagasaki coast - Glover appears centre front of the group, legs outstretched and completely relaxed. The only suggestion of concern is the rifle he is cradling in his arms.

He was in trouble with his Consul again that summer - this time for installing a battery of cannon in the hillside garden one level beneath his home. The shogun's representative complained of this breaking of the Treaty and demanded the cannons' removal.[15] What these instances show is that he was still a prime target for assassination and that he was augmenting his bodyguard with his own forms of defence.

But life in Nagasaki was normal enough for Alex Glover to marry in the middle of that year. His bride was Ann Finlay of Newhills near Aberdeen and the ceremony was performed in Nagasaki on 1 June 1866. It is not clear if Alex met Ann in Aberdeen prior to going out to Japan and later sent for her after he had established himself in his brother's company. Another possibility is that Ann went out east to visit her sister Isabel who was married to a James Smith of the Imperial Chinese Customs service. On the visit she may have met and fallen in love with the good-looking, fair-haired brother of fellow Aberdonian Tom Glover. In any case, what turned out to be their stormy marriage had begun.

In June 1866 the shogun's armies at last invaded Choshu territory and the long-expected civil war began in earnest. Glover's persistence now paid off and Sir Harry Parkes announced his intention to visit the Satsuma clan in Kagoshima. Admiral King, Lady Parkes, Dr William Willis and several other officials made up the British group which left Edo for the Satsuma capital on three warships of the Royal Navy. Glover, recognised as the organiser of the trip, was to join the party in Nagasaki.

Admiral King travelled south ahead of Parkes and stayed for some time at Glover House. The Scot was at this time being spied on by the French as well as the Japanese. French policy in Japan was broadly pro-shogun. Their Minister in Edo was Leon Roches, 'a handsome swash-buckler', who was advising the shogun to crack down on the rebels.[16] Parkes and Roches reportedly 'hated one another and were as jealous as a couple of women'.[17] Whatever was the case their policies were entirely different.

French Consuls and agents helped to keep their Minister, and through him the shogun, informed of the comings and goings at Nagasaki. The French Consul in the port reported on King's arrival:

"The English commander came here on the *Princess Royal* and is expected to stay here, at the home of Glover, for a month. The Minister is also due. Choshu is receiving many weapons through Satsuma assistance in Nagasaki and others are being imported through Glover and other Englishmen. The small steamer *Otento Maru*, with English officers aboard, has headed for the Ryu Kyus, but is now speeding here again. It is probably going to be handed over at Nagasaki for Shimonoseki."[18]

Sir Harry and his party landed in Nagasaki on 9 July. The three British warships - *Princess Royal, Serpent* and *Salamis* - left a few days later for Kagoshima.

Shortly after Glover and the British delegation had left, the French Minister arrived in Nagasaki, anxious to find out what Parkes and Glover were up to. He was approached by some Satsuma men who cordially invited him also to visit Kagoshima. He refused.[19]

'The sun shone from a clear sky, and the sea was calm and beautiful, on the 27th July 1866, when HMS *Princess Royal*, followed by the *Serpent* and *Salamis*, steamed into Kagoshima harbour.' This memory of the historic visit was recorded by an officer on one of the British ships.[20] He noted that Sir Harry and Lady Parkes were aboard the *Salamis*, while Glover and some others remained on the *Princess Royal*. A salute of fifteen guns was fired from the Satsuma shore battery and the officer remembered his last visit to Kagoshima three years before when the guns were firing in earnest. Satsuma's 'Prime Minister' and other dignitaries came on board. Later a party of the British went on shore, including Sir Harry, and were greeted by thousands of locals, most of whom had never seen a European.

Glover had prepared well and the visit was a resounding success. One dinner lasting five hours had forty different dishes and was served with British beer, sake and foreign wines.

According to Glover:

"Parkes and I travelled to Kagoshima on the British warship *Princess Royal*. We stayed there for several days. We went hunting and they showed us military exercises, they treated us very well. When Parkes met Shimazu Saburo [Regent and effective ruler of the clan] for the first time, the Satsuma Lord said, 'What happened in the past should be forgotten. Let us be friends from now on.' They gave Sir Harry and Admiral King splendid presents, which was a very exceptional thing for them to do. But we didn't have anything to give them back, so we sent Shimazu a gun.

Later, after the visit to Shimazu was over, Parkes said to me, 'I've been a fool. I never believed what you said but now I realise what the Japanese daimyo have been thinking. The reason the daimyo and Britain did not get together was that the Tokugawa [shogun] and his officials came between them.'"[21]

Glover was not exaggerating his influence which during this period was paramount. It is verified in a letter - none too complimentary to the Scot - dated 30 September 1866. The letter was written home by Dr

Willis, a member of the British delegation and a house guest of Glover's in Nagasaki on a previous occasion:

"There is a merchant at Nagasaki named Glover who supplies the intelligent and simple-minded natives of this part of the world with arms and many other useful and dangerous appliances. Now the prince [Satsuma daimyo] is deeply in debt to the House of Glover & Co. and as this is a great lever, and as our chief [Parkes] is always ready for anything, Mr Glover arranged an interview [the Kagoshima trip] and, as far as I could see, he was by far the most important visitor, Minister and Admiral included."[22]

Willis' letter contains barely concealed contempt for the Satsuma leaders - particularly for Shimazu whom he considered to be a scoundrel, the man who had ordered Richardson's murder in 1862. This perhaps explains his bitterness towards Glover, the driving force behind the moves to bring together the British and the Satsuma.

Despite the reservations of Willis, there had been some straight talking between Parkes and the Satsuma leaders. The British Minister was well known for his bluntness and he told Takamori Saigo, when that Japanese criticised the bakufu, that the shogun was a problem for the Japanese to solve, that foreigners should not become involved. But the overall result of the talks was an increase in understanding, even friendship, between the British and the rebels although Parkes was not told of the recently signed agreement between Choshu and Satsuma. A decided shift in British policy towards the rebels after the Kagoshima trip is clear. It is fair to say that the trip struck a death-blow to the bakufu. The boost to the rebels of establishing formal contact with the then British superpower cannot be exaggerated - or the effect of the visit on any potential rebels at that time still undecided on which course of action they should take.

Reinstalled back in Edo, Parkes as usual was frank at a meeting with Leon Roches, telling him what had happened at Kagoshima. Roches wasted no time in warning the shogun that Britain was now backing the rebels. He urged the shogun to crush the Choshu rebellion quickly. He promised that if arms were needed, the French would help.

After preliminary skirmishing, serious fighting had broken out between the armies of the shogun and Choshu clan on 18 July. The Choshu rifle units, heavily outnumbered but well armed by Glover and also well drilled in European tactics, proved to be the decisive factor. They held and pushed back the initial thrust of the shogun's dispirited troops in the battle which came to be known as the 'Four Borders War'.

At sea Glover's *Union* was heavily involved in naval battles between the ships of the shogun and Choshu on 28 July.

Choshu, too, had requested a visit from Parkes through Glover, but the outbreak of war had necessarily cancelled this. Parkes asked Tom to go in his place but for some unknown reason Glover refused. Later that year Admiral King made the trip to Mitajiri and there met Mori, the clan daimyo, and his son. King sent Glover photographs taken at his meeting with the Choshu daimyo.[23]

By the late summer of 1866, the shogun had been humiliated by his forces' failure to crush the Choshu rebellion. The whole fabric of the bakufu now began to crumble.

Sir Harry Parkes' report on his visit to Satsuma was a neutral one. But Japanese newspapers saw the visit as the first step towards the moves advocated by Satow in his articles earlier that year - the beginning of the end of the office of shogun and of the bakufu as a system of government. Glover almost certainly was the newspapers' source. Significantly, he is not mentioned by Parkes or Admiral King in their official reports, nor is there any mention of his behind-the-scenes work in his correspondence with Jardine, Matheson at this time. He was on his own, doing what he thought was best for Japan.[24]

The young shogun Iemochi died on 19 September 1866 of beriberi. No immediate successor was named but the shogun's death brought about an uneasy truce in the war with Choshu which was going so badly for his armies. Iemochi died in Osaka - the first shogun to die outside Edo since his family had assumed the title 200 years before.

The arms trade at Nagasaki continued to increase - now even more so with fear of the shogun's displeasure no longer valid. The rebels could now become bolder and the British, though still nominally neutral, were more or less openly backing them. There were dissenting voices among the British diplomats - the Consul, Abel Gower, continued to argue the case for a strong central government, shogun-led or not. He felt that the overthrow of the shogun would lead to the formation of states within a state - that the daimyo would become little shoguns, all controlling their own territory and that trade would suffer. Glover disagreed entirely and the two argued violently - the Scot perhaps feeling he was more aware of Japanese thought than the Consul.[25]

In the latter part of 1866 Glover became involved in a ritual Japanese suicide and the memory of the event lived with him into his old age. The man concerned, Shojiro Uesugi, was one of the tight group of twenty or so renegades formed by Ryoma Sakamoto who had based themselves in Nagasaki. Like many of the other anti-shogun rebels, their original intention had been to rid Japan of all foreigners. Sakamoto's group had gone further than most by making a blood oath to achieve that end.

But the situation in Japan had changed rapidly and many of the rebels no longer felt there was the same pressing need to expel foreigners. They felt that there was much to be learned from the Westerners - for the good of Japan. Uesugi was one of these.[26]

He had been influenced by a pro-Western samurai and friend of Glover - Komatsu of Satsuma. Perhaps jealous of the dispatch of the 'Satsuma Nineteen' to Europe the year before, Uesugi pleaded with

Japanese merchants dealing with Tom
Glover, Nagasaki, early 1860s.
*(Courtesy: Dr Sharp)*

Glover House, Nagasaki, 1863. Tom is
standing far left, next to the seated Edward
Harrison. Jim Glover is seated on the right.
These were dangerous days, note the rifle
held by Tom's guest.
*(Courtesy: Dr Sharp)*

Sir Rutherford Alcock, first British Minister in
Japan. From Charles Glover's collection.
*(Courtesy: DGO Carmichael)*

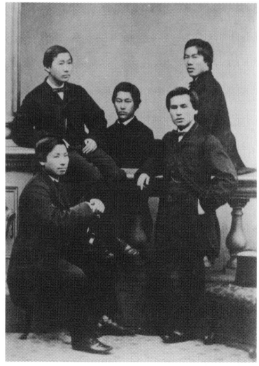

The Choshu Five, taken in the London studio of
William Maull & Co. In 1863 and presented to
Thomas Glover on the return of Ito and Inoue to
Japan. Back three: Kinzuke Endo; Yakichi Nomura
later Viscount; Hirobumi Ito (later Prince). Front
two: Kaoru Inoue (later Marquess); Yozo Yamao
(later Viscount). *(Courtesy: Nagasaki City Hall)*

HMS Cormorant in Nagasaki harbour, early 1860s.
*(Courtesy: DGO Carmichael)*

The *Kagoshima*, built through the Glovers in Aberdeen for the Satsuma Clan, 1866.
*(Courtesy: Aberdeen Maritime Museum)*

The *Ho Sho Maru* in Aberdeen harbour, late summer 1868. The funnel of the warship has still to be fitted.
*(Courtesy: Aberdeen Maritime Museum)*

LOG of the "*Ho Sho Maru*" from *Aberdeen* Bound for *Nagasakie*

| H. | K. | F. | COURSES. | WINDS. | Lee Way. | REMARKS on *Wednesday* the 5th day of *Sept* 18 |
|---|---|---|---|---|---|---|
| 2 | | | | | | The Steam Ship "Ho Sho Maru" left Aberdeen dock at 2 P.M. |
| 4 | | | | | | to sail out to Nagasakie under Canvass drawing 9 feet |
| 6 | | | | | | 3 inches Aft and 9 fet 2 inches forward, Commanded by |
| 8 | | | | | | Capt Henderson and twelve of a crew of whom are |
| 10 | | | | | | the following, William Leslie Chief officer, Alexander Topper |
| 12 | | | | | | Second officer Robert Johnston Carpenter James Davidson |
| 2 | | | | | | Steward Samuel Ritchie Cook. John Kenedy. William |
| 4 | | | | | | McLachlan. John Ledingham. Wm Law. William Thatch |
| 6 | | | | | | John Thatch Able Seaman. James Hare & John Gun Ordnary |
| 8 | | | | | | Seamen. Ship intending to go South by the English Chl |
| 10 | | | | | | Robert Souter Pilot. Tacked twice in the Bay |
| 12 | | | | | | at 4 P.M. left the bay Wind at South by West |

| True Course | Distance. | Departure. | DIFFERENCE | | LATITUDE. | | LONGITUDE. | | | VARIATIONS. | | Barom. | Thermom. | Symples. | Bearing. | Distance. |
|---|---|---|---|---|---|---|---|---|---|---|---|---|---|---|---|---|
| | | | Latitude. | Longitude. | By Account | By Observa. | By Account | By Chronom. | By Observa | By Account | By Observa | | | | | |
| | | | | | | | | | | | | | | | | |

Master. *William Leslie* Mate.

| H. | K. | F. | COURSES. | WINDS. | Lee Way. | REMARKS on ............ the ...... day of ......... 18 |
|---|---|---|---|---|---|---|

The first page of the log of the maiden voyage of the *Ho Sho Maru* from Aberdeen to Nagasaki. The original log is held in Aberdeen Central Library's Local History Department.
*(Courtesy: Aberdeen Central Library)*

The giant, ultra-modern *Jho Sho Maru,* later re-named *Ryujo Maru,* Victoria
Dock, Aberdeen, 1869.
*(Courtesy: Aberdeen Maritime Museum)*

Rifles, cannon and samurai guard. The garden of Glover House, Nagasaki, 1866. Tom Glover is sitting
centre, facing camera. Mounting these cannon infuriated the Governor of Nagasaki.
*(Courtesy: Yomigaeru Bakumatsu)*

Nagasaki's foreign community at a picnic on Nezumishima Island, near Nagasaki, in 1866.
Tom Glover, aged 28 and the leader of the residents, is lying down, front centre, cradling
a rifle. Alex Glover is sitting fourth from left, second row.
*(Courtesy: Yomigaeru Bakumatsu)*

Original caption reads *Prince Satsuma and two brothers.*
Mid 1860s, Kagoshima. From Charles Glover's collection.
*(Courtesy: DGO Carmichael)*

Admiral King with Mori, the Choshu Daimyo, and son,
Shimonoseki, 1866.
*(Courtesy: Yomigaeru Bakumatsu)*

The last Tokugawa Shogun, c. 186?
*(Courtesy: Yomigaeru Bakumatsu)*

Tom, second left, drinking tea in the garden of Glover House, shortly before leaving for
Aberdeen in the spring of 1867. Brother Alex on extreme right.
*(Courtesy: Yomigaeru Bakumatsu)*

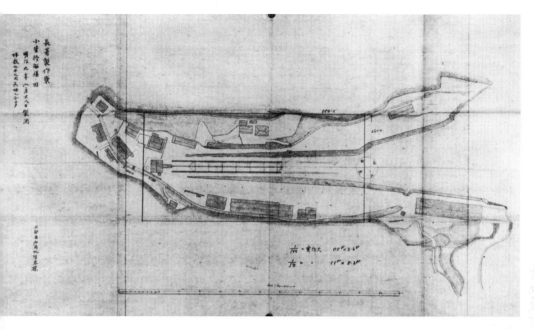

Nineteenth century Hi-Tech. The plans for Kosuge Dock.
*(Courtesy: Nagasaki City Hall)*

Kasoge Dock, Nagasaki, after installation. Made in Aberdeen for the Japanese.
*(Courtesy: Nagasaki City Hall)*

Aberdeen, summer of 1867. Only known photograph of the six Glover brothers together, taken during Tom's trip home that year. Standing, left to right: Alfred, Charles, Alex. Front: left to right: William, James, Thomas. James died, aged 33, in September of the same year.
*(Courtesy: Nagasaki City Hall)*

Takashima Coal Mine, 1870s. Glover – in blac[k] hat in centre truck – supervising operations.
*(Courtesy: Nagasaki City Hall)*

Nagasaki, lit up for the Royal visit, 1869.
*(Courtesy: Yomigaeru Bakumatsu)*

Komatsu to ask Glover to help him get abroad to study. Komatsu did approach Glover eventually and the Scot agreed to help the young samurai. He gave him money and arranged a passage for him on a Glover & Co. ship which was scheduled to leave for Europe. Uesugi had been very grateful to Glover and promised him his samurai swords in thanks and as a reminder of him. Presumably the two precious swords would not be needed by Uesugi while in Europe.

On the day planned for Uesugi's departure, the wind was blowing in the wrong direction and after boarding his ship in Nagasaki harbour he was told it could not sail. Glover went out to see him:

"I said to him, 'You will soon be leaving home, why don't you go back ashore and have a good time? You will only have to return to the ship by tomorrow morning.'

Uesugi got off the ship and went into a tea-house.[27] At that time Mutsuoki was in the tea-house.

While Uesugi was drinking in the tea-house, Sakamoto Ryoma came in and said to him, 'You are unforgivable. We made an oath. We even sealed our promise with our blood. How can you run away?'

'Goodbye,' said Uesugi.

Next morning Sakamoto came to me and told me what had happened. Sakamoto had made Uesugi admit that he was [now] against the expulsion of foreigners and that he had forced him to commit ritual suicide ... They told me that Uesugi had commited suicide very bravely.

I asked Sakamoto why Uesugi had to kill himself.

He said, 'We made an oath. He died because he broke that oath.'"

Glover was clearly upset about the young samurai's death and his bitterness is apparent, even when reminiscing on the events as an old man.[28] Perhaps he blamed himself because he had sent Uesugi ashore from his ship. He remembered Uesugi's promise of his swords as keepsakes:

"'All right,' I said. 'Uesugi gave me his word that I would get his swords. So, will you give them to me?'

They said they couldn't.

'This is ridiculous,' I told them. 'You made Uesugi kill himself because he broke his word. You are responsible for what happened. I have to get those swords at all costs.'

Sakamoto's face went blue and he said he would think about it. Later he brought me the large sword but not the small one."

Glover kept Uesugi's sword in his various homes over the years until it was destroyed in a fire.

By the end of 1866 Glover's two Aberdeen-built ships - the *Owari* and *Kagoshima* - had arrived in Japan. These were not obsolete, former Chinese coast tubs; they were state-of-the-art merchant ships, vessels of which any nation could be proud. There would rightly have been a stir in the shipping world of Japan on their arrival. Glover & Co. were expanding in Japan and in China too. The company had a staff of seventeen Europeans in Nagasaki, five in Yokohama and four in Shanghai.[29] The total now employed in all the company's various enterprises was in the hundreds and in the tea business alone in the thousands. At this stage Glover could well have dreamed of challenging the giants of the trading world - even Jardine, Matheson and the Netherlands Trading Society would have been in his sights. Ryle Holme, the young adventurer who had escorted the 'Satsuma Nineteen' to Europe the year before, had returned and become a partner in the firm. And it was not predominantly trading in arms that Glover saw as his company's future strategy; there was now a decided shift in his business towards the industrialisation of Japan. It is certain that Glover sensed the end of the civil war was not far away and that Japan would soon settle into its own industrial revolution.

On Christmas Day 1866 in Nagasaki, Alex Glover's wife of six months, Ann, gave birth to stillborn twins. Shortly before this the brothers had heard of the birth of Jim Glover's son Lindley in Old Aberdeen that September. It was a busy end of the year for Glover. Two days before Christmas Admiral King and Ernest Satow had arrived in Nagasaki on the *Princess Royal*. They were on a fact-finding visit for Sir Harry Parkes, who wanted to make clear to all concerned the British position of neutrality in the civil war.

One of the facts Admiral King would have discovered was that Glover was again in trouble with the Japanese authorities. On Christmas Eve the shogun's governors of Nagasaki wrote to the British Consul there protesting at Glover having sent three more students 'to Hong Kong and England' earlier that month. The ban on foreign travel had been lifted but a passport from the shogunate was now required and Glover had ignored this. When he had been questioned by officials of the governors he had replied 'that he allowed them to leave without waiting our decision because the steamer could not wait'.[30] Glover was suitably reprimanded by the Consul but appears at this stage to have been a law unto himself.

Many years after the events of 1866, Glover mused on the whole affair and of his involvement in bringing down the shogun.[31] He claimed that he did not do what he did simply to make money, 'that was not in his nature'. From the evidence of his relentless and highly dangerous trips in 1865 and 1866, trying to bring together the rebels and the British, as well as gun-running, there must have been some conviction on his part that the rebel cause was right. On a strictly business basis, it would have been infinitely easier for Glover to have dealt with the shogun and his supporters - his Armstrong guns deal with them is a good example. Discussing the period later, Glover commented:

"Anyway, the person who was most helpful [in the whole affair] was Harry Parkes and the best thing I ever did was to break down the wall between Satsuma and Choshu.

Tom Glover was a rebel, certainly. He had been in Japan long enough to appreciate the finer points of *bushido*, the code by which the samurai lived. In many ways he had began to think like a samurai:

[During those years] I dealt with most of the southern daimyo. I dealt in millions of Yen. But what I want to say is that in all the business I did [with the daimyo] there was never any bribery, not even for one sen ... no one did such a thing. There were one or two exceptions, like Aoki Gunhei [who Glover claimed had tried to kill him], but even they did what they did with the spirit of a samurai. It is important that no samurai used a bribe. Even if they had wanted to, they couldn't."

Clearly Glover was influenced by the code of the samurai. He concluded:

"Up to now, for the past five or six years [the interview was given around 1910], many people have come to ask me about those times. I've thought about it for a long time and of all the rebels who fought against the Tokugawa [shogun], I was the greatest."

Glover's claim to have been the 'greatest rebel' is more than simply an old man's bravado. He was instrumental in bringing down the last shogun. He had become a Scottish samurai.

# Chapter 13

# ENTREPRENEUR

The fifteenth and last Tokugawa shogun was installed on 10 January 1867. Yoshinobu Tokugawa took up the post reluctantly - he was an able and intelligent thirty-year-old, well aware of the precarious state of the Shogunate. He was in close touch with the French Minister, Roches, and clearly had been convinced that the traditional power of the shogun could be revived.

Glover's attention was at the time on other things. He owed Jardine, Matheson more than $100,000 but appears not to have been over-concerned about it.[1] With complicated arms and ships deals taking up his time, this apparent lack of concern is understandable. Between 1864 and 1867 Glover sold twenty ships in Nagasaki alone for a total of more than $1.17 million.[2] He had become rich and famous. But the signs of a slackening in the arms trade had certainly been noted and acted on.

For some time he had been talking to officials of the Hizen or Saga clan about the development of the Takashima coal mine near Nagasaki. The mine was situated on Takashima island where the Hizen clan dug the surface outbreaks of coal until sea-water ingress halted their progress. This primitive process had gone on for many years but the point noted by Tom was the high quality of the coal. By early 1867 he had at least a mental list of what was required to bring this mine up to date. Glover did not have a technical background but he did know that the lie of the Takashima coal seams was very steep and that hauling machinery was vital to even start to realise the mine's potential, and that forced ventilation and reliable pumps to keep out the sea water were essential. For these things and for advice on development of the mine he would have to go to Britain.

Then there was the slip-dock planned for Kosuge on the Nagasaki waterfront, just below and to the west of Glover House. Glover and the Satsuma daimyo - the owner of the land - had decided to go ahead with this massive project and excavations began that year of 1867 at Kosuge to accommodate the planned facility. The excavations were reputed to be costing Satsuma $10,000. It had been agreed between Glover and Satsuma that the dock and its steam machinery would be constructed in Aberdeen, then disassembled. This method would require a specially designed cargo ship to bring out all the components to Nagasaki for reassembly. They planned for a dock capable of accommodating ships of up to 1,600 tons on a carriageway 220 feet long.[3] The capacity and dimensions of Glover's planned dock would have had Nagasaki buzzing with excitement. Perhaps after all it wasn't a dream to imagine Japan as a country capable of building and repairing ships or as the coal-mining centre of the Far East.

Glover had firm commitments, too, for ultra-modern warships to be built for the Japanese clans. The first of these orders - from Choshu - was already in his hands.

The mine, the dock, the warships - it was all happening and these plans clearly show the shift from a merchant dealing in quick-profit war materials to an entrepreneur with the vision to see Japan as an industrial and maritime power. He began thinking of a trip to Aberdeen to get these projects off the ground.

Glover's decision to go back to Aberdeen at this time may well have been brought on by the death of Emperor Komei on 3 February 1867. Komei had never concealed his anti-foreign feelings but the new emperor, his fifteen-year-old son Mutsuhito (later known as Emperor Meiji), promised to be more tolerant. With the new shogun's future uncertain and a new Emperor in Kyoto perhaps Tom felt he could now concentrate his attention on the beginnings of an industrial revolution - and this meant a trip to Aberdeen.

Business continued to grow in the early part of the year - despite the Jardine, Matheson debt. Near the end of March he sold a warship to the Tosa clan's agent in Nagasaki, Shojiro Goto, a samurai with whom Glover would have many dealings over the years; the second-hand gunboat *Nankai* brought in $75,000. Another Tosa man arrived in Nagasaki on behalf of his clan on 10 April, just as Glover was preparing to leave for Aberdeen. Yataro Iwasaki was a low-ranking samurai, sent to run Tosa's Nagasaki trading station. Iwasaki and Tom became firm friends - the Japanese would go on to found the Mitsubishi Empire.

Another reason for Glover's trip home could have been the return to Nagasaki of Kenneth Ross MacKenzie. The older Scot, now in his sixties, had left a twenty-three-year-old laddie still learning his trade. He came back looking for a position with the firm founded by the young man he had left behind, now one of the leading companies operating in the Far East. MacKenzie had come back with no capital to invest in Glover & Co. His business in China had collapsed after six years - the last two of which he called 'years of woe'.[4] Yet with the very experienced MacKenzie to run his Nagasaki head office, perhaps Glover felt he could now go and conduct the business which could not be done by mail.

Alex and Ann Glover accompanied Tom on the trip home. Ann would have been recovering from the loss of her stillborn twins the previous December - she would never return to Japan. The day before the Glovers left, 27 April, MacKenzie wrote to James Whittall of Jardine, Matheson. Presumably he wanted to prepare the multinational for Glover's ideas for Japan's first modern coal mine and dock - ideas which would require the kind of investment only Jardine, Matheson could supply. Part of the letter reads:

"My friend T.B. Glover leaves this tomorrow for England and will see you in Hong Kong with a view for arranging with you if possible for a credit on your London friends for a good round sum or for sterling paper.

... I feel much pleased at having the opportunity of joining my young friend after all the trouble and woes of the past two years in China, and I hope you will continue to give G. & Co. the countenance and support you have long accorded them."[5]

MacKenzie goes on to say that Glover planned to stop off at Kagoshima on his way to Hong Kong where he hoped to collect Satsuma's outstanding debt.

No record has survived of Glover's meeting with James Whittall in Hong Kong early in May that year but presumably he received the necessary backing for his projects. Glover's enthusiasm and confidence was infectious and the two brothers and Ann would have left Hong Kong in buoyant mood. As well as the business angle Tom was still not yet thirty and both his parents were alive and well and he had been gone close to ten years - there must have been a personal element involved in his decision to go home.

Tom, Alex and Ann Glover arrived in Aberdeen early in July 1867. The voyage of about sixty days would have been a time for reflection and planning. It was probably Glover's first real chance to relax since he had arrived in Japan in 1859.

Tom's mother would have noted the change in his appearance. He remained tall and angular but his hair was now shorn close to his head and already thinning. Famous in Japan and well on his way to his first million dollars, he could have basked in the limelight as the family gathered round him and Alex and Ann in the lounge of their mansion. Tom brought with him to Aberdeen at least one gift which has stood the test of time - four Japanese walnut tree seedlings were planted in the garden of Braehead House that summer.[6]

There would have been a ritual round of visits to family and old school friends for Glover to complete. A photograph of the six Glover brothers taken in an Aberdeen studio in July or August that summer has survived. It would be the last time that all the Glover boys and Martha would gather together with their parents. But with visits to Jardine, Matheson's London office, Glasgow and the shipyards of Aberdeen all lined up there was little time for socialising.

In Glover Brothers office in Marischal Street he would have unveiled, excitedly surely, his plans for the ships, the dock and the mine to Charles and Jim. Young Alfred had been barely seven years old when

Tom had left but he was now in his final year at the Gymnasium and ready to start work. William was also at home and the six Glover brothers were actively involved in all of the Japan projects. The beneficiary of the efforts of the Glovers in the summer of 1867 would be a very grateful Japan.[7]

Appointments were essential with Alexander Hall & Co.'s shipyard management to discuss plans for the dock and the warship. Suggestions were made by the Hall & Co. technical staff and the projects from start to finish thrashed out. Whether the innovative idea for building the dock in sections for shipment to Japan for reassembly came from Glover or others is not known. But it would appear from all the evidence of his other projects that he was an 'ideas' man, that the original conception was his but that the detailed engineering side was left to Hall's specialists. Meetings were held with the Hall, Russell & Co. management, too - there the Glovers negotiated the order for the specially designed ship necessary to carry Tom's dock and its machinery to Japan.

Enquiries were started into where the latest mining equipment could be bought - this was done most likely in Glasgow - and where mining experts for overseas contracts could be hired. These enquiries would have to be followed up, although possibly much of this could be left for Charles, Jim and Alex to handle after Tom went back to Japan. It was an exciting and hectic summer for all the Glover brothers. Tom had approached Charles and Jim - and possibly his father - for a loan of £20,000 to help fund the projects.[8] They obliged through the City of Glasgow Bank. Things looked promising and they were all convinced they were on their way to making a fortune.

Glover's company in Nagasaki was not idle in his absence. In mid-July it shipped '4 boxes of treasure' containing Japanese silver coin, 79,200 *ichibu* worth around $25,000, to Jardine, Matheson in Hong Kong. MacKenzie asked for the money to be relayed 'at once' to London

"to the credit of Messrs Glover Brothers Aberdeen in accordance with an arrangement made with our senior (when passing through Hong Kong in May last) and your Mr James Whittall."[9]

Clearly Glover & Co. were pulling out all the stops.

There was little time for Tom to spend with his nephew, one-year-old Lindley Glover, son of Jim and Jane, or with Martha's three-year-old boy and baby girl. Of his home 'village' of Old Aberdeen, Tom would have seen the continued encroachment by its 'big brother'. Aberdeen was still growing and would soon swallow the burgh where Tom had spent much of his youth.

It had been settled that Alfred, his youngest brother now sixteen, was returning to Japan with him and the lad would surely have been in a state of excitement at that prospect. It had also been agreed that Alex Glover would stay on in Aberdeen. Perhaps his wife Ann had not got over the loss of their twins six months before and wished to be near her family in Newhills. Alex in any case was personally familiar with the situation in Japan and could be usefully employed in the various enterprises going on in Aberdeen and elsewhere in Britain.

Another Braehead House resident and Gymnasium pupil with whom Tom would have enjoyed long talks that summer was the young Japanese, Nagasawa. It would have been an opportunity for the Satsuma samurai to speak his native language again with Glover in his adopted home. Not that the Japanese would have had any problem communicating in English. He was a star pupil at the Gymnasium, shining in Scripture Studies, French and Writing - good enough, in fact, to gain a mention in a June 1867 issue of the *Aberdeen Journal*. For a lad who two years before most likely could speak no English at all, he was very bright indeed.

Nagasawa was only one of several young Japanese studying in Aberdeen at that time, many of whom were staying at Braehead. Fragments of details only have survived but one of the Japanese was the son of the Tosa clan lord, another 'the son of the chief minister of the daimyo of Shimonoseki'. There was also a Mr Murata, who qualified that summer as an 'extra master' in the merchant service at the Board of Trade Navigational School in Aberdeen. All of the Japanese students in Scotland were sponsored by Glover. His sponsorship covered secretly arranging their escape and the expense of getting the young men to the other side of the world, most probably travelling on his own ships. School fees and living expenses Glover most likely paid through his family and later recouped from his business dealings with their clans. Clearly his involvement in their escape strengthened his ties with the clans. Diplomats then tended to look down on merchants. Laurence Oliphant, in a letter written to a friend at this time, mentions that he was worried about the young Japanese staying with the Glover family at Braehead, 'these merchants care for nothing but money'.[10]

Yet another young Japanese Glover would have met in Scotland was Yozo Yamao - one of his original batch of samurai, the 'Choshu Five', who had come to Britian in mid-1863. In the summer of 1867 Yamao was apprenticed at Napier's shipyard on the Clyde and was attending evening classes at Anderson's College (present-day Strathclyde University) in Glasgow.[11] It would seem likely that Tom would have fitted in a visit to see Yamao in Glasgow - perhaps when he went there on the hunt for mining equipment - or that the Yamao would have been invited to Aberdeen. All the Japanese then resident in Scotland may well have got together that summer with Glover in Braehead House. The garden of the mansion slopes down the steep bank of the Balgownie gorge to the edge of the swift and black river Don. It would have been an ideal spot for after-dinner talks in the extended bright summer evenings and nights of Aberdeen. Glover could have briefed them on the recent momentous happenings in their homeland.

Charles Glover, unmarried and at thirty-seven the oldest of the Glover boys, was going out with Margaret Mitchell of Foveran, a village just north of Aberdeen. From the evidence of the 1867 photograph Charles was at this time tall and heavily built and a successful businessman in his own right in Aberdeen. Margaret Mitchell's well-to-do family surely would have visited Braehead House to meet the famous Glover brother home from Japan.

As Tom and Alfred began their preparations for the trip back to Japan, Jim Glover became suddenly and seriously ill. He was moved from Old Aberdeen to Braehead - perhaps his illness was too much for his young wife to cope with and look after their baby. Jim died of 'chronic diarrhoea' in his parents' home on 28 September 1867. The death was registered by Jim's father - a 'Royal Navy Half-Pay Officer'.[12]

Jim had come back to Aberdeen from Nagasaki early in 1865, married his Manchester bride the following year and was dead the year after, aged thirty-three. This traumatic event would have brought the Glover family back to earth after the high of Tom's return home. The Glovers, Donnells and Mitchells gathered round his grave in the newly acquired Glover family plot in St Peter's graveyard off King Street on the day of his burial. The plot lies against the north wall of the cemetery and his remains were the first of the Glover family to be placed there on that early autumn day of 1867.[13]

The death of his brother may well have delayed Tom's return to Japan. But as the days shortened and grew cooler it was time to go. It has been suggested that a broken romance in Aberdeen, perhaps the revival of an earlier affair, prompted Glover to leave when he did, but no evidence of this has survived. Certainly he may well have planned to return to Aberdeen when his fortune was assured in Japan. It was the done thing at the time for those who had made fortunes in trade overseas to return home - to become a Member of Parliament or perhaps take a part in local politics. His distraught parents no doubt hoped that Tom would do likewise, but it was not to be. Already there were indications that his life and future were inextricably linked with that of Japan. As he left for the Far East for the second time it was not the naive, optimistic eighteen-year-old who had left ten years before. He was now a hardened businessman and budding industrialist, his name known, respected and discussed in the highest circles of power in Japan.

# Chapter 14

# the shogun's surrender

Shortly before Glover left to return to Japan the last shogun, Yoshinobu Tokugawa, handed over power to an Imperial Council of daimyo. The events leading up to this historic event in November 1867 had been relatively bloodless - although among the dead was the renegade Ryoma Sakamoto with whom Glover had strong links in Nagasaki. But as he headed back, the power struggle in Japan had still not been resolved. The shogun's most conservative supporters had not accepted his fall from grace.

Early in the new year of 1868 the rebels decided to act. On 3 January Satsuma troops led by Takamori Saigo took over the Emperor's guard at Kyoto. The rebels announced the restoration of imperial rule and the formation of a new government and order in which no followers of the shogun would be included. Even the title of Shogun was to be abolished. On 6 January the shogun and his followers retreated to Osaka where four days later he met the representatives of the foreign powers. He had apparently accepted his demise but some of his most ardent supporters had not. Near the end of the month serious fighting broke out at Toba-Fushimi between the rebels and the conservatives. The troops of mainly the Satsuma and Choshu clans - now fighting as the Imperial Japanese Army and armed by Glover with the latest weapons - were the clear winners. The defeated shogun had to disguise himself to escape capture and make for Edo. The Imperial Army prepared to follow. This was the position as Glover's ship was dropping anchor in Nagasaki after his long voyage back. What he had fought for years to achieve was now within sight.

Business had continued to go well for his company in his absence but the struggle to make tea profitable was a continuing worry. Never short of ideas, Glover had earlier come up with the suggestion that steam power should be used to sift tea in his company's three Nagasaki plants. Part of the British Consul's *Report on Trade* in Nagasaki for 1867 reads:

"A novelty in the tea firing way has been introduced by Messrs Glover & Co., one of the principal British mercantile firms established at this port. They have recently erected on their premises a machine which is so constructed as to enable them to sift tea by the aid of steam machinery. This was invented and made on the spot. It has been in working order for some time and answers remarkably well. A better constructed and finished machine is now on the way out from England, a notion of which appeared in the *Engineering* paper of January 3rd. It is a great saving in manual labour which is a great consideration in an establishment where 1,600 hands are generally employed during the tea firing season."

Again there was the state-of-the-art technology and its 'on the spot' introduction in Japan. Some, at least, of this inventiveness and drive of Glover clearly rubbed off on the budding Japanese businessmen and industrialists of the day - and has been carried on into the late twentieth century.

Shipping, though, had remained his company's major money-maker. Shortly before he left for Scotland Glover had sold the gunboat *Nankai* to the Tosa clan for $75,000. A month later the British Consul, Marcus Flowers, was protesting on behalf of Glover & Co. to the shogun's governor. He claimed that somehow permission had been witheld for Goto to take possession of the gunboat. With Glover on his way to Aberdeen, Kenneth MacKenzie would have had this headache to handle.

Another hot potato landed in MacKenzie's lap during Glover's absence. On 11 May Jardine, Matheson wrote to Glover & Co. telling them of the arrival of 907 cases of guns and ammunition from Armstrong's - the shogun's order - and an invoice for nearly £20,000. With the volatile and fast-changing political situation in Japan, Tom's colleagues would have been at a loss as to what to do with these arms - they had been ordered two years before when circumstances were entirely different.[1]

Near the end of 1867 Glover's plans for starting new branches of his company in Kobe and Osaka were coming close to reality - these Japanese ports were scheduled to be opened on New Year's Day 1868. His agency business was also going from strength to strength. He was acting for the prestigious Lloyd's and six other insurance companies as well as the major Chinese banks.

Yet despite all the successes, clouds were beginning to gather on Glover's horizon. The demand for ships and arms, formerly his company's life-blood, was now certain to drop off. Had his switch of strategy to a more industrial base been quick enough?

Tom and young Alfred Glover arrived in Nagasaki near the end of January 1868. His first letter to Jardine, Matheson on the 27th of that month complains of the hold-up of the transfer of £15,000 from Matheson & Co., London, to his partner Edward Harrison also in London 'for the building of some steamers'. Tom had taken up the mantle of Glover & Co. again - at his usual breakneck pace he was leaving for Osaka 'the day after tomorrow' presumably to supervise the opening of the new branch there and 'effect the sale of one or more of your steamers'.[2] He makes no mention of the fighting or political situation so it is most likely that at this stage no word of the battle of Toba-Fushimi or its aftermath had yet reached Nagasaki.

But by mid-February Glover was well aware of the political and military upheavals further north and no doubt was very happy with them. Again he wrote to Shanghai, optimistically forecasting 'Peace for some time to come' - in their guarded reply Jardine, Matheson asked for 'full details' of the political situation.[3]

Events in Aberdeen continued apace. The *Helen Black* was launched on 25 January - just as Glover was arriving in Japan.[4] This specially constructed five-masted clipper went down the slipway at Alexander Hall's Footdee yard that winter morning and began fitting out for its main purpose - transporting the sections of Glover's slip-dock to Nagasaki. The dock and its machinery had been built next door at Hall, Russell & Co.'s yard and Charles and Alex Glover would have been watching closely as the parts were loaded aboard the *Helen Black*. William Blaikie, a yard superintendent with Hall, Russell, supervised that job and, like the Glovers, would have some say in Japan's future as a shipbuilding nation. Skippered by A McCallum, the *Helen Black* set out on its voyage of close to three months with William Blaikie on board accompanying the sections of the dock.

Charles Glover was surely relieved to see the *Helen Black* leave. But there was much more on his plate. There was the progress of the warship ordered by Glover the year before, for example, now named the *Ho Sho Maru*. This gunboat was the first new warship specifically built as such for the Japanese and it was on order from a rebel clan, the Choshu. There had been other, second-hand Dutch or American warships in the possession of the Japanese before the *Ho Sho Maru*. Many of these had simply been merchant ships with a few light cannon added for use against pirates. In some cases the Japanese had added bigger guns but found by experiment that the ship could not take the recoil of firing. The *Ho Sho Maru* was modern and fast and would not suffer from any of these deficiencies. It was well into construction in late January 1868 and at one stage would have been side by side with the *Helen Black* in Hall's stocks.

Glover had taken another risk in having the *Ho Sho Maru* built. At the time he placed the order the Choshu clan was in open rebellion against the Japanese government which was recognised by Britain. This was a flagrant breach of neutrality and did not go unnoticed. It was perhaps a simple matter to trade in materials of war in far-off Japan but this was Victorian Britain. Later, in 1868, one of Glover's skippers was called before the Lords Commissioners of the Admiralty where he explained that he had been appointed 'through Messrs. Glover & Co. to take command of an iron-plated corvette being built in Aberdeen for the

Japanese'.[5] As the Japanese revolution was to all intents and purposes over by the end of that year Glover's disregard for British neutrality became an academic point only.

Charles was involved also at this time in the ordering of a second warship for Japan, the massive *Jho Sho Maru* whose keel was laid down in August 1868. But he had other things to think about - he married his sweetheart Margaret Isabella Mitchell in her home village of Foveran on 21 May. The marriage was a big occasion, held in her home Ythan Lodge that early summer afternoon. Charles is listed in the Register simply as a 'shipowner', while his father-in-law is a 'landed proprietor and shipowner'.[6]

In Japan the rebels appointed one of their own men as governor of Nagasaki on 15 February, replacing the shogun's representative in the port. The new government acting in the name of the adolescent Emperor Meiji acted quickly and decisively. The shogun's troops were pursued to Edo and the new Imperial Army occupied the capital in May. The deposed shogun had been living in a Buddhist monastery in Edo's Ueno district since March but was now forced into exile in Mito, a town about sixty miles north-east of the capital in an area of Japan having strong connections with a branch of the Tokugawa family. There was apparently a move for him to be executed - led by Takamori Saigo of Satsuma - but Sir Harry Parkes talked the rebels out of going that far. The remnants of the shogun's forces retreated even further north and the civil war was all but over. The rebels - armed, guided and encouraged by Glover - were now running the country.

Glover made several trips to Osaka and Kobe in the first half of 1868 to establish his company – he felt that 'an immensely large trade' would be done there, that it was the place where 'all the monied merchants of Japan' lived.[7]

Takayoshi Kido was a hero of the shogun's overthrow. This Choshu samurai, with the two Satsuma leaders Saigo and Okubo, directed the armies which had forced those of the shogun to scatter and flee north in the early part of the year. Kido was also the renegade hidden by Glover in the summer of 1866 before being smuggled out of Nagasaki on one of the Scot's ships. He met Glover again in Nagasaki on 12 May 1868. They talked over the events of the previous three years. They had a lot to say, according to Kido, after such a long time and Tom presented him with a pistol before the Japanese left at 2 p.m. - certainly there was no mention of the fighting in the north on this occasion.[8]

A week before his meeting with Kido Glover had finally negotiated an agreement on the development of the Takashima coal mine with Genzo Matsubayashi, the Hizen clan agent. Hizen owed Glover & Co. $43,750 - an unpaid debt for the steamer *Eugenie*. Glover's firm had been selling Takashima coal for some time to pay off this debt and he had long been interested in obtaining a share of the mine - what he now saw as perhaps the biggest potential source of wealth in Japan.[9] He was correct in his view of Takashima. Perhaps it was not his most spectacular development - it is difficult to make the business of a coal mine glamorous - but modernising Takashima was the biggest single contribution he made to the economic development of Japan. The mine supplied much of the energy which fuelled the industrial revolution in Japan and its exports provided the crucial foreign currency necessary to pay for it. Glover felt it necessary to use an interpreter during the long and difficult negotiations for the mine - perhaps an indication of his anxiety to get control for his own Japanese was now more than adequate. He chose Joseph Heco for the job, a Japanese-American and sometime employee of Glover & Co., who later claimed that the Glover/ Hizen contract was the first-ever instance of a partnership between a native Japanese and a foreigner.[10] Another indication of Tom's anxiety was the one-sided nature of the contract - it was heavily weighted in favour of Hizen, as will be seen.

Early in June Glover met Kido again in his Nagasaki office - Joseph Heco and Godai of his 'Satsuma Nineteen' were there also. They discussed the fighting which was still going on in isolated incidents despite the shogun's exile. Tom showed him a Yokohama newspaper which carried two articles on the 'defeat of the Imperial Army'. Kido rightly ignored the newspaper stories, but was worried about 'the fighting near Edo' and sent letters that day regarding this to the other rebel leaders. He discussed leasing a warship from Glover who replied positively and another meeting was arranged.[11]

Events swung that summer of 1868 between Aberdeen and Japan. The *Ho Sho Maru* was launched from Alexander Hall & Co.'s lower dockyard on Saturday, 4 July. The local newspaper described it as a 'fine vessel, carrying two 110-pound and two 60-pound guns on deck'.[12] A Miss Mitchell named the ship, probably a sister of Charles Glover's wife of two months, Margaret.

In Nagasaki Glover had further meetings with Kido on 5 and 10 July, but his attention had now moved to another major project - the purchase of the Hong Kong Mint for the new Japanese government. Although there is no mention of the Mint in Kido's diaries, he may well have been involved in these discussions.[13] Glover's Osaka office was handling this sale and had arranged for 238 tons of Japanese copper to be sent to Hong Kong in payment, the first load of 79 tons was expected to be shipped 'by an early steamer'.[14] By the end of the month he had arranged for the steamer *United Service* to ship the plant to Kobe and he was 'hoping to obtain from the Japanese government the full cost of transporting the Mint .. to Japan in addition to the cost of $80,000'. The net profit as usual was to be split with Jardine, Matheson.

The scene now moves back to Aberdeen where in the late summer of that year the controversial *Ho Sho Maru* was preparing to leave for

Japan. The building of this ship had already alerted the British Admiralty and to compound the matter the skeleton of her giant sister, the *Jho Sho Maru*, was beginning to form on the stocks of Alexander Hall.

On 22 August the *Ho Sho Maru* on sea trials had:

"left harbour about 12 noon, returned about 4 p.m. First half hour after leaving harbour, she made 8 knots - then second half 9 knots - this was before the wind. After she was put about she steamed under bare poles [no sails], as nearly as possible into the teeth of a stiff breeze, at the rate of 7 1/2 to 8 knots, but neither then or before were the engines put to their full speed."[15]

Hall, Russell & Co. had supplied the engine for the *Ho Sho Maru*. Considering that the firm had started the production of steam engines and boilers only four years before in 1864, they were now well established. In this period of great change from wood and canvas to iron and steam, the *Ho Sho Maru* had the best of both worlds.

Two weeks later, at 2 p.m. on 5 September 1868, this famous Japanese warship left dock in Aberdeen for its long voyage to Nagasaki.[16] The skipper, Captain John Henderson, had to tack twice in Aberdeen Bay before swinging the ship south and setting the heading for the English Channel. A crew of twelve was carried and the trip was made under sail - the engine only being 'turned over' as required.[17] Significantly, the last sight of Aberdeen harbour for the crew may well have been dominated by the burgeoning *Jho Sho Maru* in its cradle at Hall's - shortly to follow them to Japan.

There was more than enough to keep Glover occupied as he waited for word of the departure of the *Ho Sho Maru*. He was disappointed in Osaka - the bonanza he expected there had failed to materialise but his natural optimism kept him going. He had splashed out on the best available lots in the sale of land there, paying the highest prices of all in the auction.[18]

But his earlier hunch that trade in Japan was dramatically changing was proved right. Glover & Co.'s six-month circular for the first half of 1868 complained that trade had been 'limited to arms transactions' - and even these transactions were quite clearly dropping off. Even with some shogun diehards still on the loose, a post-war trade depression was settling on the country. He had banked on his new branches in Kobe and Osaka picking up business - Nagasaki was beginning to look a little isolated with the war all but over and the shift in political, military and commercial emphasis now in the east of Japan. Thirteen ships were sold in Nagasaki in 1868 for just under $700,000 - against $1.2 million in sales the year before. The British Consul would comment:

"This important transaction in the sale of vessels has vastly diminished, owing to the impoverished state of the Daimios engaged in the internecine war."[19]

But it was not all gloom and doom. Glover had his stake in

Takashima, and the *Helen Black* had arrived with the long-awaited slip-dock by the autumn of that year. Assembly had already began under the superintendence of William Blaikie.

Glover's dock brought Japan the latest in technology from one of the then top shipbuilding centres in the world. The site for the dock had been well chosen - 'expressly designed by nature for the purpose' was the way one newspaper put it. The article in that paper went on:

"A great portion of the ways are on solid rock, it being necessary only to pile about 150 feet of the deepest portion. They are warranted to support a vessel of 1,200 tons, which we think will be quite sufficient for the port. The whole of the plant and the incliners, together with the vessels to bring it out, was made by Messrs Hall, Russell & Co., of Aberdeen, and it will, doubtless, be gratifying to that well-known firm to hear of the unqualified success of the undertaking."[20]

The construction of the dock was another leap forward in the development of Japan - with Glover again at the forefront - and further proof of his faith in the future of the country.

The civil war ended in November with the surrender of the Aizu clan, the last of what had been the shogun's allies. It appears to have been of academic interest only to Glover who was working comfortably with the new Meiji government, many of whom he knew intimately. Meiji officials in Nagasaki were chasing up the Armstrong guns - bought for the shogun by Tom's company but now stored in a Glover & Co. warehouse in the port. This was embarrassing for the British Consul there who had to maintain neutrality until the Meiji government was recognised as the legal government of Japan. A number of letters passed between the new Nagasaki governors, Glover & Co. and the Consul on this matter during 1868.[21]

Government officials had also approached Tom to supply precious metals for the manufacture of Japanese coin at the new Mint in Osaka. This was big business - he was asked to provide, monthly, 35 tons of San Fransisco silver and 5,000 bars of Beijing gold. Glover was a little hesitant - surprisingly - at the amounts involved at the start, but remained convinced that the supply of gold could be very profitable. As well as supplying the Mint Glover had been offered private contracts for 100 or 200 bars of gold at around $247 a bar.[22]

Severe fluctuations in Japanese currency now began to seriously affect trade. Despite the dock and the offer to supply precious metals to the Mint - and, of course, the warships, one of which was already en route to Japan - Glover's firm was in trouble. Debts continued to pile up - his company now owed Jardine, Matheson $86,000.[23] This was only half of what he owed a year before but now the situation had changed, the war was over and the daimyo had overstretched themselves in their efforts to overthrow the shogun. It would be difficult in the short term to get paid at all and in the longer term the value of Japanese currency had been weakened by the war. Clearly what Glover needed at this stage was time and capital to see him through the post-war depression. Unfortunately at this time he had neither.

The year ended on a low note for Glover. The partnership which had brought about the phenomenal rise of his company broke up. Glover, Groom, Harrison and Holme went their own ways, failing to renew their agreement after 31 December.[24]

Glover's tea expert, the Englishman Frederick Ringer, also split from the parent company at this stage. On 2 November Ringer set up a new firm in Nagasaki with fellow Briton Edward Holme, a relative of Ryle Holme of Glover & Co. This new organisation, Holme, Ringer & Co., would have a long and illustrious connection with Japan.[25]

The Shanghai branch of Glover & Co. - run by Francis Groom and a staff of six Europeans - had in its control the very successful Union Steam Navigation Company. It used the name Glover, Dow & Co. to continue its business after the break with Tom, presumably the name Glover meant something as there was no longer a Glover family connection.

It was said later that the reason for the disintregation of Glover's company at this time was the differences of opinion between the various branches of the firm. These differences were almost certainly over the company's interests in 'certain ventures'. And these 'ventures' almost certainly involved Glover's dealings in warships and arms. The partners in his company most likely did not appreciate the debts their senior Glover had run up in his rush to supply the rebels at the height of the civil war.[26]

Glover continued his business now solely in Japan. He was back in partnership with MacKenzie. Almost ten years and several fortunes had passed since Glover and the old Scotsman had formed their first partnership. At this time Glover lost his usual optimism, at least for a while, being reported as 'entering into the new partnership [with MacKenzie] with a heavy responsibility on his shoulders'. The new partnership took on the debts of the old company - now standing at $223,411. Perhaps Glover had good reason to be depressed.[27]

He had his problems admittedly but there were bright spots too as *Oshogatsu*, the Japanese New Year of 1869 approached. There was the imminent arrival of the *Ho Sho Maru* and the good reports of the building of the giant *Jho Sho Maru* from Charles and Alex in Aberdeen. And, of course, the construction of his slip-dock at Kosuge was just about complete. There was also what he now considered, rightly, to be the biggest moneyspinner of them all - the Takashima mine.

The year of 1868 was a watershed in Japanese history. Edo, the former stronghold of the Tokugawa shogun, had been renamed Tokyo, the 'eastern' capital. The Japanese calendar would record the year as *Meiji Gan Nen* - the first year of the reign of the fifteen-year-old

Mutsuhito, later called Meiji, or enlightened, Emperor. This young man had left the 'western' capital of Kyoto and was now occupying what had been the shogun's sumptuous palace in Tokyo. Glover's rebels - men such as Ito, Inoue, Kido, Iwasaki, Okubo and Saigo - would form the new Emperor's governments and their clans would supply the political, industrial and military leaders of Japan for the next fifty years. One of the marching songs used by Glover's rebels that year would later be adapted and used by Gilbert and Sullivan in *The Mikado.* But the beginning of the reign of the real Mikado, or Emperor, Meiji was a turning point for Japan and also for the young man from Aberdeen who had done so much to put him into the palace he now occupied in Tokyo.

A young girl moved into the Glover household in Nagasaki in this period. The girl, Tsuru Yamamura or Awajiya, was even at seventeen a divorced mother of a baby girl. Her family background is unclear. It has been said that she was the daughter of a poor samurai.[28] But perhaps like many others of her day she was simply a young girl forced into a form of prostitution by her family's poverty. Whatever was the case she is unlikely to have had any say in her own future. Some say Tsuru was introduced to the Scot by Genzo Matsubayashi, the Hizen clan agent in Nagasaki who negotiated the Takashima mine agreement between Tom and his clan. There was nothing particularly unusual about the arrangement - as has been seen many of the resident bachelors had a live-in musume.

Tom may well have gone through some kind of marriage ceremony with Tsuru, as he did with Sono seven years before. No record of marriage between them can be found in the Japanese or British Consulate records, and inter-racial marriage in 1868, at least marriage in the conventional, Western sense was for most still unthinkable. But a contract of some kind, possibly involving a simple verbal ceremony, was made and the couple would remain together for more than thirty years. This would suggest that it was, or grew into, more than just an 'arrangement'.

Tom was not faithful to Tsuru over the years, but there was clearly a bond between them which overcame their problems and kept them together. In any case Tsuru, like most Japanese women at that time, would not have been expecting a husband who would not stray. She was prepared to remain behind the scenes and it would be many years before she would be accepted in public as Glover's wife. She apparently tolerated one of her husband's affairs which would later prove to be semi-tragic and may well be at the root of all the speculation behind the *Madam Butterfly*/Glover stories.

# Chapter 15

# BİRTĐ OF A NAVAL POWER

The *Ho Sho Maru* arrived in Nagasaki on Sunday 24 January 1869, passing a number of fishing boats on the way in and 'turning over the engine', according to its log-book, as it glided into harbour. Japan's first custom-built warship was ready for delivery. This was a leap into the latest marine technology for Japan - a deep-sea fighting ship which any nation would envy.

Tom most likely watched from the garden of Glover House as his Aberdeen-built warship dropped anchor against the background of his Aberdeen-built dock. The dock had opened only the week before, on 19 January, attracting people from miles around to see the first ship being hauled out of the water by steam winch and landed on to the ribbed skeleton of the dock. Glover had retained Aberdonian William Blaikie to superintend the working of his dock. Perhaps for a while, in the glow of his dock's success and the arrival of the *Ho Sho Maru*, Tom's problems of debt could have been forgotten.

Captain John Henderson presented himself and his ship to Glover and presumably handed over any messages and news from the Aberdeen-based Glovers. This would have included the progress of the *Jho Sho Maru*.

Glover was impressed by Captain Henderson. He kept him on the Glover & Co. payroll on a nominal salary of $150 a month till the end of March 1869, using his expertise to train the Japanese seamen who would be taking over the running of the gunboat.

Henderson skippered the *Ho Sho Maru* to Mitajiri for final delivery to the Choshu clan. On 5 April Glover wrote a letter of reference for Captain Henderson, praising his ability and regretting that there was no command available for him 'out here', but that he was writing to 'friends' in Aberdeen. These friends would provide the skipper with the first vacancy on any ship or steamer coming 'out here'.[1]

From the tone of the letter the impression is given that a virtual procession of ships from Aberdeen was expected. Perhaps this is just another example of Glover's basic optimism. Certainly the *Jho Sho Maru* was nearing completion in the early months of 1869 and that pleasant thought would have been occupying his mind. Tom had sent one of his captains, J.M. James - called before the Admiralty to give evidence on the breaking of British neutrality the year before - from Nagasaki to Aberdeen to supervise the building of the *Jho Sho Maru* and the installation of its armaments. Alex Glover was also involved at the Aberdeen end in this biggest of projects. Captain James was set to command the warship for its maiden voyage to Japan.

Charles Glover was the registered owner of the *Jho Sho Maru* and his company was heavily in debt for its building. He, too, was concerned with the progress. It was a massive ship for the day. At almost 1,500 tons and 207 feet long it would require a crew of more than 300 men. The contract price with Alexander Hall & Co. was £46,032. Glover had arranged to sell it to the Higo clan for $360,000 (£80,000). Even with the cost of fitting out added to the contract price it looked like a very profitable operation for the Glovers. That is if Tom was paid for his ship...

Charles' attention would have wandered for the birth of his first child, a daughter, named Margaret Isabel at their home at 2 Albert Street, Aberdeen, on 3 March 1869. The imminent launching of the *Jho Sho Maru* was at the same time causing great excitement in the city. A newspaper article complained of Aberdeen's lack of a graving dock and of its distance from iron mines. The lack of these items was giving shipyards further south, such as the Clyde and the Tyne, a great advantage over Aberdeen, the paper argued. That advantage was emphasised in this period of change from wood to iron. Perhaps Aberdeen's costs were less and its reputation for beautiful and well-made clippers supreme - in any case the choice of Aberdeen to build this highly prestigious, steam-driven warship for the Japanese seemed to indicate its continuing prosperity.[2]

In a speech to gathered dignitaries after the launch of the *Jho Sho Maru* on 27 March 1869, quoted in the *Aberdeen Journal* four days later, Charles Glover had some comments to make himself on Aberdeen's shipbuilding future:

"Mr Glover, in the course of his response, said he felt obliged for the complimentary way in which Mr Hall referred to his name. He (Mr Glover) was a man engaged in business, and he had never yet refused an order when he had thought it to his advantage to take it. (Applause) But whilst it was true he looked on orders from a business point of view, he believed he could say with truth, that he took such an interest in Aberdeen, that he would bring every order to it that he had in his power. (Applause) The orders he had already been the means of bringing in this direction, had given such satisfaction, that, he believed it was to the interest of those for whom the orders were executed to have been brought here."

Charles Glover's words were quickly backed up with action. An order had come through for a *third* Japanese warship to be built in Aberdeen.

The launch of the *Jho Sho Maru* was a big occasion in Aberdeen. The *Aberdeen Herald* (3 April) commented on the large crowd and the worry that the size of the ship would cause it to hit the opposite bank of the river Dee - as it turned out the chains held and the warship was afloat and a source of pride for the whole city. The *Herald's* report reflected this:

"Although this firm bears a world-wide reputation for their building powers, they have never till now turned out anything to compare with their latest effort, in the construction of which they have combined the greatest skill with the most unfaltering energy."

The launching ceremony was performed by Charles Glover's wife Margaret shortly after noon that Saturday in late spring. Captain James was to be assisted in his command by the chief officer, Lieutenant James Ingleback. The crew of the *Jho Sho Maru* would number 300 officers and men and the warship was expected to leave Aberdeen for Nagasaki 'two months hence'.

Heavily armed with the latest weaponry it was a very fine warship indeed and even at this early stage in the development of what would become the Imperial Japanese Navy, the Japanese were signalling to the world their intention of becoming a first-rate naval power. The *Jho Sho Maru* was now tied up at Aberdeen's Victoria Dock for its final fitting out. There it had many admirers with its Japanese sunburst radiating across the bow anchor ports. The engines were tested successfully - they could provide up to 1,000 hp. The ship's three decks were spacious and airy, the lowest of which provided the quarters for the crew. The Glover company flag flew proudly from its topmast.

The news of the launch would have been telegraphed to Shanghai and from there most likely brought by sea to Glover in Nagasaki. It was good news for him, but the Takashima mine was now beginning to dominate all of his affairs.

The agreement with the Hizen clan regarding the mine was unfavourable to Glover, perhaps a reflection of the little time he had given to the negotiations the previous year. At the time of the signing Glover was as usual juggling with several major projects. But it was signed and was scheduled to last for seven years - he had a half-stake in a mine which could be producing vast amounts of coal in the months ahead. The sale of coal or the working of his dock was not politically volatile - if he was only given some time to get his mine away his problems were over.

But Matsubayashi had struck a brilliant deal for his employer - the Hizen daimyo, Nabeshima: Glover was to supply all the modern machinery required to develop the mine. Much of this equipment had been ordered on his trip to Britain in 1867 and cost Glover between $70,000 and $80,000. The deal was that profits from the mine were to be shared equally between Hizen and Glover, but a royalty of 66 cents for every ton mined was to be paid to Hizen. And the daimyo's steamers had to be supplied with coal at cost price. The clan was to put up the cash for half the cost of the new machinery, but they did not have nor could they raise the money. Glover loaned them $48,000 to cover this - on top of the $40,000 still owed his company by Hizen for the steamer *Eugenie*. The agreement was that the loan was to be repaid out of the mine's profits. And, of course, at the end of the seven-year contract the mine would revert entirely back to Hizen. If no profit was made the clan still had the mine and the machinery. It was a 'Heads I win, Tails you lose' situation. It has been argued that this was the only agreement that could have been wrung out of Hizen and it was only Tom Glover who could have got this far with a national asset like the mine. But this would ignore Glover's earlier business coups. The impression is left that Tom was preoccupied with other matters when he agreed to the Takashima conditions.

Already one year of the seven-year agreement had passed and Takashima's No 1 Shaft had only now been sunk. In May 1869 an eight-foot-thick coal seam was struck at a depth of 150 feet so there was some cause for cheer for Glover. He would have felt some gratification at the find - to have entered into such a one-sided arrangement with Hizen he must have been absolutely certain of the mine's prospects from the start. Glover & Co. were now, in fact, the mining company, supplying everything that was necessary except the miners and the officials to administer the new island community that would be needed to support the modernised mine.[3]

Glover, of course, did not have the cash to finance this huge project on his own and borrowed heavily from Jardine, Matheson. On 9 June he wrote to them explaining that he had sunk all his available funds into the mine and requested off-payment he was due them on a loan. He was expecting his new machinery to be working in a few weeks and

"...no doubt ere this year [1869] is over we shall, independently of the security you hold, pay you all the money we owe ... All Glover and Company need is time."[4]

But it was impossible for Glover to give the mine the attention it now needed. He was back in Osaka at the end of June, presumably trying to pick up new business. He met Kido again while there and his old sparring partner, the Consul, Gower, with whom he had argued vehemently over the shogun. Kido questioned them closely on their past differences and 'came to understand what each had in mind'. They lunched together at one o'clock, 'then went our separate ways'.[5]

Around this time Glover would have been given news of a near-disaster in Aberdeen. His warship was undergoing a very extensive fitting out at the Victoria Dock, mainly because of the modern arms it would carry. Near the end of May a fire broke out close to where the ship was moored. The report of this incident in the *Aberdeen Journal* (2 June) conveys the scene well. The article was run under the heading 'Death of Mr James Hall':

"Between 2 and 3 o'clock on Saturday morning fire broke out in the saw-mill of Messrs George Milne & Co. on the Inches, & the Messrs Hall, as usual on such occasions, were the first to be appraised of the situation. Mr James, on getting the alarm, which he did from the watchman on the *Jho Sho Maru*, proceeded with great alacrity to the spot as that vessel was lying only 20 yards from the saw-mill where the fire was reported. Meanwhile the bell on board the vessel was rung, and every moment increased Mrs Hall's anxiety for her husband's safety, especially as, when arriving at the dock gates, he found the Bridge open, and was thus detained for some time before he could get across. Notwithstanding this detention, he arrived at the fire when it was still in a smouldering state, and only two or three people were collected. No sooner had he begun to give some orders, and while in the act of directing the water hose with his own hands, than the flames burst thro' the floor at his feet, and without word or sign, he dropped down and instantly expired. We understand his medical adviser attributed the death to a choking of blood to the heart, produced by the excitement and the haste with which the deceased gentleman hurried to the scene of the fire."

James Hall was sixty-five and the second son of Alexander Hall, the founder of the shipbuilding company. He was prominent in shipping affairs in Aberdeen and well known to the Glovers. His quick action had saved the *Jho Sho Maru* from going up in flames by ordering it to be pulled out into midstream from the blazing Victoria Dock side. The *Journal* went on to report that since James Hall's death on the Saturday previous, all the ships in the harbour were flying their flags at half-mast and that the tragedy was 'the only topic of conversation in the town'.

In August 1869 John Henderson, skipper of the *Ho Sho Maru*, was back in Aberdeen and enquiring at Glover Brothers office in Marischal Street for work. There was nothing available for him at the time but Tom's third Japanese warship the *Wen Yu Maru* was taking shape at Hall Russell's yard, only the third or fourth all-iron ship built by the firm.[6] Perhaps there would be an opening for Captain Henderson there later in the year.

On 10 August Tom was telling Jardine, Matheson that trade at Osaka was 'completely flat due to currency fluctuations'.[7] Four days later the *Jho Sho Maru* left Aberdeen for Nagasaki carrying a crew of ninety. Alex Glover, a Lieutenant Hawes and a D. Peapigna were the only three listed passengers. Alex and his wife had remained in Aberdeen when Tom and young Alfred had gone back to Japan sometime in November the year before. Ann was pregnant again, seven months gone when Alex left her to return to Nagasaki on the *Jho Sho Maru*.

The trip out was an eventful one. One report in Nagasaki the next year stated that the *Jho Sho Maru* had arrived in Nagasaki 'from Galway'. Why Captain James should have taken the ship from Aberdeen to the west coast of Ireland is not known. A report in the *Aberdeen Journal* (15 Dec. 1869) followed the next part of the warship's progress:

"On the 19th October, the screw steamship *Jho Sho Maru*, 1,490 tons, Captain James, from Aberdeen, 14 August, bound for Japan put in for coals. In making for Table Bay, this vessel narrowly missed being wrecked near Cape Point in a fog. The vessel, after taking in a supply of coal, sailed for China."

Alex Glover's wife would have read that report in the *Journal* with some interest. In her family home in Newhills she had just given birth to their only son, Ryle Alexander Glover, on 30 November 1869. The choice of the unusual Ryle for the first name of her son would suggest he was named after Ryle Holme of Glover & Co., Nagasaki.

Only a week before she read of the progress report on the voyage of the *Jho Sho Maru*, Ann would have read of the launching of the last of the three Japan-bound warships with which her husband had been closely involved.

The *Aberdeen Journal* (8 Dec. 1869) reported it thus:

"There was launched from the building yard of Messrs Hall, Russell & Co., on Thursday last, a composite screw gunboat, called the *Wen Yu Maru*, of 360 tons and 80 horsepower, and carrying four guns of large calibre.

[It is] expected to prove a very fast and powerful gunboat ... intended for the Japanese government, and has been constructed through Messrs Glover Brothers. ... will be commanded by Captain Gibson, whose lady gracefully performed the ceremony of naming the vessel."

So Captain Henderson didn't get his Glover ship and there would be no more Aberdeen-built warships for Japan. An era was passing. The three warships built in Aberdeen would train a generation of Japanese seamen/samurai. As their Navy grew the Japanese would have to turn towards the Tyne and the Clyde for their ships - ships far beyond any size Aberdeen could handle. And eventually the Japanese would absorb the technology and build their own. But in the beginning Aberdeen's contribution was enormous. At the very least, the Japanese had the excellence of the Aberdeen-built ships as a model for which to aim.

Tom Glover's slip-dock was sold to his friends in the Japanese government in 1869 for $130,000, already a great success. The sale brought a much-needed $60,000 profit to the beleaguered Glover but was probably Japan's biggest ever bargain.[8]

Glover was under increasing pressure from Jardine, Matheson as the year came to an end; his letter of 21 December shows it all - the optimism overcoming the fact that his company was running out of time:

"I have not had this pleasure for some time having been absent from the office since my arrival from Osaca superintending the completion of our Coal Mine. ... we have had a continual drain of our funds towards the completion of our coal venture to which besides a loan of some $50,000 we have paid away between 40 and $50,000 which has kept me very short and prevented me making you any remittances long ere this. Things have now changed, our mine being now completed and today we make our first credit entry, a month or two's production will I have no doubt enable us to reduce very much, if not entirely pay off what we owe you."[9]

Talk of Glover's dock and warships perhaps dominated the social event of the year of 1869 in Nagasaki - the visit of Queen Victoria's son Albert, the Duke of Edinburgh. Tom was among those invited to a lunch at the British Consulate in honour of the Royal visitor. An 'illumination' of all foreign property in the port was part of the celebrations. Nagasaki had been downgraded from a city to a town by the new government but to counteract this loss of status a street lighting system was in the process of being installed. The number of foreign residents in Nagasaki had fallen for the first time since the opening of the port ten years before - a good indication of how deep the depression in trade had become.

# Chapter 16

# ȚAKASHİMA ȚROUBLES

The depression in trade appeared to ease early in 1870 and Glover's prospects began to pick up. By mid-January his mine at Takashima was producing 90 tons of coal per day and this was expected to increase quickly to 200 tons. He had brought out from Britain two mining experts who were prediciting that production could reach as much as 500 tons a day - and that no new machinery was necessary to attain that figure. James Whittall of Jardine, Matheson had inspected Tom's mine and his company's books and was impressed. The multinational believed that they were Glover's only debtor.

The *Jho Sho Maru* had arrived finally on 7 January. The Aberdeen crew under Captain James were remaining for a spell to train the Japanese sailors and samurai in the latest technology the warship carried. It was a pleasant interlude for Glover who had been under some pressure from Jardine, Matheson to repay his outstanding debt.

It had been an eventful trip out for the new warship. After the near miss in the fog off South Africa, the *Jho Sho Maru* spent a month in Cape Town, 'unavoidably detained'. This was followed by heavy gales in the Indian Ocean on the next leg of her voyage. The officers on board told the *Nagasaki Express* reporter that these events proved 'her to be as fine a sea boat as ever floated'.[1]

The trip had been made mostly under sail but the ship had steamed when required. Thirty-five tons of coal a day had provided 11 knots. Her best one-day run had been 264 miles. The *Nagasaki Express* was very impressed by this ship, 'built on the latest principles as adopted by the Royal Navy'.

Japan was no longer lagging behind the West in naval technology. Significantly the *Jho Sho Maru* had arrived in Nagasaki with the Glover & Co. flag flying high on its masts. It was yet another wonder to be viewed from the shore by crowds of people. Its steam-driven launch, 46 feet long and itself capable of 10 knots, was buzzing round the harbour under test. As were the other seven boats carried on board. The chill January air would not have cooled the excitement in Nagasaki brought on by the arrival of this ship.

Alex Glover arrived back in Nagasaki on the *Jho Sho Maru*. With

Captain James he had seen the project through from its conception. On the arrival of Alex in the port, Tom most likely told his younger brother of the birth of his son in Aberdeen the previous November - if he did not already know. Certainly the news was announced in the *Nagasaki Shipping List* of 5 February that year. But Alex would neither see his wife, nor his son again. Their marriage had for some reason collapsed irretrievably while they were both in Aberdeen.

The first anniversary of the opening of Glover's dock at Kosuge was celebrated on 19 January 1870. During that first triumphant year thirty ships of various nations had been docked. The largest ship handled was a steamer of 1,150 tons. The success of the dock had encouraged the Japanese government to start construction of a huge dry dock on the other side of the harbour. The government now owned Glover's dock and it would be used to train a generation of shipbuilders and engineers. They also retained William Blaikie to superintend the dock's operation. His expertise was used to the full. He was sent to Kigatsu on the island of Hirado in January to check on the wrecking there of the steamer *Governor Higginson*. The government wanted him to assess the chances of refloating the ship.[2]

Yet despite the glory Tom could not sit back and relax. He was becoming bogged down in the business of the mine. In February Jardine, Matheson were shocked and puzzled by the latest twist in what was turning into an extremely complicated transaction with Glover. He asked them for a loan for *any* further sum he might require. For this blank cheque, and for putting off any payments he was due on existing loans to them, Glover was offering them 25 per cent of his stake in the mine. Jardine, Matheson not unreasonably wondered why. After all, his mine was in good running order - James Whittall himself had verified this in mid-January - and he claimed he had no other debts. Why then would he want to sell a part of his stake? To further puzzle them he had also claimed profits of £15,000 on the gunboat and $60,000 on the sale of his dock to the government. The company assumed that despite what he had told them, Glover had other pressing debts, the £20,000 borrowed from the City of Glasgow Bank for the *Jho Sho Maru*, for example. The company did not take him up on his offer and, in fact, their suspicions were further aroused. The correspondence between Glover and Jardine, Matheson in the first half of 1870 reflects this growing impatience with him.

The foreign community in Nagasaki had been stunned in late January by the sinking of the US corvette *Oneida* after a collision with a British steamer, P & O's *Bombay*, near Yokohama Bay. A large number of the American ship's officers and crew died in the accident and at a meeting of the foreigners in Nagasaki on 14 February an Address of Condolence to the US Consul was signed by all of the expatriates. Alex and Alfred Glover, Frederick Ringer, J.C. Smith, Henry Gribble and other past and present members of Glover & Co. were among the signatories. Tom Glover could not. Now desperately trying to save his business, he had left Nagasaki for Shanghai on 25 January on the steamer *Lightfoot*. He was not back in the port until late February.

Tom's spirits would have risen in early March. As well as the news of the *Wen Yu Maru* leaving Aberdeen on the 5th, production at the mine had reached 300 tons a day and he was still hopeful of achieving the magical figure of 500 tons a day. He calculated, as it turned out optimistically, that the coal cost only $2 a ton to produce and could be sold in Nagasaki for $4.50. At a production rate of 300 tons a day, in a twenty-day month, he would be making $15,000 a month profit.

The market was certainly there. The American, French, German and Russian Navies would queue with some of the best-known shipping companies in the world for Glover's high-grade coal. Hizen was not to receive his 66 cents royalty until the clan paid off the almost $90,000 they owed Tom. The first year's profits were projected as high as $200,000, allowing Hizen to clear all his debts quickly and from the second year on claim their annual half-share of the profits in addition to their royalty. But although Hizen could pay off all his debts rapidly, it soon became clear that Tom Glover could not pay off all of his. Things now started to go seriously wrong for Glover. Jardine, Matheson's suspicions regarding the £20,000 City of Glasgow Bank loan for the *Jho Sho Maru* were well founded.

With the company refusing his offer of a stake in the mine, Glover took the plunge and attempted to go public by selling his share in the mine to the businessmen of Yokohama. This would suggest the first signs of panic by Glover. He was hoping to raise $370,000 from the sale. There were no takers. An approach was then apparently made by Glover to the Meiji government where many of his friends had positions of real power, but it looked as though all the potential buyers were being influenced by Jardine, Matheson's decision not to buy. It was felt in general that Glover's affairs had become very complicated; that he had lent vast sums to the rebel clans who could not now repay; that he was in a spot and that his mine deal with Hizen was one-sided and unfair. Much of this Glover could not deny.

Jardine, Matheson were now beginning to think that Glover's brinksmanship with the mine had gone far enough and that even after ten years of close dealing with the young Scot, they would have to withdraw their financial support.

Glover fought on. Earlier in the year he had made an approach to A.J. Baudiun, the Nagasaki agent of the powerful Netherlands Trading Society (NTS), to take care of the now pressing £20,000 City of Glasgow Bank loan. The Dutchmen had dealt with Glover for years and, like Jardine, Matheson were owed substantial sums by him. Baudiun decided to take a chance. He agreed to Glover's proposal, but made conditions. These included Glover's share in the mine and the modern equipment he had installed being transferred to the NTS as surety. It is clear that the Dutch felt that they were already out on a limb with Glover and that he deserved another chance. Tom had no choice but to agree to their conditions and gain a short breathing space.

His March 1870 correspondence to Jardines follows the drama.

To FB Johnson in Shanghai on the 3rd:

"I find it no easy matter to keep things going ... I am very anxious indeed to have some money sent to my brother, say 20 or $30,000 as G & Co. have kept him out of his money too long, could you not anticipate Mr Keswick's reply and on the security of our plant and an offered share of a 1/8 let me have say £5,000."

On 7 April the *Jho Sho Maru* was formally handed over to the Higo daimyo's principal retainer at a ceremony in Nagasaki attended by Glover. It would have been a welcome break from the worries and frustrations of the Takashima coal mine. The *Nagasaki Express* reported on the handing-over ceremony on 9 April:

"On Wednesday last, the 6th inst., the armour-plated corvette *Jho Sho Maru* was inspected by officers of the Prince of Higo, who proved by the thorough way in which they went about their work that they were well acquainted with all that is required for a first-class man-of-war. The inspection proved quite satisfactory, and on Thursday the *Jho Sho Maru* was formally handed over to the *Karro* [daimyo's retainer] of the Prince, and the flags were changed under a salute from her guns. We hear that the vessel will remain in harbour for about three weeks longer (during which time the crew will be well drilled in the European system) and will then proceed to Kumo Moto, to be there inspected by the Prince, after which she will proceed to Yedo and be handed over to the Mikado. She will certainly make a fine addition to the Japanese fleet."

The training of the Japanese crew did not require Captain James. Some weeks before he had already written to Jardine, Matheson in Shanghai looking for another command.[3]

Perhaps the lowering of the Glover House and Union flags that day in April 1870 was symbolic as well as ceremonial. Now the war was over the Higo daimyo could magnanimously offer his warship to the service of his Emperor. But he could pay only in grain to Glover the $360,000 he had bargained for the ship. Glover had written to Jardine, Matheson the previous month:

"I am in a hole ... about this payment as I find the corn which Higo intends to pay in will from the depreciated state of our currency ... be less by some $15,000 than I expected ... if the Bank will not discount this paper and I cannot use it as payment on the £20,000 I am in a complete fix and know not what I can do ... Everything goes well with the mine and all I require is time ... "[4]

Higo was not the only daimyo owing Glover at this time. The debts of the other clan lords could not be covered for very much longer.

The distraction of the *Jho Sho Maru* ceremony would have been a pleasant but very short interlude for Glover. He was soon back at work, now personally managing the mine, for the first time giving it his undivided attention. And it began to show. A Jardine, Matheson report could now update the situation, saying that Glover & Co. ' ... had an undoubted source of wealth in the Takashima coal mine if properly looked after as it is commencing to be now'.[5]

Things did appear to be looking up. Improvements were being made to the mine on an almost daily basis. A second steam engine had been installed to pump out the mine, freeing the first engine to haul out coal exclusively. The galleries in the mine had been enlarged, allowing the use of trucks. When loaded, the trucks would be lifted in cages and transported to the tramway at the side of the pier. There the trucks would fill the waiting barges. Glover had organised nineteenth-century coal production technology at its very best.

On 12 April the brother of the Higo daimyo had visited the Takashima mine to see this wonder for himself. The *Nagasaki Express* of 23 April ran a report on his visit. In part it said:

"He expressed himself very much pleased with all he saw, and paid a well merited compliment to Mr T.B. Glover for his energy and perseverance; and further, expressed his regret that his countrymen had not adopted the European system of mining, years before."

This Japanese appetite for the latest in technology would become insatiable.

Despite the glowing reports, Jardine, Matheson's uneasiness with Glover remained and in mid-1870 they finally decided to withdraw their support. From apparently nowhere the NTS stepped in, again rescuing Glover from disaster by paying off his debts to Jardine, Matheson. The Dutchmen were commited to Glover now to the tune of over $400,000. The size of this debt would indicate that Glover had been borrowing heavily from the NTS for some time and not only for investment in his mine. This was now Glover's last chance of independent survival and he battled desperately to get the mine into maximum production.

The Nagasaki regatta of May 1870 would have been another welcome relief. Tom was stroke in a five-man crew which rowed the *Pluck* to victory that year. Frederick Ringer was cox and Alex Glover and two others made up the winning crew. Twenty-year-old Alfred Glover's *Flirt* came third in the sailing race. The Glover brothers' years of sailing experience in their father's Coastguard boats was again evident.

Back at the mine the three Glovers battled on. There were no new shipping orders to be had but the *Wen Yu Maru* arrived in Nagasaki from Aberdeen on 18 July. Commanded by Captain Gibson, it was destined for the Choshu clan. This was a temporary arrangement - the feudal clan system in Japan was dying - and like its two sister ships, the *Wen Yu*

*Maru* would form part of the nucleus of the Emperor's Imperial Japanese Navy.

The all-iron gunboat's trip out was a lot less eventful than that of the *Jho Sho Maru*. Leaving Aberdeen on 5 March it had run into gales rounding the Cape, but came through with no problems. The *Wen Yu Maru* dropped anchor in Nagasaki harbour in the stifling heat of mid-July 1870 on time.

As he grappled with the problems of the mine, now his only hope, it would have been doubly frustrating for Glover to read of his slip-dock break another record. That same month it docked the steamer *Nautilus*, at 262 feet and 1,160 tons the largest and heaviest ship it had yet handled. The *Nautilus* was only one of twenty-four ships docked that year. The Japanese government were getting a handsome return from their purchase of Glover's dock. And William Blaikie was building a small steamer on the slip, only about 100 tons, but yet another first for Nagasaki. All that was required to complete Blaikie's ship was the engines he had ordered from England.[6]

Glover read the *Nagasaki Express* issue later that month, in which, referring to 'incoming passengers', it noted 'Captain Forbes and 10 Chinese', landing in Nagasaki from Shanghai on the steamer *Tapang-Nyo*.[7] This mysterious Captain C.J. Forbes had some say in Glover's future. The end came for Glover & Co. in August 1870. Captain Forbes had demanded $35,000 owed him by Glover, he claimed, for the construction of a gunboat. With over $350,000 in liabilities, Forbes' $35,000 was small beer - but it was enough for the Netherlands Trading Society. Like Jardine, Matheson before them, they simply had reached breaking point with the young Scot. Glover & Co. was declared bankrupt at the Nagasaki British Consular Court on 22 August 1870.

Glover's letters of the period to Jardine, Matheson for the first time show a depth of feeling in the man:

"Dear Mr Johnson, I am very sorry to have to tell you that Captain Forbes has pressed my Firm into Bankruptcy, notwithstanding I had done all I could to prove to him that with time he as well as any other would be paid in full.

The Dutch Trading Co. have volunteered to accept a small payment monthly ...

Mr Gribble has started on his own account and once our affairs are settled I would take it as a giant favour your giving him your agencies. It is impossible that I can leave the mine ... and by and by I trust that in due course you will again give me the support of your Firm.

... I am sorry to say that [in] my anxiety to satisfy all our pressing creditors I prevented any money being sent to my Brother and he stands now at the mercy of creditors for £40,000."[8]

In a later letter to the company Glover again unusually involves his family:

"I have done all I can to pay off the old Firm's debts and I have made the money raised on the Mine go as far as it would go, to pay debts...

... of the money lately raised from the Dutch Trading Co., I have not paid my Father and my Brother one dollar and my present Firm has used none of it."[9]

A meeting was arranged of Glover's creditors at the British Consulate on 16 September 1870. The Consul formally opened the meeting and the creditors elected Julius Adrian of the NTS as chairman. The NTS were Glover's biggest creditors and their agent made it known that the Society were prepared to carry on the working of the Takashima mine. In fact, they wanted to develop it further by sinking a second shaft and investing more in the project. And they were sure that the expected profits from the mine ' ... would be sufficient to pay off all the creditors in full, without interest, within the space of two years.'[10]

The *Nagasaki Shipping List*'s report on the second meeting of Glover's creditors, held at the Glover & Co. offices on 19 September, says in part:

"that at the public meeting held at the Consulate [on the 16th], Mr T.B. Glover, enthusiastic to the last, has voluntarily offered his services gratis to superintend the practical working of the mine, he himself has thus apparently small doubt of ultimate success."

But no matter the future success of the mine, this was the end of a ten-year line for Glover's company and no amount of enthusiasm could alter that fact. The 1860s had seen the company rise from nothing to become a major shipowning and trading concern. The Glover flag had flown on the masts of many ships in many seas and oceans. Glover & Co. warehouses still adorned the docksides of Japan and China but already these were being renamed. The train, the dock, the warships and merchantmen were all Glover enterprises and would not be forgotten. Neither would the mine - perhaps the cruellest blow of all - only now beginning to show its true potential. The coal, the tea, the silk - all were major Glover initiatives for the Japanese export trade.

At one point Glover & Co.'s rapid expansion would have had even the giants such as Jardine, Matheson and the Dutch sitting up and taking notice of this new phenomenon in the trading world of the Far East. His company's star had burned brilliantly before being snuffed out. More than anything else it was his basic lack of working capital, his constant but necessary juggling of the limited resources he did have, which brought him down. Glover just could not sit still and let his wealth accumulate. His drive propelled him from one grand project to the next. He had won and lost several fortunes - there had been no real planning, events in Japan had moved too quickly. His fortunes were won - and lost - in haphazardous style. He acted instinctively and compulsively at times - either in extending loans to the rebels or in his constant switching of business priorities. Ironically, his mine would prove to be an 'undoubted source of wealth' and finance and fuel much of Japan's industrial revolution; his slip-dock and merchant ships were the start of Japan's eventual world dominance in such matters; and his warships were the nucleus of the mighty Imperial Japanese Navy which would in time spread its tentacles throughout the Pacific and beyond.

With his business complete, Captain Forbes left Nagasaki as mysteriously as he had arrived. Near the end of September he boarded the *Golden Age* for Shanghai and London.

The summer of 1870 had been long and hot, even for Nagasaki. Into early October the temperature remained in the high 80s, hot and sticky enough for the locals to worry about the approach of a typhoon.

Glover sweated with the others in the opressive heat and pondered on what might have been after the collapse of his company and presumably his dreams. Sitting brooding in his Nagasaki office he could see his latest innovation, a very basic telegraph system, the first in Japan, linking his head office in town the seven miles or so to the offices of the mine on Takashima. He was down, but he was not out. He was still only thirty-two years old. He would work and clear the debts and start again.

# Chapter 17

# Dutch Masters

G lover, by 1870, owed $500,000. He had assets of just over $200,000 and the value of his stake in the mine. There are entries in Glover's Accounts, presumably for this period, referring to the outstanding debts owed to *him* by the now emerging young leaders of the New Japan, many of them helped abroad by Glover in the 1860s.[1] Among those listed as owing Glover money are Hirobumi Ito, Endo, Matsuda and Sano, all well-known names in Meiji Japan. It would seem certain that many of the young students he helped owed him thanks for more than advice and the provision of transport and contacts.

Glover's list of creditors is interesting. The most notable is the Netherlands Trading Society, as would be imagined, but more than $125,000 was owed to his brother Charles' company, Glover Brothers, Aberdeen.[2]

The agreement finally reached at the creditors' meeting was that the NTS would operate the mine as trustees in order to regain their money. This was in addition to taking over the administration of some other Glover concerns. The Dutch were shrewd enough to see the value of retaining Glover to run the mine - he would need little motivation to maximise its efficiency and in this way clear his estate. Ideally for Glover the mine could be sold later as a highly profitable concern, giving him part of the buyer's lump sum. He had offered his services free to the Dutch so convinced was he that the mine would very quickly reach its production target. The NTS agreed to pay him a derisory $200 a month for his expertise, knowing well that no salary incentive was necessary in this case.

His partner, MacKenzie, was now a very old man and Glover took over his share of their company's debts. He would have been planning, with the help of Alex and Alfred, to improve the working of the mine now that the bankruptcy hearing was over. It would appear that his optimism had returned at this stage. Alfred was not yet twenty, and in just over two hectic years in Japan had amassed a tremendous amount of business experience. And in that critical year of 1870 a fourth Glover brother joined the three Nagasaki residents. William was back in the port again - this time as skipper of the *Kagoshima*.

Things were changing for the foreigners in Japan. The British Consul wrote to Nagasaki's governor thanking him for the new regulation which barred 'all persons wearing two swords' - the samurai - from entering or leaving the foreign quarter.[3] This new ruling would have pleased Captain Hewitt, RN, who had complained to the Consul of 'being rudely pushed aside' by the Japanese guards 'who parade the streets of the settlement'.[4]

After his bankruptcy much of Glover's trading business was taken over by Holme Ringer. The same company took on many of his redundant employees, including J.C. Smith, one of his brightest young men. Henry Gribble was another Glover man who founded his own company in August 1870. Gribble was advertising former Glover & Co. insurance agencies in the Nagasaki newspapers within a month of Glover's bankruptcy. Ryle Holme, after whom presumably Alex and Ann Glover had named their son, joined Gribble in this new venture. The plum agency of Lloyd's went initially to Alt & Co. It was not simply a case of vultures picking the carcass of the dead Glover & Co. - on the contrary, many of these people had strong personal and family ties with Glover and he would retain an interest in some of what had been his Nagasaki operations. He had asked Jardine, Matheson, for example, to appoint Gribble as their Nagasaki agent. His friendship with Frederick Ringer was cemented even more when Ringer House was completed at No.2 Minami Yamate in 1868, next door to Glover House at No.3.[5]

Glover now buckled down to the job of managing the mine on behalf of the Dutch, assisted at this time by Alex and Alfred. Acting for the NTS he would give the mine more of his attention than he ever did as its owner. A report on the mine, commissioned by the Dutch and dated 26 August 1870 reckoned that:

"the workings are laid out without any system or view to facilitate the work ... The management was very defective ... The machinery ordered from Europe had not been properly planned, requiring expensive alterations on its arrival."

Much of the criticism was valid and Glover could not deny it. He had sunk Takashima's No.1 Shaft with one priority only - to extract the coal sell it as quickly as possible. His policy had been successful - 30,000 tons of coal, valued at $126,000, were exported in 1870. But clearly there had been no careful planning for further shaft sinking, drainage or ventilation. Glover had succeeded in modernising the mine and making it profitable quickly. He had seen a future for a modernised Takashima while most were unaware that coal existed in Japan. But he had not made it profitable quickly enough to save his company. Certainly what was required now was some careful planning. What was certain, too, was that the arms trade had all but dried up. In the year of Glover's bankruptcy, the value of imported arms fell to less than $40,000.

Early in 1870 an affair of Tom Glover with a Japanese woman resulted in her becoming pregnant. On 8 December this woman, Maki Kaga, gave birth to a son in Nagasaki. She recorded the birth of her baby and the baby's name as Shinsaburo on her *koseki*, the official Japanese register of births, marriages and deaths.[6]

Thomas Glover was the father of the child and freely acknowledged this. One researcher has come across five instances of children fathered by Glover in Japan to different mothers, but this male child was somehow different from the others. Glover would lavish money and attention on this little boy far in excess of what was normally expected. He had married, or at least formed a permanent relationship with, Tsuru Awajiya by this time. Maki, then, was his mistress and was expecting his baby by the spring of 1870.

Babies born in these circumstances were not uncommon and, sadly, were not normally accepted by the Japanese or by the Westerners. But this child was different - perhaps because at thirty-two Glover had come to accept that he would not return permanently to Scotland. Whatever was the case, Maki approached Glover when she became pregnant, telling him that she was carrying their child. Apparently at this stage he rejected her, insisting on remaining with Tsuru who had at that time not yet become pregnant by Glover. It would appear that some kind of promise had been made to Maki, a promise she felt had been broken. Maki and her baby boy went to live alone at this stage, supported by Glover. What can only be guessed at is the reaction of Tsuru. It would not have been unusual for a Japanese of similar status to Glover to keep a mistress and child more or less openly. Certainly Tsuru knew of the baby and accepted the situation with her Scottish husband. The birth of this baby boy may well have been the beginning of the *Madam Butterfly* story.

# Chapter 18

# MEIJI MUSCLE

A British mining engineer, Frederick Potter of Derby, was chosen by the Dutch in early 1871 to expand the workings of the Takashima mine. It was hoped he would exploit the ten-foot seam which was known to lie beneath the area then being worked. Potter felt that it was there the real potential lay. He was not long in criticising Glover and his brothers, saying that the No.1 pit had been 'greatly misrepresented, it being no doubt the policy of the Glovers to represent it as of *immense value* when near their bankruptcy'.

Potter was new to Japan and at this stage perhaps not aware of the many problems there were in managing the mine. The productivity rate of the Japanese miners was only a fraction of their European counter-parts. Attempts to introduce the light European pick, for example, had been bitterly resented by the Japanese who wished to retain their traditional digging tools. Time was needed to train the miners.

The opinions of Glover's workforce had to be regarded, if only to make them perform. They were organised and disciplined, surprisingly so for labourers born into a feudal system. What they certainly were not was compliant slave labour. At one point Glover tried to lower production costs by cutting their pay rates but they petitioned Matsubayashi, Hizen's agent, over Glover's head and had the cuts restored. On another occasion the isolation of the island had forced the miners into having to buy necessities at what they thought were excessive prices. This caused a riot which required extra police to be sent from Nagasaki to control. But it would be wrong to think of Glover at this time other than as a very hard and forceful manager at Takashima.

The price of coal took a short but dramatic drop in mid 1871. Glover had been steadily paying off his debts but it now looked as though the coal price collapse would put a stop to his plans. He tried to renegotiate with Matsubayashi the 66 cents per ton royalty which had to be paid to Hizen. He proposed that the clan accept 60 per cent of the profits of the mine and cut-price coal for their steamers in return for the royalty being dropped. The Dutch thought Glover over-generous, reasoning that the coal required by the Hizen ships 'may be so great that Takashima may lose all its profits for the purpose of seeing Hizen's steamers burn its coal'.

But the mine was not occupying all of his attention. In this period of fundamental change in Japan he found time to philosophise on the future of the country. In a revealing letter to the British Consul, Marcus Flowers, dated 30 December 1871, he admitted he was reasonably happy with the working of the Treaty to date.[1] Inevitably the merchants' old chestnuts were raised in the letter. He complained of the high taxes on 'inferior' Nagasaki tea and of the excessive land rents. He added a third complaint - the perennial problem of unfair competition from Chinese merchants. For a bankrupt businessman paying off his debts by managing a coal mine, Glover in this letter indicates that he was very much keeping his finger on the pulse of events in Japan.

Of course, his main interest at that time was in mining and he pleaded the case for Japanese coal replacing British on the markets of the Far East:

"... but it is against all the laws of trade to bring 'coals to Newcastle', in other words - to make it necessary to furnish our steamers, both navy and merchant, with fuel from distant countries, while Japan can produce it in quantity and quality to supply the whole East, if proper facilities are granted, and encouragement given to capitalists to invest, and engineers to manage the opening up of the mineral districts of this country. In countless ways would it benefit the Japanese as well as the foreigners."

He had a plan for making use of many of the now redundant samurai, warriors no longer required in the New Japan:

"Native engineers and mechanics in great numbers would find suitable occupation and good wages. This in itself is very important to Japan at the present moment, and will be so for a long time, until the immense body of idle samurai are employed; and from the writer's personal notice no work is so inviting and suited to that non-merchant class, as the management of machinery, supervision of coolies, and the numerous other posts of responsibility connected with mining."

At this stage he thought that in manufacturing Japan 'from its extent' could not compare with China but that its minerals could be made of immense value to all nations:

"To the Japanese nation, with its acquired taste for expensive form of Government and necessary naval and military requirements, it would supply, from present stony and barren lands, an immense increase in revenue, and be the means of raising large and flourishing villages, where at present but the fisherman's hut exists ..."

He felt that Japan was not yet ready for unrestricted opening to foreigners. There were several reasons for this, he argued, the central point being the effect on many of the still innocent Japanese in some districts of the country:

"but only those who have witnessed the lawless acts of many of our countrymen, know what would be the result of misbehaviour perpetrated in some of the districts of Japan, where nothing but Japanese custom and quiet have reigned."

The British diplomats, he felt, should ensure the quality of Britons now arriving to help develop Japan, and 'uneducated and unprincipled assistants and teachers may bring a curse on our countrymen'.

His final point regarded Christianity in Japan. His adopted country had come in for severe Western criticism for its treatment of its native Christians. He asked for caution in this potentially explosive issue:

"Let the present [Japanese] government refrain from all persecution, but prevent all steps on the part of our Ministers to preach religion, or attempt to make converts, and Japan will have Christianity when the state of the country, and the minds of the people are ripe for it."

In late 1871 Tom learned of Emperor Meiji's official visit to the *Jho Sho Maru* off Shinagawa. In November of that year the Japanese sovereign was welcomed on board Glover's ship, now renamed *Ryujo Maru*, and the pride of the Japanese Navy. A Western-style military band played and a twenty-one-gun salute was fired by the ship in the Emperor's honour. This was further evidence for Glover of Japan's rapid change to European ways. The officers and crew of the *Ryujo Maru* were very nervous throughout the Royal visit. This would have been something entirely new - the Imperial presence actually within touching distance and aboard their ship. Nearer the end of the month Emperor Meiji was back on board again - this time for a visit to Yokosuka harbour.[2]

Another point of great significance to the future of Japan's Navy was the dispatch of Heihachiro Togo to Britain in 1871. As a sixteen-year-old Satsuma samurai Togo had helped defend his clan's capital city Kagoshima from bombardment by the Royal Navy eight years before. Now a sub-lieutenant in the rudimentary Japanese Navy, Togo was being sent to England to be trained by the Royal Navy, the first of what would be a procession of Japanese naval cadets over the years. Togo was an acquaintance of Glover and had begun to learn English only the year before.

Another letter written by Glover to the Consul, Marcus Flowers, at this time suggests that perhaps his wheeling-and-dealing days were still not over; with his usual flourish and writing in gold-coloured ink, Glover applied for a passport to travel to Kobe. The Treaty regulations still required this formality. He wrote:

"As my Medical Adviser has ordered me to try the Sulphur Baths of Higo for my rheumatism, I shall feel obliged by your granting me a Passport for that country."

Flowers passed on his request to the Nagasaki governor, recommending that the passport be granted.[3] The suspicion that Glover was making the long journey to the developing business community of Kobe for more than a visit to the 'Sulphur Baths' is impossible to contain.

But speculative trading ended in 1871, at least as Glover had known it. The arrival of the Great Northern Telegraph Company's cable in

Nagasaki that year would take, to a great extent, the guesswork and gambling out of trade. There would be no comparison with the 1860s, when the markets in Europe and America were months away. At thirty-three Glover had become an old-timer, a veteran of Far Eastern trading. He would have gained no satisfaction from hearing that Francis Groom's venture, Glover, Dow & Co. of Shanghai, had collapsed in bankruptcy that year. The exploits of the brightest young men and adventurers of the trading world of the 1860s were coming to an end.

And even as the previous decade became a memory, the new team of Glover-sponsored decision-makers were consolidating their power in Japan. His resolution to help abroad young rebel samurai was beginning to pay dividends as early as 1871. Hirobumi Ito was Emperor Meiji's Minister for Public Works and was beginning to exert great influence on how the country was run. He was later joined at his Ministry by another Glover protégé, Yozo Yamao. This was the same young member of the 'Choshu Five' that Tom met in Aberdeen or Glasgow during his trip home four years before. He had completed his study of shipbuilding and engineering in Glasgow and was fired by what he had seen there. These two young Japanese began drawing up plans for an engineering school to train the army of technical people needed for the industrialisation of their country. This was the beginning of the Imperial College of Engineering, Tokyo, which would become in time Tokyo Daigaku [Tokyo University or *Todai*], Japan's Oxbridge.

Significantly, the engineering school would be very much based on the Scottish system of practical training. Later the same year Ito was included in the Iwakura Mission, a group of high-powered Japanese government officials and students who would visit the United States and Europe to gain even more knowledge of the West.

In July 1872, Emperor Meiji visited Nagasaki in what was now his Aberdeen-built Imperial vessel or Royal yacht, the *Ryujo Maru*. The visit was part of a three-month tour of western Japan. There were seven other warships accompanying the Royal yacht and these carried many of the leading figures in the new government, including the Satsuma clan's Takamori Saigo. Saigo was now chief of the Meiji armed forces. From 19 to 22 July the *Ryujo Maru* remained in Nagasaki but it is not known if Glover met the Emperor on this occasion. Certainly the Japanese sovereign visited Glover's slip-dock where he watched a ship being berthed.

Glover's overriding concern in the early 1870s remained the mine at Takashima. A good idea of how he had organised the operation and how the mine ran in those days is given in a report by Alexander Jones, a US Consul in Nagasaki at that time.[4] Jones describes Takashima as 'rocky and barren rising abruptly from the water as if suddenly and violently thrown up from the sea'; praises Glover as being the sole impetus behind the mine's development; and calls him 'an English gentleman of sagacity and enterprise'.

Jones noted that about 4,000 people were employed in and about the mine,'...which includes a very competent staff of mechanics'. The coal was conveyed to Nagasaki from the island by a fleet of about 100 native junks 'being pulled to and fro by the Company's steam tug boat'. The village housing the Company's employees was 'considerable' and most of the needs of the workforce and their families could be supplied - 'by the company at cost price' - without having to journey the ten miles or so to Nagasaki.

The working day was a day or night shift of eight hours, initially, for a twenty-day month, hours as good as that of British miners of the day. Jones noted wryly that there was no expense incurred in clothing the miners - 'a straw sandal being usually the only garment'. Women and children were employed in the mine at a lower rate than that of the men.

There was a depot at Nagasaki where a further 800 were employed unloading the barges at the coalyard and coaling the steamers. This was done from junks which drew up alongside the ships to be coaled. The method was simply a human chain passing small baskets of coal from the junk up the ships' ladders and down into the bunkers in a 'marvellously rapid fashion'.

It was later noted that the Japanese carried out the coaling with 'never-ceasing merriment and cracking of jokes' - most of the jokes being directed at the wide-eyed foreigners watching the whole operation from the side of the ship. They were amazed even more when they saw the loaders, operation over, wash their almost naked bodies clean of all coal dust and unashamedly pull on 'a clean chemis'.[5]

It puzzled Jones that the Japanese of Nagasaki, 70,000 to 80,000 of them, with so much coal readily available, did not use the fuel at all in their homes and did not even have chimneys on their houses. For heating in cold weather and for cooking throughout the year, they preferred the charcoal-burning *hibachi*.

Tom Glover, his skill being perhaps more inclined towards the marketing of the coal, shuttled between the mine's offices on the island and his own office in Nagasaki. Supervising this massive undertaking involving almost 5,000 workers would have been a demanding job. The expatriate mining engineers lived in European style on the island, with occasional trips into Nagasaki.

By the summer of 1872 the mine's No.2 Shaft was producing coal. A visitor at this time to Glover's house was a Major W.M. Bell. He thought the view from Glover's garden 'exquisite' and Nagasaki Bay 'a mingling of Killarney and the Trossachs'.

A visit to the mine was arranged for the Major. Glover's earlier plan for employing some of the redundant samurai - the 'two-sworded men' - was apparently now beginning to work well. Major Bell reported:

We went down the mine by a shaft of some 160 feet, and found a splendid seam of coal eight feet high, very good for steam purposes. The colliers were chiefly two-sworded men, who, when we arrived, bowed in the peculiar manner of the country, rubbing their knees with the palms of their hands; and when they came up from their grimy occupation took a hot bath in open day.[6]

The mine was running very well and two years after Glover's bankruptcy, in September 1872, the Dutch had recovered all but $95,000 of the $400,000 owed them by Glover. The high price of coal and Glover's skilled management had allowed him to pay off more than three-quarters of what he owed in two years. The question will never be answered of what would have been if Jardine, Matheson had continued to back him in 1870.

All Glover's energy and attention was now concentrated on the mine and it showed in its success. That same month his hopes would have soared again. The Meiji government sent delegates to negotiate the outright purchase of the mine. That event would have been a dream come true for Glover - a buyer when the mine was booming - and perhaps the capital for him to completely clear his debts and start again. But on the brink of completing the deal, the Japanese suddenly pulled out.

The clan lords of Japan, the daimyo, were obliged at the end of 1872 to surrender all their estates to the Emperor Meiji. The Hizen daimyo, like all the others, obeyed. The Japanese interest in the mine then turned from Hizen and Matsubayashi to a government department, the Mining Department of the Ministry of Works. The Dutch, Tom Glover and Frederick Potter would now have to deal with this department. The Japanese at the time were employing expatriate British civil servants in key positions until their own people gained experience. These British expatriates immediately let Glover know that they did not regard any previous arrangement with Matsubayashi binding on them.

The change from Hizen to Meiji authority on Takashima brought about a major incident. The Hizen officials had left, but their Meiji replacements had failed to show up by mid-December 1872. The labourers were upset at the upheaval. They formed a mob and soon drove the British engineers and staff from the mine. The rioters stopped the mine's pumps, putting the expensive No.2 shaft in danger from flooding. The British realised that things had got out of hand and that they were in serious danger. They fought off the mob with rifles, killing and wounding several of them. It is not known if any of the three Glover brothers were involved in this incident - they were all prominent members of the mine's staff and it would seem likely that one or more of them was on the island at the time. It proved that Nagasaki even in 1872 was still a very dangerous place in which to live.

If Nagasaki then was still displaying shoot-outs more in line with what was going on at the time in the Wild West of the United States, elsewhere in Japan things were becoming distinctly more civilised. Construction of a railway, financed, engineered and built by the British, had begun in 1870. The first line to be laid was between Tokyo and Yokohama. Hirobumi Ito had been prominent in pushing for the building of this railway and the first service between the two cities began in 1872. Glover could have smiled ruefully at the news of this great 'first', considering his *Iron Duke* had run along the Oura waterfront in Nagasaki seven years before. The Tokyo/Yokohama service was operated by British crews and it would be several years before the Japanese would be considered sufficiently skilled to take over the running of their own railway.

Things settled down at the mine in 1873 and Glover in his uneasy alliance with Potter and the government department continued to manage the mine and pay off his now fast-diminishing debts. The miners' wages had risen considerably since 1870 and there was a temporary peace on that front. Glover learned that year that Japanese coal - overwhelmingly that mined at Takashima - had completely replaced British coal on the Shanghai market. Only eight years before, the British had supplied 50 per cent of the coal to Shanghai, the great coal market of the Far East. This Japanese enterprise of the early 1870s, very much orchestrated by Glover, would be repeated a century later in various other markets previously dominated by the British. The Japanese were superb pupils for Glover.

The following three years, 1873-6, Glover appears to have spent quietly managing the mine. He managed a steady growth in profits from Takashima, despite the occasional dip in the price of coal. It would seem certain, too, that he had other business enterprises going on in Nagasaki and elsewhere during this period. These would most likely have been carried out in conjunction with some of his former employees. He would have been available, in any case, for consultation to Henry Gribble, Frederick Ringer or any of the others whose new businesses were beginning to expand. Glover's knowledge of Japanese trade and politics would have been unequalled in the Far East.

His old friend and fellow Scot Kenneth Ross MacKenzie died at Glover's house in Nagasaki on 5 November 1873 aged seventy. Glover's affection for the old man is apparent. He would certainly have led the mourners at MacKenzie's funeral and later burial at Oura International Cemetery. MacKenzie died far from his native land. His final resting place lies in the cool of a Nagasaki hillside, not far from Glover House, a place which in beauty could match the glens of his native Scotland.

The foreign community in Nagasaki at this time numbered around ninety and they appear to have been a closely knit bunch. There was an active social life, confined mostly among the foreigners themselves although Glover had many close Japanese friends. Perhaps the more isolated community at Nagasaki did not have all the facilities available to the foreigners resident in the now large settlement of Yokohama. But in March 1873 Nagasaki's own horseracing course was opened at Isahaya, a flat area of land about fifteen miles inland from the port itself. The *Nagasaki Express* reported on the long procession of foreigners on their ponies going to and from the racecourse on the day of the opening causing 'considerable commotion amongst the natives in the villages en route'.

Nagasaki's foreigners did have their own Amateur Dramatic Society, the Olympic Theatre and the annual regatta as well as the other social occasions where they entertained themselves.

Variety shows were part of the Dramatic Society's repertoire. In a *Nagasaki Express* report of that era a show put on by the 'Tourists - a minstrel party, containing a lady and four gentlemen performers' is highly praised. The report complains, though, of the poor turnout at the show of the port's residents, only the presence of visiting seamen filled most of the available seats in the theatre. Intriguingly, the report also mentions 'Mr Glover's Masks and Faces' as being 'well executed and highly appreciated'. Which of the three brothers was involved is not mentioned.

Glover House, though, was the venue for most of Tom's social activities. Dinner eaten, his guests would wander out on the patio in front of the house. There, under the camphor trees in the balm of a Nagasaki evening, they could have viewed the lights of the ships in the bay below shimmering on the darkening water. The seemingly incessant chirping of the cicada would have supplemented any background music. Tom was well known as a generous host and his guests were plied with after-dinner drinks as they gathered in these fairy-tale surroundings.

He entertained lavishly. A contemporary tells of one occasion when the band of the US Navy's Asiatic flagship played in the garden of Glover's house while a tennis match was staged there. Glover wandered around among the guests seeing that everyone was being looked after. He asked one naval rating if he had what he wanted.

'No, sir', replied the young seaman, 'I should like a bottle of sarsaparilla.'

Glover was apparently taken aback at his staff being unable to supply the young sailor's needs.[7]

Tom also entertained his guests with the story of a Scottish-built steamer he had supplied to the Hizen clan some years before. He had sent instructions to the shipyard, he said, on how the ship should be decorated, and enclosed a copy of the Hizen clan crest to be copied by the yard. On arrival in Nagasaki the ship was inspected and sure enough the Hizen crest appeared everywhere - even being woven into the carpets in the saloon. Some Hizen samurai were sent by their daimyo to inspect the steamer before the clan took delivery. Glover could still laugh years later at their attempts not to stand on their clan's crest as they made their way through the saloon. The offending carpet was removed.[8]

On a more serious note the main topic of conversation of the early 1870s was Japan's headlong rush for Westernisation - a rush led by many of Glover's friends now in high places. Japan's samurai had their special privileges as warriors withdrawn in 1873. National Service had been started and this would lead to the formation of a standing Imperial Japanese Army and Navy. This flexing of the Meiji government muscle led to resentment by many of the dispossessed samurai.

The following year of 1874 an anti-government rebellion broke out in Saga, about 100 miles from Nagasaki, led by Shinpei Eto. This uprising was put down ruthlessly and quickly. Eto was executed in the aftermath. The *Ho Sho Maru* was in action with the newly formed Japanese Navy in its operations in North Kyushu helping to put down this insurrection.

Another samurai leader unhappy with the way things were going in the New Japan was Takamori Saigo. His position in the Satsuma hierarchy had involved him in many dealings with Glover before, during and after the turbulent years of the rebellion against the shogun. Now Saigo was disillusioned. He was a giant of a man for a Japanese, a massively built six-footer, and had fought against the shogun because he had seen that rebellion as a catalyst for a return to all that he thought best in traditional Japanese values. He had resigned from his position in the Meiji government and returned to his Kagoshima home because for one thing he felt that Japan should be more militarily adventurous and, for example, invade and colonise Korea. The returning members of the government's Iwakura Mission in 1873, fresh from Europe and the United States, felt differently. They thought that it was a time to consolidate and strengthen Japan domestically. Saigo now became the exiled conservative hero, promoting old-time samurai values. He began to build a strong following in the south of Japan.

But in Nagasaki more mundane problems were concerning Tom Glover. In January 1874 the Japanese government bought out the Dutch and became the owners of the Takashima mine. The reported price was $400,000 and it is generally accepted that there was a pay-off to Glover on top of this. One writer claims that Glover's cut was also $400,000, but this amount appears excessive.[9] In any case the transfer of the mine to the Meiji government brought Glover back into contact with Shojiro Goto. He had dealt on and off with this Tosa clan hero for many years - Goto was well thought of by British diplomats and was a shrewd and ruthless businessman. The Japanese had been a member of the first provisional Meiji government in 1868 but had resigned in 1873. Perhaps as a sop to the politically troublesome Goto, the government offered to sell him the mine at a knock down price. It also fell in with their general policy of privatising major enterprises. And it would presumably keep Goto quiet and far away from Tokyo in Nagasaki. He was familiar with the port, of course, where he had been a Tosa agent. He had bought from Glover in early 1867 the gunboat *Nankai,* the ship the shogun had attempted to impound. Whatever the reasoning behind the government's actions, Goto became the owner of the mine in September 1874.

Glover and Goto had long discussions on the mine and its workings, now providing clear profits of around $400,000 a year. It had been necessary for the Japanese once more to involve Jardine, Matheson in the mine - only a company like the multinational had the kind of funds available for this kind of investment. Goto entered into a fifteen-year agreement with them, allowing him to borrow from them the $200,000 in cash he needed for the purchase of the mine from the government. Jardine, Matheson were to be repaid with a half-share of the mine's profits plus interest on their loan. It was a good deal for Goto and Jardine, Matheson now had a guaranteed supply of coal for their steamers, and a stake in the development of Japan. As well as that, the mine was simply a very good investment at that time.

Perhaps Jardine, Matheson were advised in their dealings with Goto by Alex Glover. Tom's brother had left Nagasaki in 1874, almost certainly for a position with the company in Shanghai. There had been no reconciliation for Alex and his wife who now lived in Aberdeen with their son Ryle. The Glover brothers' connections with Takashima, in any case, were beginning to slacken about this time. Tom and Alfred continued to work there but the bankruptcy debts were almost clear and the lump sum Tom had received earlier in the year was another cushion for them. They could start to look elsewhere.

The temptations of the bright lights of Tokyo proved to be too much for Goto. After only a few months in Nagasaki he returned to the Japanese capital, apparently bored with his new acquisiton. Jardine, Matheson now became the de facto operators of the mine, with occasional interruptions from Goto in Tokyo. New boilers, pumps and hauling equipment were imported from Britain in the summer of 1875 and were in operation by September of that year. The company had invested heavily and it began to show - production was almost doubled in a couple of months.

Glover struggled with the problem of selling this surfeit of coal. At the price they charged he could not sell all of the coal now available. He sweated over whether he should cut the price or production. By the end of 1875 the problem was solved for him. In early December a huge explosion devastated the mine and, for the first time, Japan experienced some of the horror that an industrial revolution could bring. Forty-four died, twenty-four were injured and five disappeared entirely in the disaster. Earlier that year sea-water ingress had been continuous and dreaded fire damp had been encountered but little had been done about these problems. This was Japan's first industrial disaster and a first of which Glover was not proud.

By March 1876 Takashima was back in full production. This was a temporary situation as in July a small fire in the west workings got out of control and Glover's engineers had to reverse their pumps and flood the mine to put out the fire. More problems and delays arose and the second half of 1876 proved to be a financial disaster for Takashima. Goto's debts were building in the meantime and Jardine, Matheson's frustrations were increasing at the same rate.

With these mounting problems and with the cavalier Goto now the owner of the mine, 1876 was a good time for Glover to sever his connection with Takashima. For more than six years he had been involved in its running, both as owner and manager. But now other openings were becoming available. His original seven-year contract with Hizen in any case had been honoured. His bankruptcy debts would be cleared officially and honourably the next year. It was the perfect time to move on. And the time was right not only for a move by Tom. His brother Alfred joined Henry Gribble & Co. the same year. Alfred was twenty-six in 1876 and already a nine-year veteran of Japan. Another former Glover & Co. man on the move was Ryle Holme, who left Ringer's to become Jardine, Matheson's representative and Nagasaki agent for the Takashima mine.

Although it is unclear exactly how it came about, at around this time Glover was asked to go to Tokyo as an adviser to Yataro Iwasaki, founder and head of the burgeoning Mitsubishi concern.[10] In his forty-second year, Iwasaki was four years older than Glover and had become very close to the Scot during the frenetic 1860s in Nagasaki. Like Goto, Iwasaki was a Tosa man and had headed that clan's office in Nagasaki from April 1867. When the civil war ended Iwasaki had transferred his clan's shipping interests into a new concern which he owned and which he called Mitsubishi Shokai. Iwasaki's relationship with Glover was strong enough for one Japanese historian later to describe them 'as if they had been real brothers'.[11] It would seem most probable that Iwasaki wanted to use Glover's talents in this period of great expansion for his company. Glover's knowledge of foreign trade and connections with the leaders of New Japan would be invaluable to Iwasaki.

Glover accepted the offer and prepared to move to Tokyo with Tsuru and their newly born daughter Hana. Going with them would be Tom's son by Maki Kaga. Mitsubishi's head office and base was in Tokyo but there was no bridge-burning by Glover. He kept Glover House and many of his other interests in Nagasaki. In particular, his friendship with his new neighbour Frederick Ringer remained strong. A new life awaited them in Tokyo but they had not seen the last of Nagasaki.

On 8 August 1876, Tom and Tsuru's baby girl Hana was born. After the birth of their daughter, Tsuru became more accepted as the permanent partner or wife of Glover. She had moved into Glover House some years before and was still only twenty-five when their baby was born.

Glover's son by Maki Kaga, now renamed Tomisaburo, was six years old in 1876. By this time he had moved into Glover House as the unofficially adopted son of Tom and Tsuru. For those first six years of his life he had lived separately with his mother, supported by Glover. Why Maki now let go the son she had conceived with Glover is not known.

There are many possibilities. It is likely that she was approached by Tom or Tsuru who had failed to produce a son of their own. An entry in Nagasaki's British Consular Register of Births for the previous year, 1875, further complicates matters. It lists a John Glover, son of Thomas, the birth of the boy being recorded a couple of months after the event by an associate of Glover. The whole entry has at some stage later been deleted by hand. What is clear is that at this point Maki was coldly asked to surrender her child to Glover and Tsuru, perhaps breaking some kind of promise she had been given. According to one source, she then attempted suicide, first blindfolding her little boy and then slicing open her own neck. Almost certainly this dramatic scenario became the inspiration for the tragic ending to the story, play and opera *Madam Butterfly* many years later. This attempted suicide story has persisted over the years and the only fact that is certain is that Maki survived. But in the aftermath she did give up her son to the rich and famous Thomas Glover and the little boy was welcomed into Glover House.[12]

Tom had kept tabs on the boy since his birth. The offer from Iwasaki to move to Tokyo may well have spurred Glover into pressuring Maki to hand over their son. Perhaps he did not want to leave his little boy behind in Nagasaki and in this sense he differs from the majority of Western fathers who ignored their children born to Japanese women. In this respect he ignored the convention of the day, freely acknowledging his son.

Maki Kaga now becomes a shadowy figure, until recently totally unknown, but perhaps the true model for the immortal Madam Butterfly.

Thomas Blake Glover, c. 1890, Japan.
*(Courtesy: Nagasaki City Hall)*

Thomas Glover with Yaonosuke Iwasaki,
chairman and younger brother of the founder of
the Mitsubishi company.
*(Courtesy: Nagasaki City Hall)*

This photograph was captioned in Japanese *Thomas Glover with leading members of the Mitsubishi Company.* Taken c. 1890. On Glover's left is Yaonosuke Iwasaki, chairman of the company.
*(Courtesy: Nagasaki City Hall)*

*Thomas Glover entertaining Mitsubishi people at his Nagasaki home –*
the Japanese caption on this 1890s photograph.
*(Courtesy: Nagasaki City Hall)*

Glover's face being used to advertise Kirin beer – *"The beer he loved"*.

Tokyo, November 1905, in the grounds of the home of Yaonosuke Iwasaki, chairman of Mitsubishi. The occasion – a reception for Admiral Togo (seated, centre, with short white beard), victor in the annihilation of the Russian fleet at Tsushima several months before, the crucial sea battle of the Russo-Japanese war of 1904-5. Thomas Glover's presence directly behind the admiral at this occasion speaks volumes for his status in the New Japan. Iwasaki is seated two from the right of Admiral Togo. *(Courtesy: Nagasaki City Hall)*

Braehead House (Cottage), the Glover family home 1864-1890.

Reception at Glover House, Nagasaki, for Hana Glover's wedding to Walter Bennett in 1897.
Immediately behind the groom is Tsuru with her daughter from a previous marriage and on their right
Alfred Glover. Behind Hana to the right is Martha Glover and on her left Tomisaburo.
*(Courtesy: Nagasaki City Hall)*

Glover family group, mid 1890s, Glover House, Nagasaki. Sitting to the left of Thomas is Martha;
daughter Hana and wife Tsuru standing in centre and Alfred Glover between two unknowns in back row
*(Courtesy: Nagasaki City Hall)*

Thomas Glover and his
daughter-in-law, Waka,
1890s, Tokyo.
*(Courtesy: Nagasaki City Hall)*

Glover and Japanese friends, early 1900s, Tokyo.
*(Courtesy: Nagasaki City Hall)*

Madam Butterfly statue with child in
Glover Garden, Nagasaki.

Madam Butterfly programme cover.

Glover family group, Tokyo, around 1910. Left to right; Waka (wife of Tomisaburo), Glover, Glover grandson Thomas (son of Hana), Tomisaburo, Hana. *(Courtesy: Nagasaki City Hall)*

Unknown location – some believe this photograph was taken on a later visit to Aberdeen – Thomas with young Japanese woman and friends. *(Courtesy: Nagasaki City Hall)*

In the grounds of Glover House, Nagasaki, early 1900s. Thomas entertaining family and friends. Sitting in centre is his daughter Hana, on her right her husband Walter Bennett. Directly in front of Hana sits Alfred Glover. *(Courtesy: Nagasaki City Hall)*

omisaburo on his visit to North East Scotland in 1903. The photograph was captioned Fochabers 1903. Seated in the centre is Charles Glover's widow with her daughters, son-in-law and grandchildren. *(Courtesy: DGO Carmichael)*

Signed photograph of Hirobumi Ito given to
Thomas Glover around 1900. Ito was Japan's
first prime minister – he served five separate
terms in that office – and a life long friend.
*(Courtesy: Nagasaki City Hall)*

Thomas Blake Glover, aged 70 in 1908,
displaying the medal awarded to him that yea
by Emperor Meiji.
*(Courtesy: Nagasaki City Hall)*

Glover graves, Sakamoto International Cemetery, Nagasaki.
*(Courtesy: Nagasaki City Hall)*

# Chapter 19

# ADVISER TO MITSUBISHI

The Glover family set up home in Tokyo near Shiba Park in 1876. Many of Glover's friends of long standing were now among the leading members of the Meiji government and would have welcomed his arrival in the capital. He was now resident near the seat of government, even in a position to advise and influence his proteges of the wild years.

His main occupation was advising the Mitsubishi conglomerate. He was driven in a fine horse-and-carriage daily to the company's offices in the city.[1] From the evidence available it would appear that Glover was very keen on the trappings which went with his new position. In the heyday of Glover & Co. in Nagasaki it had been ornate House flags and crested notepaper. Here the fine house, numerous servants and carriages reflected his professional and social prestige. His position would appear to have been unofficial, although extremely well paid and recognised. One report states that his salary was 20 per cent more than that of the Mitsubishi chairman.[2]

Mitsubishi was much favoured by the government and was expanding rapidly at this time. Iwasaki had managed to secure the services of Glover at the best possible moment for his company. In matters of shipping and shipbuilding - Mitsubishi's first major enterprises - the practical advice and counselling of Glover would then have been of crucial importance.

And as Mitsubishi's tentacles spread into other business activities, again Glover's experience and contacts could be utilised. The extremely shrewd Iwasaki had struck gold - the right man in the right place at the right time.

As he did in Nagasaki, Glover entertained well in his new home. His guests included many VIPs and members of the oligarchy then ruling Japan. It was from these connections that he would have learned of the sinking of his Aberdeen-built all-iron gunboat that year. The *Wen Yu Maru* - now known as the *Un Yo Maru* - went down off the coast of Wakayama prefecture.

Glover's new house now became a principal meeting place for progressive Japanese, a place where they could mix with influential foreigners and where ideas and opinions could be floated freely. It is difficult to imagine at this time Tom Glover harbouring any thoughts of a permanent return to Aberdeen. As was the case with most long-term expatriates, he would now have become more of an alien in his own home town than he was in his adopted Japan.

Certainly his thoughts would have turned to Aberdeen when he heard, most likely by telegraph, of the death of his brother Charles in Old Aberdeen on 14 April 1877. Charles had died of cancer at the age of forty-seven, leaving his wife Margaret, two daughters aged six and eight, and his only son, Thomas Berry, then aged four.

Charles Glover's fortunes in Aberdeen had dipped at the same time as Tom was hitting his lows in Japan. He had moved from 37 High Street, where the town houses of the gentry lined the road, to a much less grand home at 44 Don Street, Old Aberdeen, in 1875. It was in his Don Street house that he died. It is impossible not to speculate whether the trauma of the collapse of Glover & Co. in Japan and the consequent problems of debt that brought to Charles Glover - he was owed $125,430 by his brother's bankrupted firm - did not bring on or accelerate his ill health and death. Charles is buried close to the west wall in the churchyard of St Machar's Cathedral, in the most beautiful and peaceful part of Old Aberdeen and only yards from his last home in the burgh.

A second brother, Captain William Glover, also died in 1877. Aged only forty-five, William had spent most of his life at sea and died far from Aberdeen or Nagasaki where he had spent extended periods. Presumably while in charge of a ship, he died in Port Elizabeth in South Africa. The deaths of Charles and William in 1877 seem to follow a pattern which affected the whole Glover family - a high point or triumph in their lives would suddenly and dramatically be followed by a tragedy.

There was much to discuss at the Glover gatherings of 1877 in Tokyo. The Minister of Home Affairs, Ito, briefed Glover on the Satsuma rebellion which had broken out that year. This uprising was the last conservative military reaction to the new order in Japan. It involved Takamori Saigo who had become the focal point for those with severe misgivings about the direction in which Japan was going.

Saigo's followers, centred in Kagoshima far to the south and west of Tokyo, had become more strident and the government feared an all-out insurrection. It was decided to pre-empt an uprising and an attempt was made to confiscate arms and munitions in Kagoshima. These factors had been enough to spark off the rebellion and Saigo found himself leading the anti-Meiji rebels on a march to Tokyo. At Kumamoto in central Kyushu they were halted by the town garrison and the government in Tokyo gained the time they needed to send reinforcements south. The rebellion raged on for a further six months but the Saigo-led samurai got no further than Kumamoto. Things then turned against them and they were gradually forced back on their base of Kagoshima.

This uprising was a watershed in Japanese military affairs. The new,

Westernised conscript army were trained in and armed with the latest weapons. Saigo's army fought with swords and rifles, the last samurai army, fighting to keep what they saw as the traditional values of Japan. Modern communications and a Navy which included Glover's ships operating off Kagoshima helped the government's land troops win the conflict.

The Saigo rebellion was finally and crushingly put down at Kagoshima that September of 1877. A modern army of 60,000 conscripts had defeated an army of samurai - the impact of this fundamental change to the strictly ordered society of Japan is scarcely imaginable. Saigo took the traditional warrior's way out and commited hara-kiri on the battlefield, following the final defeat. The uprising was over and it was the last attempt to steer Japan away from the course on which it was set. The same year the samurai lost their centuries-old right of carrying swords and indeed it must have felt that an era had passed. Saigo remains a hero in his country, the perfect example in Japanese eyes of unselfish nobility, even in defeat.

The news of the outcome of the battles in the six-month-long rebellion was relayed to Tokyo and dominated the Meiji government's actions during the period. Tom was well informed and, in a sense, in a quandary as he knew the affable and popular Saigo as well as he did the leaders of the New Japan. In mid-1866 Glover, Saigo and the Satsuma daimyo had plotted the downfall of the shogun, placing their own lives in jeopardy. Now one of the insurgents had rebelled and paid the ultimate price.

The uprising affected most of southern Japan in one way or another. Glover's former concern, the Takashima mine, suffered more than most with many of its labourers being tempted away by higher wages to build fortifications for the Meiji forces. When the fighting ended in September they returned to Takashima, some of them infected with cholera which spread at a devastating speed; 163 were dead from the disease by November. Glover would have been relieved to be in the relative safety of Mitsubishi's Tokyo office throughout that second half of 1877.

Glover was forty years old in 1878 and had spent half of his life in Japan. His father died that year in Aberdeen, aged seventy-three, at Braehead House, and was buried in the family plot in St Peter's King Street graveyard beside the remains of his son James. A photograph of the grave was sent to Glover in Japan. His mother Mary was now living at Braehead House with her daughter Martha and Martha's two children. Martha's husband James George appears to have died somewhere around 1870 for at that time she vacated their house in the Chanonry in Old Aberdeen and moved the short distance to her parents' home.

The future Admiral Togo arrived back in Japan in 1878 after his seven-year stint with the Royal Navy in Britain. Now thirty-one years old, Togo returned to be given the routine but important job of surveying parts of the Japanese coast for development as naval bases. Togo's day had yet to come. His friendship with Glover was renewed in this period.

In Tokyo Glover continued as Mitsubishi's adviser. He had left Takashima at the right time, the explosion of 1876 and the Satsuma rebellion of the following year having seriously affected production. His old sparring partner Goto, still nominally the owner of Takashima, was in a spot. He had not paid the miners for three months and in July 1878 the rioted in protest. Things got completely out of hand and the foreigners based on Takashima spent a terrifying night hiding out on the island in the hills above the mine. The miners burned the Westerners' houses and their belongings. Only the arrival of boatloads of armed Nagasaki police the following morning stopped the problem from worsening. On hearing of this outbreak of trouble that summer, Glover worried about the besieged foreign staff, many of them hired by himself. Certainly Alfred was now working in the town of Nagasaki with Henry Gribble and Alex was in Shanghai most likely with Jardine, Matheson and so well clear of the danger. But Glover was familiar with most of the Takashima-based people. Life in Tokyo was a lot quieter than being at the sharp end of business life on Takashima. Perhaps Glover felt a little nostalgia for the wilder life he had left behind in Nagasaki.

Alex Glover was the owner of the *Star Queen* which was lost off Nagasaki in January 1879. Alex had been based in Shanghai since 1874, but like his brother he had retained interests in Nagasaki. His ship left Nagasaki in the late afternoon of 21 January carrying a cargo of Takashima coal to Shanghai. Angus Mackintosh was the ship's Scottish skipper and with crew and passengers the total on board was thirty-three. On the night of the 21st the *Star Queen* ran into a south-east gale and was blown up on the rocks of Oshima Island. The lifeboats were washed away and twenty-two of those on board were killed. Two women and children were among the victims as well as Captain Mackintosh who was struck by a falling mast and died instantly. Mackintosh was later buried in the European cemetery at Oura.[3]

Alex Glover sent orders from Shanghai to Nagasaki's auctioneers to sell the wreck of the *Star Queen* and it was advertised for sale in the *Nagasaki Express* at the beginning of February. Alex was a frequent traveller between Shanghai and Nagasaki and was fortunate not to have been a passenger on his ship's last voyage.

Alfred Glover left Henry Gribble & Co. in 1879 and took up a post with Frederick Ringer's Holme, Ringer & Co. This was Alfred's last career move and he would remain with his new firm for the rest of his life. Despite his switch of employers, Alfred found time to compete in the 1879 Nagasaki regatta. On 8 May he won a tankard as a member of the *Beautiful Maiden* crew. Alfred was stroke and his new employer Frederick Ringer cox.

Japan's rush to catch up with the West continued during 1880. Tom and his young family were by now well established in Tokyo, daughter Hana four years old and Tomisaburo ten. But back in Nagasaki the once-flourishing Takashima mine was beginning to run into serious difficulties.

As usual Goto was heavily in debt with Jardine, Matheson that autumn of 1880. Because of his record of bad debts the Japanese could not get much-needed equipment and stores for the mine unless he paid in cash, and even then he had to pay the suppliers more than 30 per cent over the going rate. The price of coal had fallen as a result of overproduction and this added to his problems. As was his custom, Goto simply stopped paying his miners when things got tight. Early in November the miners went on strike in protest at this and sabotaged enough of the mine machinery to put it out of action for a month.

Goto's opinions of his miners are quite revealing. In a letter to Jardine, Matheson on 24 September 1880 he wrote:

"These miners are not people to be looked at in the same light as ordinary mankind, as they are animals like beasts or birds which begin to seek for food and drinks when they feel hungry or thirsty and know today but not tomorrow; and therefore if they were paid as their works were done and plentifully supplied with food and drinks, they would have one by one ran away and most probably you would not have been able to find Takashima in the present flourishing state."[4]

Goto was a samurai businessman and from the evidence of this letter, more samurai than business inclined. In any case his animal-like miners had had enough of Shojiro Goto.

Jardine, Matheson, too, had had enough, and early in 1881 they sold their interest in the mine for $200,000. There were additional payments for the mine's equipment but it should have been more. The company, in the end, were glad to be shot of Goto and they knew that they would have little or no chance of recovering their loss in a Japanese court.

Mitsubishi took over Takashima in the spring of 1881. It is inconceivable that they were not advised by Glover on this matter. Iwasaki dispatched Glover back to Nagasaki to assume the commercial management of the mine. He was forty-two and in his prime when he reappeared on the Nagasaki scene. It was not surprising Mitsubishi bought the mine. They were now Takashima's best customers because of their expanding fleet of steamers. The deal probably cost Mitsubishi $1.5 million in all. As their adviser Glover was more aware than anyone of Takashima's past and its future potential and would have been acting for Mitsubishi from the outset of the negotiations.

Mitsubishi was a government favourite. Their steamship division NYK was a major success and it was good business for them and for the government that they owned the mine. Tom, reinstalled in Glover House, began to arrange getting the Takashima coal on to the markets of Nagasaki and Shanghai in a way that would ensure top price was paid.

Iwasaki would have been well aware that his mine could not have been in better hands.

Away from the business of the mine, Glover was able to resume his favourite outdoor sports - sailing and pheasant and snipe shooting - now that he was back in Kyushu. On occasion he would now go over to Korea to hunt bigger game. Friends of Glover were often surprised by presents of game delivered to their doors.

He now moved into the diplomatic world. He took over as Portuguese Consul in Nagasaki from Willie P. Magnam, the US Consul, who had held both posts there until mid-1881. An official Ball was held at Glover House to celebrate the Portuguese king's forty-second birthday later that year. This spectacular event attracted more than sixty guests of various nationalities.

Alex Glover, too, was back in Nagasaki in 1881. Still apparently connected with Jardine, Matheson, he was most likely involved with its agency regarding coal sales to China though few details have survived. Alfred, now thirty-one and a long-time Nagasaki resident, continued with Holme, Ringer & Co. The three brothers would have been reunited in Nagasaki for a good part of that year.

Young Tomisaburo Glover, aged eleven, was installed in Nagasaki's Chinzei Gakuin school that year of 1881. The school had only just been founded by the American missionary couple, Dr and Mrs Long, who had arrived in Japan eight years before with their daughter Sarah Jane. Tommy Glover - Tomi-san to the Japanese - was one of the new school's first pupils and initially was doing very well there. This was another example of Glover's acknowledgement of his son by Maki Kaga - privileges for mixed-blood children were previously unknown. As the son of Thomas Glover he would have been the school's best-known pupil.

# Chapter 20

# POLITICAL host

The next few years appear to have been another period of relative calm and consolidation for Glover. Back at the helm of the mine there was more than enough to keep him occupied and there were trips to Mitsubishi's Tokyo office as required. But Takashima was Mitsubishi's jewel in the crown and so Nagasaki was where Glover was based. He would have noticed his slip-dock was now well established. In 1881, alone, five ships had been built on it, earning the yard $326,000. The dock had earned the name in Japanese *Soroban Docku*. The soroban is the Japanese abacus and the ribbed shape of the dock resembled the Japanese counting tool. The dock is within a short walk of Glover House and Tom is likely to have viewed the goings on there with some interest. The slip-dock was still owned by the government but it would not be long before this thriving enterprise, formerly owned by Glover, was taken over by Mitsubishi.

Sir Harry Parkes wrote to the Foreign Minister, Inoue, on 24 February 1882 confirming official British approval for Glover's appointment as Portuguese Consul in Nagasaki. Glover and Inoue were old and intimate friends but Parkes, familiar with both men, wrote his letter in the diplomatic language of the day.

Business trips to Mitsubishi in Tokyo were not the only journeys Glover made in this period. A report in the *Rising Sun & Nagasaki Express* (29 July 1882) tells of another journey Glover made, this time with brother Alex:

"Mr T.B. Glover, accompanied by his brother, Mr A.J. Glover, left by the *Nagoya Maru* last night *en route* for Oregon. We understand he will return to Nagasaki in about six months' time, the trip being partly for relaxation from business, and partly with a desire to investigate on the spot the resources of the Far West. Mr Glover's name has so long been associated with Nagasaki, and he himself the centre and active agent of every movement for the social welfare of residents and visitors, as well as in other ways having done so much for the improvement of the port, that he will be widely missed. We only wish to join with almost every other resident of Japan in wishing him *bon voyage* and a safe return."

Tom and Alex landed in Spokane in the State of Washington in 1882.

There the brothers invested in land and for a spell Tom enjoyed the novelty of a farmer's life. But the call of Japan proved to be too strong for him. He transferred all of his interest in the American land to Alex and made plans to return to Japan. Alex remained in the United States and it is there he is reported to have died. There was to be no reconciliation with his wife Ann and son Ryle Alexander back in Aberdeen. Exactly what became of Alex Glover is not known. He was in his early forties when he left Japan for the last time. The next year, 1883, Tom was back in Nagasaki with his family. The New World of the United States or the Old World of Scotland would not tempt him to settle permanently again. Japan was now his home.

In the autumn of 1884 Glover sent his son to Tokyo's Gakushi-in, or Peers School, for a secondary education. As well as being another example of the attention he lavished on Tomisaburo, it was another honour for Glover as the school was intended exclusively for the children of the Japanese Emperor's family as well as the peerage. A Western-style peerage system had been created that year and many of Tom's intimate friends, including the leading former rebels, had been honoured. Young Tommy, while attending his new school in Tokyo, lived at the home of Yataro Iwasaki, founder of Mitsubishi. It was necessary for Glover to have some strings pulled at the very highest level to have his son admitted to this school. The fourteen-year-old Tomisaburo would remain a guest of the Iwasaki family during his terms at the school over the next few years. All of his classmates here were Japanese, many the sons of people helped earlier by his father.

Mitsubishi continued to expand. The government in its privatisation mania encouraged Iwasaki to take over newly built government shipyards in Honshu in 1884. The yards at Nagasaki would follow three years later. The main aim in the move was to end Japan's reliance on foreign shipping and shipbuilding. It is certain Glover would have been consulted on these major acquisitions.

Hirobumi Ito became the first prime minister of Japan in 1885 - the same Ito who twenty years before as a rebel on the run from the shogun had stayed at the home of Glover's parents in Aberdeen. With the new peerage system now in force, Tom could now boast of famous and titled visitors during his stays in Tokyo. Count Mutsu, Marshal Oyama and the prime minister, Ito, were regular callers. Glover was now a famous man in his own right, being consulted by those at the very pinnacle of power in Japan.

Yataro Iwasaki, who had been given the title of Baron, died in Tokyo in 1885. Iwasaki was fifty-one, Tom forty-seven, and Glover mourned the loss of his old friend, the founder of Mitsubishi. He had worked and fought with Iwasaki during the wild 1860s in Nagasaki. Iwasaki's Mitsubishi did not die with him, this future *zaibatsu* was still in its infancy but growing at a prodigious rate. The founder's younger brother

Yanosuke took over the running of the company, retaining Glover at his right hand.

A French warship visited Nagasaki that summer of 1885. On board was a thirty-five-year-old lieutenant, Julien Marie Vaud, later better known by his pen-name of Pierre Loti. His ship was stationed in Nagasaki for a spell that summer and Loti, like so many before him, took a Japanese 'wife' for the duration of his stay. Loti's impressions of Nagasaki and his 'marriage' would begin the *Madam Butterfly* saga and indirectly affect the Glovers. It is intriguing to wonder if Glover and Loti met during that long hot summer, particularly as Tom often entertained visiting mariners at Glover House.

# Chapter 21

# RED-FACED DEVIL

As the disillusioned Loti headed back to France with his squadron, Takashima continued to cause problems for its owners and management. It was, of course, one of Japan's first great industrialisations. In November 1885 a young Japanese journalist had found employment at the mine in order to report at first hand on the working and living conditions of the miners. When published, this reporter's revelations caused a storm. Two thousand of the mine's workers were crowded on to the small island, he wrote, many in bad health and in terrible conditions. Many were illiterate agricultural workers made redundant by the depression of 1885. The most prominent of those who then began taking up the cause of the miners was Tsuyoshi Inukai, writer and budding politician and later a Japanese prime minister. Inukai conceded that the miners were hard cases requiring strong discipline and that Mitsubishi were not aware of the problems caused by the recent and rapid expansion of the workforce. As commercial manager of the mine Glover was involved in this matter to a certain extent. To make the mine more profitable he had earlier advised squeezing the miners' piece rates, an action which would surely have made a bad situation worse. But the whole affair was a lesson to Mitsubishi at the start of that company's operations in the importance of looking after its workforce.

Despite the recurring accounts of Tom Glover's pleasant personality and generous nature, there was undeniably an ugly side to his character. Although generally amiable to his employees his dark side surfaced occasionally.

Jisaburo Matsuo was a mechanical fitter who worked at Takashima between 1883 and 1893. His son later wrote in a Nagasaki magazine, recalling what his father had told him, while a small boy, of Glover and the mine in those days.[1] Matsuo began in the mine as a 'boy' and personal servant to Glover. He was a favourite of Tom's and his friends and workmates made fun of him because of this. Guraba-san was a hard taskmaster, apparently, with a very short fuse indeed and a virulent temper. He was known to flare up very quickly and even to beat the miners with his walking stick when he flew off the handle. On these occasions the workers called him *Aka Oni*, the red-faced devil - the reddening of his face apparently being the sign of an impending outburst. Presumably Glover was not aware of his nickname.

According to Matsuo, Glover's walking stick got him into more trouble. Once while walking through Nagasaki Glover was pestered by a dog which first barked at him, then began snapping at his leg. Glover brought down his stick on the head of the dog and killed it. The ensuing fuss eventually involved the British Consul and, it was said, resulted in Glover being forbidden to carry his stick.

These reminiscences of Matsuo ring true because of his obvious respect and deep affection for Glover - his anecdotes were not intended as criticism.

The years from 1885 to 1887 were very busy ones for 'T.B.' Glover as he was now becoming generally known. He left the management of Takashima in 1885 and spent the next few years commuting between Nagasaki, Yokohama and Tokyo. His arrangement with Mitsubishi clearly allowed him a great amount of freedom. He was heavily involved in business, social, and even Consular activities. In business, his biggest concern was the Japan Brewery Company, founded in 1885.

The Dutch had introduced beer to Japan and it was a taste the Japanese took to with relish. Originally all the beer drank in Japan was imported. But in 1869 an American, William Copeland, had opened Japan's first brewery in Yokohama. Named the Spring Barley Brewery, it was a success, but on a small scale and illness forced Copeland to close down his enterprise in 1884. By the following year there were several more small breweries in operation in Japan, but even with imported beer costing twice as much as that brewed locally, more than half of the beer drunk in Japan was foreign.

Glover saw this gap in the market. What was needed was a top-class Japanese brewery on a grand scale, producing beer as good as that imported. In partnership with a fellow Briton, M. Kirkwood who worked for the Japanese Home Office, Glover bought the closed-down Spring Barley Brewery in Yokohama. Most of the money needed he raised from the expatriate community in Japan. He was back wheeling and dealing with the best of them.

In July 1885 he founded the Japan Brewery Company. Capitalised at $50,000 in 500 $100 shares, his company was registered in Hong Kong. Glover was thinking on the grand scale again. British engineers were engaged to design and build the brewery and office complex and a master brewer was found and brought over from Germany. Quality requires money and costs began to spiral. Glover found his $50,000 was not enough. To raise the $25,000 extra necessary he needed he went to his top Japanese contacts - including the Mitsubishi president. The extra money he raised saved the project.

He became managing director of the Japan Brewery Company in

1887. His close involvement with the brewery meant Tsuru and eleven-year-old Hana were uprooted from Nagasaki to join him in Yokohama. It also meant giving up the position of Portuguese Consul in Nagasaki - but the honour remained in the Glover family, younger brother Alfred taking up the post.

As well as his strong interest in the politics of Japan, Glover in this period became the honourable foreign secretary of the *Rokumeikan*, the Deer Cry Pavilion.[2] The Rokumeikan was a building specially erected in Tokyo's Hibiya district in 1883. Designed in Victorian style by a British architect, its construction was financed by the Japanese government. At its opening ceremony the Foreign Minister announced that it had been built to provide a place for international communication - for East to meet West; and perhaps a place where the Westernisation of Japan could be accelerated.

In practice, that meant a huge dining room and kitchens supervised by a French chef, with German beer, American cocktails and English cigarettes; ballrooms and promenading corridors in the best European fashion of the day; and, for a period, it led to the wives of Japan's leading citizens discarding their timelessly beautiful kimono for what was currently fashionable in the West. The push for rapid Westernisation was then at its height and if that meant doing away with traditional Japanese social behaviour then so it had to be.

Glover's thoughts on this, unfortunately, are not known. As Rokumeikan secretary he would have been involved in the organisation of the balls, concerts and meetings of East/West societies regularly held there. Certainly in the Grand Masquerade Ball of 1887 the Rokumeikan reached its pinnacle of success: all the leading members of Ito's government were there, including the Prime Minister himself in the guise of a Venetian nobleman. Various foreign dignitaries were similarly disguised.

The Ball of 1887 was another turning point in the Westernisation of Japan - the point at which many began to think that they had gone too far, too quickly. The spectacle of Japan's leading politicians disguised as they were brought on a torrent of criticism. Loss of dignity is perhaps the worst crime of all in Japanese eyes. The occasion in any case marked the beginning of the end of the Deer Cry Pavilion and the first application of a revised attitude on adopting all things foreign - be they good or bad. As in almost every revolution, the pendulum had swung too far.

With Glover in Tokyo, Alfred took on the family mantle in Nagasaki - but he was not a natural leader like his brother. Modest and quiet by all accounts, he had remained a steady and unspectacular employee of Holme, Ringer & Co. since joining the firm in 1878. But in 1886, with his brother busy in Tokyo, Alfred got the opportunity to shine. He founded the port's St Andrew's Society. The thirteen resident Scots in the port, many of whom, like Alfred, were Aberdonians, joined with twenty-three others to celebrate the Scottish patron saint's day on 30 November that year. The venue for the party was Nagasaki's Fukuya restaurant and Alfred had prepared well. The tables had been laid with real Scots food, including haggis, roast beef and cheese and there were desserts to follow with all the trimmings. It was a quite spectacular occasion, well worthy of big brother Tom. The normally quiet Alfred ended the celebrations with the proposal of the toast to Queen Victoria.

Glover's mother Mary died in Braehead House in Aberdeen aged eighty in 1887. Her daughter, Martha, registered the death. Martha, her son, Charles, then aged twenty-three, and daughter Annie, then twenty-one, were living at the Glover family home at the time of the death of the old lady. It appears that they vacated Braehead House shortly after. Charles was a clerk with the Railways and little more is known of him after this date. There is some reason to believe that at this time Glover wrote to Martha from Japan offering his sister and her children the opportunity to join him. There is also the distinct possibility that Glover travelled back to Aberdeen again later that year, perhaps to visit his parents' grave in St Peter's in King Street. He may well have then made the offer to Martha in person. For the time being at least she turned down the chance to join her rich and famous brother in the Far East but fate and tragedy would intervene. In any case, the twenty-five-year connection of the Glovers and Braehead House in Bridge of Don, Aberdeen, was broken at last.

The following year, 1888, Tomisaburo was officially adopted by Tom and Tsuru and he appears on her koseki. He had completed his four years of secondary education at the Peers School in Tokyo and left there after graduation to go and live with Tom, Tsuru and his half-sister Hana in Yokohama. He later registered himself on his own koseki as Tsuru's son. He followed this with a short trip overseas on a government mission with the statesman friend of his father, Viscount Mutsu. Back in Japan Tomisaburo began to write his middle name, A. or Albert in English, as Awajiya, Tsuru's maiden surname. He was now ready for University. He sailed to the United States that year and enrolled in Philadelphia University in Pennsylvania.

Living in Philadelphia at that time was the lawyer and author, John Luther Long. Long's sister Sarah Jane had married Irvine Correll, later another missionary principal of Chinzei Gakuin in Nagasaki, the school which Tomisaburo had attended some years before. It is not known if Long met Tomisaburo at this time or during his long stay in the American city but with the Long/Correll/Nagasaki/Tomisaburo connections it would seem likely.

# Chapter 22

# FROM KEELS TO KIRIN

The Japan Brewery Company's first beer went on sale in May 1888. Glover had been helped by Hakaru Issono, president of the Meijiya company, to get his new beer on the Japanese market. It was a lager beer, named *Kirin* after the half-horse, half-dragon of Japanese legend. The Kirin was also a symbol of good luck and was a good choice, as the brewery proved to be another great success for Glover. He continued as a director of the new company.[1]

Japan took another giant step towards Western-style democracy in 1889. The new Constitution, the brainchild of Hirobumi Ito, came into force that year. The following year the Japanese National Diet was established, a two-House parliamentary system. Even if only 10 per cent of Japanese could vote, it was still a step in the right direction. To Glover, now a thirty-year veteran of Japan, it would have been hard to accept just how far his adopted country had come in those three decades. Japan was well on the way to becoming a power in the world. Even the hated and humiliating extra-territoriality agreements, which prevented foreigners being subject to Japanese law, were being reconsidered for the first time. The Japanese military was strong, particularly its Navy which in the early 1890s was still using Glover's Aberdeen-built ships of the late 1860s. The Army, too, was well armed and disciplined.

Industrially as well as militarily Japan was expanding. Glover's spent these momentous years in Tokyo advising Mitsubishi as the corporation grew and seemingly could do no wrong. His consultancy allowed him the freedom to continue runnning the Japan Brewery Company of which he became president in 1891. As well as Mitsubishi and the brewery, there were pleasant interludes in Nagasaki.

During these years Glover's houses continued to be places where progressive Japanese and foreigners could meet and talk freely. Many important Japanese and foreign diplomats would visit him. Tourists, too, with the latest news and fashions from the United States and Europe would call and ideas and opinions were floated freely.

Glover appears to have considered himself by this time an authority on Japanese affairs. He could be scathing in his criticism of visitors who became 'experts' in things Japanese during fleeting visits to the country.

Glover's friends respected his claims to know how the Japanese thought. Perhaps in his mid-fifties he did think he knew everything there was to know about Japan. There was one recorded occasion, though, when Glover got caught out.[2]

A party of foreign residents, which included Glover, were lunching at the house of a well-known Tokyo-based Westerner, Captain Brinkley. Brinkley was a long-time British resident who regularly wrote articles for the *Japan Mail*. The table conversation got round to the then current visit to Japan of Sir Edwin Arnold, owner of the *Daily Telegraph*. Arnold was writing a series of articles on Japan for his paper and one had just appeared dealing with Japanese politics.

At the lunch Glover let fly, criticising Arnold as yet another short-time visitor who considered himself an instant expert on Japanese affairs. Brinkley broke into Glover's tirade, asking him what specifically he found fault with in the article.

"Oh," said Glover, "he may gush as much as he wants about geisha, but when he writes such rot as he did the other day on Japanese politics, it is another matter."

"Would you be surprised, Glover," said Brinkley, looking at the Scot, "to learn that *I* wrote that article?"

An awkward silence followed. Glover must have been surprised because the article had been signed in Arnold's name. But he recovered his composure and said that it did not alter his opinion of the article. The subject was quickly dropped.

As he did in Nagasaki, Glover kept well-stocked greenhouses in the grounds of his Tokyo home and now spent much of his time in them. It was said that he would have made an excellent farmer. Perhaps this is not so surprising in view of the fact that his mother Mary's family were prominent farmers in north-east Scotland. Another favourite pastime was working on the lathe in the workshop he had installed in his home; he became very skilled in its use.

The Rokumeikan, where Glover had served as honorary foreign secretary, was severely damaged in an earthquake in 1893. Repairs were calculated to be too expensive and this monument to Japan's Westernisation was allowed to die. It had been Japanese high society's meeting place during its heydays of the late 1880s. But Japan had slowed in its rush for Westernisation. The Japanese had began to take stock of where their country was going and the death of the Rokumeikan was perhaps a symbol of this reappraisal.

By the late 1880s Glover's sister Martha had become the sole surviving member of the family left in Aberdeen. Of the three living sons, Tom and Alfred were in Japan and Alex in the United States. Tom's mother, father and three of his elder brothers had died, all but the second son William being buried in Aberdeen. Martha and her two surviving children moved to a smaller property in Aberdeen after her mother's death, perhaps finding the upkeep of Braehead too much.

The death of Martha's second daughter in 1889 at the age of twenty-two was perhaps the spur she needed to take up the offer made earlier to go out and join Tom in Japan. Her son Charles remained in Scotland.

Hana, the daughter of Tom and Tsuru, was fourteen in 1890 and Martha may well have been asked out to help groom her niece in Western ways. Hana most likely served as a substitute for Martha's own two daughters, both of whom died tragically young. She left for Japan sometime in this period and took up residence initially at her brother's home in Tokyo. Martha now became the sixth of the seven children of Lieutenant and Mrs Mary Glover to arrive in Japan and to spend extended periods there.

Alex Glover's wife, Ann, died in Edinburgh in 1893 at the age of fifty-three and was buried in the Finlay family plot at Newhills near Aberdeen. Her family tradition has it that she spent many years waiting for the return of Alex Glover and was in fact a Scottish Madam Butterfly. Her son Ryle was now the last surviving Glover/Japan connection in Scotland.

And across the English Channel in France, that same year of 1893, Pierre Loti published his book *Madame Chrysanthème*. The book continued the craze for all things Japanese which had begun in Europe over thirty years before. It was an autobiographical account of a French naval officer's summer in Nagasaki and based on Loti's own experiences with his temporary Japanese wife in the port eight years before. Loti's views as expressed in the book are openly racist. His tale has no tragic end. In the final scene his Madame Chrysanthème is left checking the gold coins left her by the officer with a small hammer. Any disillusion-ment in his book is felt by the Frenchman, not by the Japanese child bride.

# Chapter 23

# hONOURED BY EMPEROR MEİJİ

J apan's war with China in 1894 over disputed Korean territory and
Japan's notable successes in that conflict began waking up the West
to the new power in the Far East. On 25 July 1894 Captain Togo
of the Imperial Japanese Navy fired the first shots of the war, almost
three weeks before the official declaration of the conflict. As they
would do against the Russians in 1904 and the Americans in 1941, the
Japanese struck first and heavily. All caution and diplomatic considerations
were thrown to the wind. Glover had retained his interest and advised
the Japanese government in the development of its Navy and would
have been thrilled by its successes in the war with China. Later Glover
would be cited by the Japanese Emperor for his 'hidden service' to Japan
during this war. It is likely that this 'service' consisted of using his
diplomatic connections to push the case for Japan. Also, as a neutral
Briton, he could have travelled to China and passed on any information
on the Chinese armed forces which he came across.

The war was over by April 1895 and the victorious Japanese forces
had employed Glover's now veteran ships with the modern units of their
fleet. His ships by this time had trained a generation of Japanese seamen.
Japan was now a colonial power in its own right where forty years before
it had been itself a possible target for colonisation. The result of the war
elevated Japan's status. The Anglo-Japanese Treaty signed by Foreign
Minister, Mutsu, in 1894 further increased its prestige. It was agreed with
the British that the hated extra-territorial laws would end in 1899, after
five years. The Japanese knew that once the British had signed, all the
other powers in the world would follow. These were heady times
indeed for the Japanese.

Tomisaburo Glover joined his uncle Alfred as an employee of
Holme, Ringer & Co. the following year of 1895. Young Glover would
remain with this firm for the next forty-five years. Tomisaburo was
financially secure and his work with Holme, Ringer appears to have
been more of a hobby than of an employer/employee relationship. His
father had brought Frederick Ringer to Japan in the 1860s as a tea expert
for his company and the two had remained firm friends. Ringer House now
shared a prominent spot slightly above Glover House on Minami Yamate.

Glover's daughter Hana married in 1897. She had been educated in Tokyo mostly, during her father's long residences there and in Yokohama. She preferred the Western way of life to the Japanese and, by all accounts, was like her father and very much the extrovert. She was also a very intelligent young woman. On 26 January 1897 she married Walter Gordon Bennett of Holme, Ringer & Co., a London-born Briton who had been working in Japan since 1890. They had met in 1894 when the then eighteen-year-old Hana and her parents were living at Glover House in Nagasaki. Walter was aged twenty-eight and Hana twenty-one when they married. It was a big occasion in Nagasaki as the wedding photograph shows; it depicts a now white-haired Glover, close to sixty years old, somehow aloof but still the proud father. Alfred, a mischievious look on his face, now forty-six with almost thirty years in Japan behind him, stands to the right of the group. Tomisaburo is there, too, as is a rather stiff-looking Martha and presumably some of the leading members of the Western establishment at the port. Tsuru, in formal kimono, stands in front of Tom on one of the very rare occasions on which they were photographed together.

Hana and her husband left Nagasaki the following year for Korea where Bennett had been appointed a branch manager with his company near Seoul.

John Luther Long published his story 'Madam Butterfly' in the American *Century* magazine in 1898. Long himself never visited Japan.

His story quite clearly was influenced by Pierre Loti's highly successful *Madame Chrysantheme* of five years earlier. But there is one crucial difference between the Loti and Long versions - the suicide of Madam Butterfly at the end of the American's story. It is this vital addition to the proposition of Pierre Loti that East meets West equals disillusionment which suggests that Long added the Maki Kaga/Tom Glover drama to the bare bones of Loti's *Madame Chrysantheme* and produced an immortal character.

There may have been other influences. Long's sister had moved to Nagasaki in 1892 and lived on Higashi Yamate - sometimes known as the Missionary Hillside and just across the Oura river from Glover House on Minami Yamate. On a visit to Philadelphia in 1897 she passed on to her author brother the story of Cho-san, the abandoned 'wife' of an American naval officer whom she had lately known while in Nagasaki. She told him of other Japanese experiences she knew of. Long was fascinated. He sat up that night writing till dawn. The following year 'Madam Butterfly' was published.[1] Long reportedly would later claim that his story was based on true incidents told him by his sister, incidents which had happened in Nagasaki some years before and that the suicide in his story, in fact, had been an unsuccesful attempt. Clearly there was more than one source for Long's story but the case for the climax of his 'Madam Butterfly' being based on the Glover/Maki Kaga drama is a strong one.

At the time of the story's publication, Glover was sixty and Tomisaburo twenty-eight. It is unlikely that they would have heard or known of it, at least at that time.

With Hana married and gone, Glover and Tsuru were pleased to see Tomisaburo and Waka Nakano become very close. Waka was the beautiful daughter of a Japanese woman and a British diplomat and had been unofficially adopted by Tom.

The wedding of the two was planned for Nagasaki in June 1899. Tsuru Glover had by then been suffering from cancer of the stomach for some time. Her death on 23 March that year came perhaps more suddenly than anyone had thought. She had remained with Glover for thirty-two years and despite their problems it does seem to have been a love match. She did know of their first grandchild before she died. Walter Bennett was born in Korea in 1897 and their second grandson, Herbert, was born the year she died. Her funeral service was a grand occasion and after cremation in Tokyo her remains were taken to Taiheiji Temple grounds in Nagasaki. This quiet spot was only a few hundred yards south of Glover House.

In another twist to the Madam Butterfly story, her gravestone was marked with her family crest - a butterfly.

Commenting on her death, an article in an English language newspaper called her 'Lady Tsuru', an indication perhaps of the Glovers' standing in the community.

The wedding of Tomisaburo and Waka went ahead as planned in Nagasaki on 12 June 1899. The same year Tomisaburo joined with his uncle Alfred in founding Nagasaki's Naigai Club, an organisation intended to promote Japanese and Western friendship and understanding. Now in his sixties, perhaps Tom was ready to take a back seat in these matters. After the death of Tsuru and the wedding of Tomisaburo, Glover moved more or less permanently into his Azabu home in Tokyo. He would still visit Nagasaki but Azabu was now his main base.

In London in 1900 the visiting Italian composer Giacomo Puccini took in the play *Madam Butterfly*, then showing at the Duke of York theatre. The play had been produced by the American David Bellasco and was a dramatised version of John Luther Long's short story. Puccini was fascinated by the play and it was said that he was so moved he could not get up from his seat at the end of the performance. Apparently there and then he decided to write an opera on the bitter-sweet 'Butterfly' theme. Puccini would spend 1902 sweating over what would become one of the world's best-known operas. In a letter to a friend from Torre del Lago, in the summer or autumn of 1902, he wrote:

"... I have had a visit from Mme Ohyama, wife of the Japanese ambassador. She told me a great many interesting things and sang some native songs for me ... I sketched the story of the [Butterfly] libretto for her, and she liked it, especially as such a story as Butterfly's is known to her as having happened in real life."[2]

In Japan the Anglo-Japanese Alliance was now in force. This was the official end of Japan's centuries of isolation, a further boost to national prestige and the military now felt much freer to act. Glover's thoughts can only be imagined in those early years of the twentieth century as his adopted country went from strength to strength. Family affairs now occupied the old man.

His first granddaughter, Edith Bennett, was born in 1901. Martha Glover George died in 1903 in Nagasaki, aged sixty one. She had spent the final ten years or so of her life with her brother Tom in Japan and is pictured with him in many of the photographs taken during those years. Nothing is known of her son Charles who would have been thirty-nine and presumably still in Britain at the time of his mother's death. After the loss of her husband and her two daughters so young and in such a tragic fashion, Martha's last years at least appear to have been happy ones. As well as grooming Hana, Martha had occupied herself with volunteer work for the church during her stay in Japan. She died in Glover House on 20 March 1903. Martha appears to have converted to Catholicism sometime after the death of her second daughter and her funeral was held in Nagasaki's Catholic church, Oura Tensho Do, literally only yards from Glover House on Minami Yamate. She was buried in Sakamoto International Cemetery and it was reported that the procession of *jinrikisha* to carry the mourners to the graveside stretched for more than one kilometre. Again this would suggest her high place in the hierarchy of the foreign community, the sister of the famous T.B. She was the first Glover to be buried in Sakamoto, the port's newly opened foreigners' graveyard. Sakamoto lies just a little to the north of Glover House, a green and peaceful glade on a steep hillside.

Another Glover granddaughter was born that year. The fourth and last Bennett, a girl named Mabel, made her appearance. As Tomisaburo would remain childless, these four Bennett chidren would become the only known descendants of Thomas Blake Glover and like their illustrious grandfather's family, the Bennetts would spread themselves over the globe.

The year of Martha's death, 1903, Tomisaburo visited his father's relations and old haunts in far-off Aberdeen. Perhaps he carried news of Martha's last days to her son and to the other Glover in-laws. He had tea with Charles Glover's widow and her children in the garden of a house in Fochabers, a small town a little north of Aberdeen. No doubt Tomisaburo had been briefed by his father in what to expect from his Scottish Glover kin. He was, after all, a Glover but despite his reported 'manners of a British gentleman and graces of a refined Japanese', in the photograph taken at Fochabers during his visit he looks somehow alien and ill at ease and entirely Japanese. Certainly it was unusual for those born in his circumstances to be acknowledged as openly as he was -

another example perhaps of his father's regard for him and there is a suspicion that this regard was tinged with guilt concerning his removal as an infant from his natural mother. The caption on the photograph calls him 'The Boodle' - presumably the then current and somehow sad word for someone of mixed blood. Tomisaburo's trip was not entirely for pleasure. Acting in his capacity as the managing director of the Nagasaki Fishery Steam Trawling Company - an offshoot of Holme, Ringer - he completed some important business too. Like his father on his historic visit to Aberdeen thirty-six years before, Tomisaburo placed orders for ships with an Aberdeen shipyard, this time for Japan's first steam-driven trawlers. He returned to a Japan on the brink of war with Russia.

Japan's war with Russia started in February 1904 and was its claim to undisputed recognition as a power in the world. The Russians on the outbreak of war looked down disdainfully on the Japanese. Cartoons in Russian newspapers lampooned the Japanese as monkeys. As they would do against the Americans thirty-seven years later at Pearl Harbor, the Japanese struck first and without warning.

Japan's daring exploits in the Russo-Japanese war of 1904-5 put the country again in the headlines of the world's press. Like the war with China ten years before it was fought over disputed territory in Manchuria. During the night of 7/8 February 1904, the Japanese launched their surprise naval attack on the Russian-held stronghold of Port Arthur in Manchuria. Leading the Japanese fleet was the newly promoted Vice-Admiral Togo on the British built warship *Mikasa*. The British and Americans were openly sympathetic to 'little' Japan in its struggle with the overpowering Russian Bear. Aberdeen shared in the early successes of the Japanese fleet. To quote from the *Aberdeen Journal* (20 Feb. 1904), shortly after the outbreak of war:

"In view of the remarkable success which has attended the dashing operations of the Japanese fleets in the Russo-Japanese war, it is a fact, of which Aberdonians have some reason to feel proud, that the first ironclad  or protected war vessel of the Japanese navy was built in Aberdeen ...

...to the honour which Aberdeen can thus lay claim to as a factor in the building up of Japan's fortunes at sea ..."

The article went on to describe the early ships built for the Japanese by Glover and even corrected a London newspaper's slip that the *Jho Sho Maru* was Japan's first modern warship. There was a sense of pride evident when it pointed out that the honour of being first went to the *Ho Sho Maru*. The article finished by also pointing out that both of these ships, built almost thirty-five years before, were still in use with Japan's Navy:

"After a long period of service the *Jho Sho Maru* was converted into a training ship, and she is still doing yeoman service in the making of

Japanese seamen and gunners."

Japan would have have been in the public eye once more in Europe that year. Puccini had produced his masterpiece at the second attempt and the reworked *Madama Butterfly* was first seen on 28 May 1904 in Brescia. The first version had gone out within days of the opening shots of the war, on 17 February. The new *Madama Butterfly* would take Europe and later the United States by storm. The innocence of the Japanese in *Madama Butterfly* can be contrasted with the ferocious-ness of the Japanese military in the war with Russia.

Glover shared in the pride of Aberdeen and Japan in the perform-ance of its Navy. The Japanese hero of the war was Togo, the same young samurai who had helped defend Kagoshima from British bombardment in 1863. But as well as the reflected glory of 1904 there was sadness, too, for Tom. He had brought his brother Alfred back with him to Japan after his trip to Aberdeen in 1867. It is likely that both Tom and Alfred made several more trips back to Scotland in the ensuing years - but no concrete evidence of this has survived. In 1904, after a thirty-seven-year residence in Japan, Alfred decided to return perma-nently to Scotland. On the first leg of this journey home he became ill and on 18 May he died in Hong Kong. His body was shipped back to Nagasaki for burial. He was buried there, at Sakamoto, on 7 June 1904 after a service in the Episcopal church in Higashi Yamate. He became the second Glover to remain permanently on that beautiful hillside resting place of Nagasaki and is buried close to the grave of his sister. Alfred is not known to have married and appears to have been the complete opposite of Tom in many ways. Quiet and introverted, he shunned the limelight in which Tom basked all of his days. Although he lived his life very much in the shadow of his famous brother, Alfred did become involved in the social life of the foreign community, particularly Nagasaki's St Andrew's Society. At fifty-four, Alfred was twelve years younger than Tom when he died and the older brother surely would have remembered the early days in Aberdeen and Nagasaki and would have known that his own days were now numbered.

The final crushing victory over the Russians came in the Battle of Tsushima in May 1905. The Japanese fleet annihilated the Russian fleet in this historic sea battle fought in the Sea of Japan. Admiral Togo led the Japanese and for a change the people of Japan had a living, victorious hero. There was no glorious but futile suicide to end this war. Togo returned to Tokyo in triumph. He was later invited to a reception in his honour at the home of Yanosuke Iwasaki, head of Mitsubishi and brother of Tom's old friend. As in the war with China ten years before, Glover's 'hidden service' and advice in the conflict had been noted and would be mentioned in the Emperor's citation some years later. Significantly, in the group photograph of Togo's officers, seamen and family taken at the Iwasaki reception stands Tom Glover. A foreigner in a sea of Japanese faces, Glover, adviser and old friend, was given a place of honour. His inclusion on this occasion of supreme pride for the Japanese nation says more than words can describe.

The war with Russia had been costly: 120,000 Japanese dead, slightly more than the Russian total. But the victory and the alliance with Britain were vindications of Glover's faith in Japan, now at last a recognised power in the world. The Japanese Navy at the beginning of the Meiji period had in total 6,000 tons of warships and half of that tonnage was made up of Tom Glover's ships. Now that same Navy weighed in at 380,000 tons. In less than fifty years the nation had risen from being a feudal, backward society to a major military and industrial force in the world. The development of Modern Japan had proceeded at a hectic pace and throughout the dramatic period Glover had been there, prodding and advising, the great innovator, truly a founding father of this new state.

Tomisaburo's natural mother Maki Kaga died in 1905. It is not known if Tom or his son kept in touch with her or even knew of her death. Ironically, the opera which she perhaps inspired was enjoying great success.

In 1906 Charles Glover's son, Thomas Berry Glover, on leave from his post with a Calcutta-based company, died in Yokohama. Young Thomas was thirty-three in the year of his death and was on a visit to his famous uncle in his adopted country. Thomas Berry Glover is buried in Nagasaki between the graves of his uncle and aunt, the third Glover to be laid to rest in Sakamoto. The date and place of his death is recorded on the gravestone of his parents in St Machar's churchyard in Old Aberdeen.

That same year Glover's former concern, the Japan Brewery Company, was sold to the Mitsubishi group. At the opening ceremony of the new firm Tom was presented with 3,000 Yen for his efforts in the initial development of the brewery; 3,000 Yen was then a large sum - a detached house with garden in Tokyo cost about 200 Yen. The Japan Brewery Company's Kirin Beer even today counts for about 60 per cent of the Japanese beer market.

In his seventieth year, 1908, Glover was recommended for a national honour or award. The recommendation came from his two old friends, now raised to the peerage, Prince Ito and Marquis Inoue. They made their views known to Emperor Meiji and he apparently agreed. The two now elder statesmen knew that their old Scottish sparring partner would greatly appreciate the honour. The Emperor was surely well aware of the assistance given by Glover to the rebellion which restored the monarchy to power in Japan.

Tom Glover was presented with the Order of the Rising Sun,

second class, by Emperor Meiji of Japan in 1908. No details of the ceremony have survived but the record of his accomplishments for Japan presented at the time runs to twenty pages of Japanese script. Pictured after the ceremony displaying his award, Glover looks a proud man. His day, at last, had come.

# Chapter 24

# The final years

Glover's last three years were spent mostly in his Tokyo home at Azabu. An extension had been added to this already large house, it was said at the expense of Hirobumi Ito. Glover lived there quietly with his staff, still entertaining, still concerned with the development of his visiting family, still advising Mitsubishi when required. The coaches of Japanese and foreign high society could still be seen parked outside his house.[1] He occasionally travelled to Mitsubishi's Marunouchi offices and remained an honoured guest of the Japanese government. He was probably the best-known foreigner in Japan and even then was regarded as one of the driving forces behind Japan's emergence as a powerful modern nation.

It was during this period Glover gave the interviews to the Choshu clan historian Kunihei Nakahara, some of which are quoted in this short account of his life. Clearly he was ill and old and a little confused when he recalled the events of decades before, but there is a ring of truth in his replies, a last chance perhaps for a dying old man to set the record straight.

On 13 December 1911 he suffered an attack from the chronic kidney problem which had plagued him for some time. The attack forced him to remain in bed. On the morning of the 16th it looked as if he was getting better. About one o' clock lunch was brought to his bedroom. He got out of bed and sat at the small table set nearby. When he had finished his soup he suddenly fell over and within minutes he was dead. The cause of death was diagnosed as Bright's Disease, kidney failure.

His funeral service was held in Trinity Episcopal Cathedral, Tokyo. Over two hundred mourners attended, led by Tomisaburo, Hana and her family, and included government ministers, business and diplomatic leaders. The British ambassador in Japan as well as his Japanese counterpart in London were among them as were the Iwasaki brothers who owned Mitsubishi. Kaoru Inoue, years before helped abroad by Glover and now a seventy-six-year-old elder statesman, sent a wreath. Hirobumi Ito, former prime minister and perhaps Glover's closest Japanese friend, had died the year before - assassinated by a Korean nationalist while colonial governor of that country. Two episcopal priests conducted Glover's funeral service and Bishop McKim and his assistants were in attendance. It was an impressive occasion and would surely have pleased the man who valued style so much. Glover's award from the Emperor three years earlier had mentioned his 'hidden service' to Japan. Perhaps the grandness of the funeral was a nation's thanks.

His body was cremated in Tokyo and his ashes brought back to Nagasaki for interment at Sakamoto International Cemetery. In a moving parade through the streets of the port where he had arrived in Japan fifty years before, his ashes were carried with his medal at the head of the procession. Some excerpts from the Japanese English-language press of the day give an idea of the esteem in which he was held:

"[Mr Glover] was on terms of intimacy with all the great leaders in the renaissance of Japan and we have heard it said that no foreigner was so greatly trusted by the Japanese, or understood them so well, as the deceased."

"Many [of the makers of modern Japan] flocked to Nagasaki in quest of knowledge or on business. Among these were the late Prince Ito, Count Okuma, Marquis Inoyue, and others. By all of these personages he was held in the highest esteem, especially so by the first-named statesman who counted him among his intimate friends."

"Nagasaki paid tribute yesterday to the late Mr T.B. Glover, who was one of the founders of the foreign settlement and for many years its leading resident.

... There was a great assembly and only a few of those present could be accomodated in the room [in Glover House] where the service took place."

"... the casket (completely hidden by beautiful wreaths and crosses) was borne to Urakami Cemetry. ... as the cortege passed through the settlement the flag at the British Consulate was lowered to half-mast and other marks of respect were shown. The decorations conferred on the deceased by H.M. the Emperor were carried on cushions before the casket."

The port's Consuls were the pall-bearers and it would appear that Glover was held in almost royal awe. Tsuru Glover's remains were moved from the temple grounds where they had lain and later reinterred with those of Thomas Glover in Sakamoto. Despite the indiscretions of Glover over the years they had remained together for more than three decades.

Glover had never been engaged in any official capacity by either Mitsubishi or the Japanese government. Even before then his efforts for the rebels in the uprising which brought down the shogun had been clandestine and in many cases not officially recorded. The references to Glover in the standard histories of the Meiji period are tantalisingly fleeting - frustratingly so. But he is mentioned in almost every one and his life in this period can be traced with reasonable accuracy. Lord

Redesdale published his *Memories* in 1915. As a young man - then simply Algernon Mitford - Lord Redesdale had served with the brilliant Ernest Satow as an interpreter and assistant to Sir Harry Parkes. In *Memories* Redesdale wrote of Satow's efforts in furthering Anglo-Japanese understanding. He goes on:

"There was another man, Mr Thomas Glover, a merchant of Nagasaki, who also rendered good, though hitherto unacknowledged, service in the same sense."

The impression is strong that Glover was involved undercover at the core of the overthrow of the shogun and that Lord Redesdale was belatedly acknowledging this. But perhaps the finest epitaph to Thomas Glover is that of his contemprory, long-time resident, journalist and Japanese scholar, W.B. Mason:

"Glover was one of the few men who found admission to the inner shrine of Japanese life in days when the stranger from abroad rarely penetrated further than the *genkan* [doorway]."

Glover's business success in the beginning had been helped in part by his family's shipping connections in Aberdeen. His fluent Japanese was another prime asset, particularly in the early days. But there was much more to it than that. He was propelled by a nervous energy and his willingness to take a chance became in time a reckless compulsion to succeed. Could this urge in the beginning have been the model for the young bloods of Mitsubishi and in time Sony, Toyota, and others, for the Japanese economic miracle? Glover enjoyed his success and the privileges that went with it, as do the Japanese of the late twentieth century. It is fortunate for the Japanese that Thomas Blake Glover was there at the start of their country's transition into the successful modern nation that it is today.

# epilogue

Thomas Blake Glover died before the upsurge of Japanese militarism which scarred the first half of the twentieth century. He died a hero. But the anti-foreign hysteria he had experienced as a young man returned to Japan not long after his death - perhaps another long-delayed reaction to the over-rapid Westernisation of the country. This xenophobia perhaps dulled Glover's fame at that time. Japan had never been a colony but like many newly independent nations the country went through a phase of playing up the contribution of its own people in its development and playing down that of foreigners.

If Glover did not live to witness the nationalism of the 1920s and 1930s, his son came through this period in relative calm. But as the 1940s began and the countries of his mother and father came into conflict in the Second World War, he must have viewed the unfolding international events with horror.

Tomisaburo had moved into Glover House shortly after the death of his father. He was independently wealthy but continued his work as an executive with Holme, Ringer & Co. He actively promoted Japan-Western understanding and enjoyed golf and the other leisurely pursuits of the pre- war elite of Nagasaki. One photograph taken in the mid 1930s shows him entertaining Japanese guests at a garden party he held in honour of the accession of King Edward to the British crown. But as the clouds of war began to gather, Glover's son found it more and more difficult to remain a 'British gentleman' and a 'refined Japanese'. A book on the Glovers - written by a Canadian ex-Buddhist monk, Brian Burke-Gaffney, long a resident of Nagasaki - goes into the life and anguish of Tomisaburo in some detail. Written in Japanese and titled *Hana To Shimo* (Blossoms and Frost), it compares the Blossom of Tom Glover's life with the Frost of that of his son.

The amiable and easy-going Tomisaburo never quite lived up to the reputation of his famous father. Clearly, his Scottish father had doted on him. He flaunted convention by acknowledging him openly and sent him to the best schools in Japan and the West. Later he used his business and political contacts to boost Tomisaburo's career. But the drive and determination of the father was not continued by the son who preferred the quiet life. For some time after the death of his father, Tomisaburo lived with his wife in Glover House. Later he moved to a smaller place - somehow symbolically lower down Minami Yamate and in the shadow of his father's home. He sold Glover House to the Mitsubishi Dockyard Company in 1939, where it was first used as a clubhouse and later a dormitory after the outbreak of war.

The attack on Pearl Harbor by the Japanese and the start of the war between Japan and the United States and Britain in December 1941 soured Tomisaburo's last years. Ironically, the Imperial Japanese Navy's prominent aircraft-carrier *Ho Sho* was named after the gunboat brought from Aberdeen to Japan the year before Glover's son was born.

Despite his Japanese citizenship he was suspected of spying for the British and hounded by the Japanese *Kempeitai* or secret police. He was taken away and interrogated several times during the war years. His wife Waka died in 1943, around the time the previously invincible Japanese military machine was beginning to collapse overseas. The sacred homeland was now threatened by invasion from the West - as it had been eighty years before. Tomisaburo, now on his own, despaired. He commited suicide in his home on Minami Yamate on 26 August 1945, almost two weeks after the atomic bombing of the city - which had wiped out the northern half of Nagasaki but left Glover House and the southern half virtually intact. He died four days before the occupying troops were due to land in the port. Another in the long line of ironies was that the ostensible target for the atomic bomb which destroyed much of Nagasaki was the Mitsubishi shipyards - the shipyards his father Tom Glover had done so much to develop. Tomisaburo and his wife were childless. They became the sixth and seventh - and last - Glovers to be buried in Sakamoto. After eighty-six years there was no longer a Glover resident in the port. Tomisaburo left all his wealth for the restoration of Nagasaki.

In the immediate years after Japan's surrender the occupying Army took over Glover House. Mitsubishi later regained possession and gifted the house and land to the City of Nagasaki in 1957. It was developed as a venue for visitors to the port - 'the house of Madam Butterfly' - and became a huge success. It remains one of the biggest tourist attractions in Japan.

Some critics scoffed at the Glover/Madam Butterfly allusions suggested by the developers but until recently most people were unaware of Maki Kaga and of the drama surrounding the birth of her son. Clearly the Madam Butterfly legend developed from several sources but the Tom Glover story is surely one of them. It is certain that Nagasaki City was not aware of Maki Kaga and simply chose the immortal Butterfly theme as a tourist draw for Glover Garden - after all the backdrop to the opera is a house on a Nagasaki hillside. There were even suggestions that Tom's wife, Tsuru, was the Butterfly model. This was certainly not the case and the arguments against the Glover drama as the inspiration for the story hinge on that fact. But if Maki Kaga replaces Tsuru as the Japanese woman involved, the arguments against Glover as the source are destroyed. It may well be that, perhaps even unwittingly, the City has been presenting the true story. This would certainly seem to have been the case. In any event the tourist guides continue to sing the Japanese version of 'One Fine Day' as they lead their groups around the statue of *Butterfly* in the garden above Glover House.

The Glover Garden complex now includes the homes of William Alt and Frederick Ringer - close friends of Tom Glover - and these places, too, have been painstakingly restored.

Mannequins in Glover House depict a white-haired 'T.B.' and his family as well as the young Tom plotting with the rebels in the mid-1860s. More than 2 million visitors pass through the complex every year.

Thomas Glover's reputation declined in the 1960s. Perhaps influenced by the atomic bombing of Japan and the post-war pacificism which swept the country, some Westerners wrote of him as Japan's first 'Merchant of Death'. Significantly, the Japanese did not join in this criticism. In Japanese history books his place is secure. This reverence for the Scot can be seen in the Senshukaku, Mitsubishi's sumptuous VIP guest house in Nagasaki. Set in a secluded, tree-lined glade in the company's vast shipyard across the bay from Kosuge Dock and Glover House, the Senshukaku houses many Glover relics. His walking stick and original cutlery from Glover House are among the treasures kept there.

Another example of his attraction can be seen in a Nagasaki advertising hoarding for Kirin Beer, the top product of his Japan Brewery Company. Glover's face can be seen beside a declaration that it was 'the beer he loved'. Few nineteenth-century figures, in Japan or in the West, could be used profitably in such a way.

The family of Tom's daughter, Hana Bennett - apparently in nature much more the extrovert like her father - settled in the United States where her descendants remain today. Tom's granddaughter, Mabel Wright, is in her eighties and in 1993 still going strong in California. Descendants of Charles Glover and of Alex Glover's wife Ann Finlay's family are living in south-east England. There is no known Glover family connection left in north-east Scotland.

Recently Glover's part in the Meiji resoration and in the industrialisation of Japan has begun to be more appreciated. In Japan two more books on the life of the Scot have been written and interest seems certain to increase. Grampian Regional Council have bought Braehead House in Bridge of Don, Aberdeen, and plans to develop the mansion and gardens as a visitor and business centre, with emphasis on the Japan connections, are well advanced. In Fraserburgh, a major Glover restaurant/heritage centre is being built. The potential is limitless, close to half a million Japanese tourists arrive in Britain each year and, developed properly, Braehead and Fraserburgh could become focal-points for many of them. Thomas Glover would have have been proud of the Councils' foresight.

Clearly, there was much more to Thomas Blake Glover than an arms merchant. He was indeed a *Scottish samurai.*

# NOTES ON SOURCES

## 1 THE COASTGUARD'S FAMILY

1 Public Record Office (PRO), Information, Records of HM Coastguard, No 8.

2 PRO, Coastguard: Records of Service (ADM 175/77; 175/97; 175/3; 175/22; 175/23; PMG 23/4; PMG 23/10; ZHC 1/2390). All Glover senior's career moves (24 July 1827 to 31 Aug. 1864) and pay and pension details are recorded in the above documents.

3 Fraserburgh 1841 Census. There is no record of the Coastguard being involved in the renting of 15 Commerce Street. The house was one of a group of four, Nos 15, 17, 19 and 21 demolished as a result of a German air raid on 26 May 1941.

4 All the early Glover family details are held in the General Register Office for Scotland, Old Parochial Registers (OPR), OPR153/5 (Fordyce); OPR/196/2 (Fraserburgh); OPR/1688/14 (Old Machar). Thomas Glover's exact place of birth is not known - the register for his place of birth states simply Fraserburgh. The baptism was held on 12 July 1838, details held in *Records of Episcopalian Births Marriages and Deaths in Fraserburgh*, Aberdeen Central Library.

5 Watt, Theodore, MA, *Aberdeen Grammar School Roll of Pupils 1795-1919*, Aberdeen, 1923. Copy held in Aberdeen Central Library's Reference Department, Local History section. Same source also has Anderson, Peter John, (ed.), *Records of the Marischal College and University of Aberdeen*, Aberdeen, 1923, which records Charles Glover's attendance there between 1844-8.

6 PRO, ADM/175/22.

7 An Old Boy, *The Gym or Sketches from School*, Aberdeen, 1885. (Copy in Aberdeen Central Library.)

8 Copies of Census Returns for Old Machar and Old Aberdeen for the years 1851, 1861, 1871, 1881, 1891, held in Aberdeen Central Library.

9 See the *Record of the Gym, Spirat Adhuc Amor*, Aberdeen, 1923, compiled by A. Shewan, copy held in Aberdeen Central Library's Local History section. This contains brief details of Thomas, Alex and Alfred Glover's schooling at the Gym.

10 Michie, A., *Englishmen in China*, (2 vols), London, 1900) vol. 1,

pp.258-9.

11   *The China Directory*, 1862, p.66.

12   Passport No. 39973 (FO611/6. 11)

13   Obituary in the *Japan Times*, 19 Dec. 1911.


# 2  FROM SHANGHAI TO NAGASAKI

1   Harriet Sergeant's *Shanghai,* Jonathan Cape, London, 1991, is an excellent history of the city.


# 3  MACKENZIE'S PARTNER

1   See *Jardines in Japan 1859-1867*, p.8, Dr. John McMaster, privately printed in Groningen (Netherlands), 1966.

2   Jardine, Matheson Archive, University Library,

    Cambridge (JMA), Japan Correspondence, Nagasaki 1859-64.

3   Dollars quoted are Mexican dollars, the standard international trading currency then in use in the Far East. The Mexican dollar was roughly equivalent to the US dollar at 4.5 to the £ sterling.

4   *Jardines in Japan*, p.11.

5   Holmes, H., *My Adventures in Japan*, London, undated, pp.10-30, quoted in *Jardines in Japan*, p.7.

6   JMA, letter to J. Whittal/JM/Shanghai, 22 Sept. 1859, signed by K.R. MacKenzie appears to be in Glover's distinctive handwriting.

7   *Jardines in Japan*, p. 12.

8   Records of US Consul, Nagasaki, 1860.

9   JMA, KR McK/Nagasaki to J.Whittall/JM/Shanghai, 8 Sept. 1860.

10   JMA, TBG/Nagasaki to JM/Shanghai, 5 Jan. 1860.

11   See Sir Rutherford Alcock, *The Capital of the Tycoon*, London, 1863.

12   W.B. Mason, 'The Foreign Colony in the Early Meiji Days: Thomas B. Glover, A Pioneer of Anglo-Japanese Commerce', *New East*, Feb. 1918, p.155.

13   *Guraba Tei Monogatari* (Glover Garden Story), Nagasaki, 1969.

14   *Nagasaki Shipping List & Advertiser*, 24 July 1861.


# 4  THE PHANTOM AND THE FANATICS

1   JMA, From HBM Consulate/Nagasaki to KR McK/ Nagasaki, 24 May 1861.

2   *North China Herald*, 11 May 1861, Notices of Firms.

3   JMA, KR McK/Nagasaki, to J. Whittall/JM/Shanghai, 18 June 1861.

4   JMA, TBG/Nagasaki, to JM/Shanghai, 19 June 1861.

5   Paske-Smith M., *Western Barbarians in Japan and Formosa in Tokugawa Days, 1603-1868*, Kobe, 1930, p. 261.

6   The exact relationship between James Mitchell and the Glovers is not known but was close. On 10 July 1862 in Aberdeen a passage for a 'Mrs Mitchell and two children from London to Hong Kong' was paid for by Charles Glover of Glover Brothers, Shipbrokers, Aberdeen (letter in Glover file, Aberdeen Maritime Museum). James Mitchell arrived in Nagasaki at the same time as Tom, late in 1859. He later became involved with Mitsubishi and is buried in Kobe. His gravestone there reads:

James Fowler Mitchell, of Aberdeen

1829-1903 Master Shipbuilder

For 44 years a resident of Japan

Formerly of Nagasaki

James Mitchell in the mid-1870s erected a statue in Oura International Cemetery, Nagasaki, in memory of his three brothers, William, George and Andrew. All of the Aberdeen-born brothers had strong shipping connections and two of them died while working in Japan. The statue survived the atomic blast of 1945 and still stands.

7   See the full report of the launching of the *Phantom* in the *Nagasaki Shipping List & Advertiser*, 24 July 1861.

8   *Nagasaki Shipping List & Advertiser* report, 24 July 1861.

9   See Oliphant's full account of the attack in *Blackwood's Magazine*, vol. 141, Jan. 1887.

10  *Nagasaki Shipping List & Advertiser*, 24 July 1861.

11  *Official Notice to British Subjects*, from F. Howard Vyse, British Consul in Yokohama, dated 6 July 1861.

12  *Return of all British Subjects resident in the port of Nagasaki*, 29 June 1861, A.A. Annesley to R. Alcock, Nagasaki, 20 July 1861 (FO262/29).

13  *Western Barbarians*, pp. 229-65, 243-4, also *Nagasaki Shipping List & Advertiser*, 10 July 1861.

14  *Western Barbarians*, p. 255.

## 5 CONTACT WITH RENEGADES

1   *Jardines in Japan*, pp. 97-9.

2   For a detailed account of Glover's struggle with the tea business, see Professor Shinya Sugiyama's *Thomas B. Glover: A British Merchant*

*in Japan, 1861-1870*, in *Business History*, vol.XXVI, no.2, July 1984 (*Thomas B. Glover*).

3   *Nagasaki Shipping List & Advertiser* report, 14 Aug. 1861.

4   JMA, JM/Shanghai to TBG/Nagasaki, 19 June 1861.

5   JMA, JM/Shanghai to TBG/Nagasaki, 10 Sept. 1861.

6   JMA, TBG/Nagasaki to JM/Shanghai, 20 Sept. 1861.

7   JMA, TBG/Nagasaki to JM/Shanghai, 9 Oct. 1861.

8   *Jardines in Japan*, p.100.

9   *North China Herald*, Notices of Firms, 22 Feb. 1862.

10  *North China Herald*, Notices of Firms, 20 Sept. and 18 Oct. 1862.

11  JMA, TBG/Nagasaki to JM/Shanghai, 5 June 1862.

12  JMA, JM/Shanghai to TBG/Nagasaki, 24 June and 16 July 1862.

13  *Western Barbarians*, pp. 261-3.

14  Cortazzi, Sir Hugh, *Dr Willis in Japan 1862-1867 British medical pioneer*, Athlone Press, London, 1985, p.21.

15  Shortly before his death Thomas Glover gave an interview to a Choshu clan historian, Kunihei Nakahara. The text of the interview was published in the Choshu Historical Society magazine, *Bocho Shidan-kai Zasshi*, no.27, in 1912, in an article titled *Cho-Satsu-Ei no Kankei* (Choshu/Satsuma/Great Britian Relations), pp. 49-72. A copy (in Japanese) is available at Cambridge University Library, open shelf, ref FD 383:2. My thanks to my wife, Sachiko, for her translation. Glover was an old man at the time of the interview, perhaps suffering from the disease which would kill him. He was remembering events of forty years before and at times his rambling answers to the interviewer's questions perhaps reflect this - yet there is a ring of truth throughout.

# 6  IPPONMATSU

1   Glover's house in Nagasaki is the oldest surviving Western house in Japan and is designated an 'Important Cultural Asset' by the Japanese government. Now part of a tourist complex - Glover Garden - it has been restored and mannequins have been placed in the rooms of the house depicting a young Glover plotting with the Japanese rebels as well as the mature Glover with his grown family. More than 2 million tourists, mostly Japanese, visit the house annually.

2   Williams, Harold S., *Foreigners in Mikadoland*, Charles Tuttle, Tokyo, 1963, p.92.

3   In albums in the possession of descendants of Alexander Glover's wife, Ann (Finlay) Glover and Charles Glover's great grandson,

both now resident in the south of England. The owners of the albums were put in contact with the author after a BBC Radio 4 broadcast on Glover in 1989. I was able to identify positively some of the people and places in the photographs of which the owners of the albums were unaware.

4   *Foreigners in Mikadoland*, pp. 109-10.

5   *Jardines in Japan*, p.32.

6   Quoted in full in *Western Barbarians*, p.254.

7   *Western Barbarians*, p.255.

## 7  ESCAPE OF The 'ChOShu FiVE'

1   Quoted in full in *Western Barbarians*, pp.155-6.

2   JMA, TBG/Nagasaki to JM/Shanghai, 29 April, 6 May, 16 May 1863.

3   *Western Barbarians*, pp.157-9.

4   JMA, TBG/Nagasaki to JM/Shanghai, 26 May 1863.

5   *Western Barbarians*, pp.160-1.

6   JMA, TBG/Nagasaki to JM/Shanghai, 17 June 1863.

7   Some say that the shogun secretly ordered the 'Five' to go and the Choshu daimyo supported them - see Grace Fox, *Britain and Japan 1858-1883*, Oxford University Press, Oxford, 1968, p.458.

8   Cortazzi, H., (ed.), *Mitford's Japan*, Athlone Press, London, 1985, p.26.

## 8  in The LanD OF The 'BARBARiaNS'

1   JMA, TBG/Nagasaki to JM/Shanghai, 4 July 1863.

2   JMA, TBG/Nagasaki to JM/Shanghai, 10 July 1863.

3   JMA, TBG/Nagasaki to JM/Shanghai, 25 July 1863.

4   JMA, TBG/Nagasaki to JM/Shanghai, 27 Aug. 1863.

5   *Western Barbarians*, p.167 - apparently the murderers were never found.

6   *Jardines in Japan*, p.115

7   JMA, TBG/Nagasaki to JM/Hong Kong, 14 Sept. 1863.

8   *Britain and Japan*, p.332.

9   Aberdeen Maritime Museum, File of Details of Aberdeen-built vessels ordered for Japan by Glover Brothers, Marischal Street, Aberdeen.

Name: *Satzuma*

Owner: Charles Thomas Glover bought her in January, then sold her to Thomas Blaikie (*sic*) Glover in May.

Master (1864) W. Glover.

Description: three-masted barque.

Tonnage: 281.90 tons register.

Length : 124 Feet.

Breadth : 24.275 feet.

Depth of Hold: 14.383 feet.

Built: Willaim Duthie Jnr., January 1864.

Destined voyage: Japan

N.B. Vessel lost June 1864 on Japanese coast

10 Aberdeen Central Library, *The Post Office Directory, Aberdeen, 1864-65*, lists 'Glover Charles T., Ship

Insurance Broker, 47 Marischal Street'.

11 'The Foreign Colony in the early Meiji Days', *New East* magazine, February 1918 p.157.

12 PRO, ADM 175/23, Establishment Book, Scotland, 1862-6.

13 Braehead House, Balgownie Road, Bridge of Don, was occupied by the Glover family from 1864 to 1890. *The Post Office Directory Aberdeen* for 1864-5, lists 'Lieutenant T.B. Glover' as chief officer, preventive station, Bridge of Don, home Braehead Cottage, Old Bridge of Don.

14 See *Britain and Japan*, p.459.

# 9 showdown at shimonoseki

1 Williams, Harold S., *The Story of Holme Ringer & Co., Ltd. in Western Japan 1868-1968*, Charles E. Tuttle, Tokyo, 1968, p.15.

2 JMA, TBG/Nagasaki to JM/Shanghai, 26 Oct. 1864.

3 *Jardines in Japan*, p.89.

4 See Conrad Totman, *The Collapse of the Tokugawa Bakufu 1862-1868*, University Press of Hawaii, Honolulu, 1986, p.212.

5 *The Chronicle and Directory for China, Japan and* Phillipines, 1864.

6 *Western Barbarians*, p.261.

7 Footnote to *Satsuma* section of Details of Aberdeen-built vessels ordered for Japan by Glover Brothers, Marischal Street, Glover file, Maritime Museum, Aberdeen.

8 Satow, Sir Ernest, *A Diplomat in Japan*, Oxford University Press, Oxford, reprinted 1968, pp.96-7. Satow, a brilliant Japanese scholar, interpreter and later British Minister in Japan, accompanied Ito and Inoue on their last-gasp peace mission to Shimonoseki. He was very

much in accord with Glover regarding the shogun.

9   Ibid., Satow, *Diplomat*.

10   *Britain and Japan*, pp.134-5.

11   JMA, TBG/Nagasaki to W. Keswick/JM/Hong Kong, 3 Oct. 1864.

12   JMA, TBG/Nagasaki to W. Keswick/JM/Hong Kong, 5 Oct. 1864.

13   JMA, TBG/Nagasaki to JM/Hong Kong, 24 Oct. 1864.

14   *Jardines in Japan*.

15   JMA, TBG/Nagasaki to JM/Shanghai, 24 Oct. 1864.

16   JMA, TBG/Nagasaki to W.Keşwick/JM/Shanghai, 31 Oct. 1864.

17   JMA, W.Keswick/JM/Shanghai to TBG/Nagasaki, 24 Nov. 1864.

18   *Jardines in Japan*, p.58.

19   *Japan Times*, 6 Jan. 1866.

20   'New Advertisments', *North China Herald*, 22 April 1865.

21   PRO, ADM/175/23.

# 10   ARMING THE REBELS

1   JMA, TBG/Nagasaki to E. Whittall/JM/Hong Kong, 2 Dec. 1864 and 5 Jan. 1865.

2   Professor Sugiyama's *Thomas B. Glover* article in *Business History*, p.123, contends that 'repectable' firms like Jardine, Matheson were not involved until as 'late as 1867'.

3   JMA, TBG/Nagasaki to JM/Shanghai, 6 April 1865. See also *Thomas B. Glover*, pp.123-4, for much of the detail quoted here - although Professor Sugiyama dates the departure of the 'Satsuma Nineteen' as *1866*.

4   JMA, TBG/Nagasaki to JM/Shanghai, 6 April 1865.

5   Jansen, Morris B., *Sakamoto Ryoma and the Meiji Restoration*, Princeton University Press, Princeton, 1964, p.212.

6   *Britain and Japan*, pp.152-3, quoting FO 46/53, Winchester to Russell, 30 January 1865.

7   *Bocho Shidan-kai Zasshi* interview.

8   See F.V. Dickens, *The Life of Sir Harry Parkes*, 2 vols, London, 1894.

9   *The Collapse of the Tokugawa Bakufu*, p.212.

10   *Thomas B Glover*, p.123.

11   Britain and Japan, p.154.

12   Ibid., p.155.

13   *Bocho Shidan-kai Zasshi* interview.

14   Mitford's Japan, p.21.

15 JMA, TBG/Nagasaki to Messrs G. Armstrong & Co., Newcastle upon Tyne, 28 June 1865.

16 JMA, TBG/Nagasaki to W. Keswick/JM/Hong Kong, 10 March 1866.

17 *The Collapse of the Tokugawa Bakufu*, p.212.

18 Full report of the incident in *Aberdeen Journal*, 23 Aug. 1865, p.2.

19 *The Collapse of the Tokugawa Bakufu*, p.212; *Britain and Japan*, pp.152-3; *et al*.

20 *Bocho Shidan-kai Zasshi*, Glover interview. Glover House in Nagasaki has a mannequin on a ladder climbing into the ceiling void depicting Glover hiding the rebel samurai. In another room a young Glover is sitting at a table with two rebels, plotting the downfall of the shogun.

21 *Britain and Japan*, p.163.

22 Ibid., p.335.

23 JMA, TBG/Nagasaki to JM/Shanghai, 11 Oct. 1865.

24 JMA, TBG Nagasaki to EW/JM/Hong Kong, 3 Nov. 1865.

25 JMA, JM/Shanghai to TBG/Nagasaki, 1 Aug. 1865.

26 *Thomas B. Glover*, pp.120-3.

# 11  SAMURAI IN ABERDEEN

1 A painting in present-day Glover House in Nagasaki depicts this historic event.

2 There is much evidence to suggest that Aberdeen, in fact, was the base for several more Japanese. The *Aberdeen Herald*, 5 Oct. 1867, for example, remarks on 'several Japanese gentlemen recently studying in Aberdeen'. Glover's old school *(The Record of the Gym)* records 'five pupils from Japan' in the period but lists by name only two - Nagasawa and a H. Heiki.

3 The *Aberdeen Post Office Directory* for 1864-5 lists Glover, Charles T., Ship Insurance Broker, 47 Marischal Street and George, James, 19 Marischal Street; for 1865-6, Glover, Charles T. is at 19 Marischal Street and at the same address Glover Brothers, Ship Insurance Brokers.

4 See *Aberdeen Journal*, 30 Aug. 1865, p.4, for a full report of the launch.

5 *Britain and Japan*, p.174. Eleven of the shogun's officials had arrived in Britain in the early summer of 1865, at about the same time as Glover's 'Nineteen'. They visited factories, shipyards, the London Underground. Later they went to France where the shogun was building a strong military connection.

6   Brief details of the marriage are contained in James Glover's death certificate, *Old Machar Deaths, 1867*, Aberdeen Registrar's Office.

7   *Britain and Japan*, p.332.

# 12  ChE GREATEST REBEL

1   *The Post Office Directory,* Aberdeen 1866, lists 'James Glover (of Glover Brothers) Chanonry, Old Aberdeen. It seems likely that at this time he was staying temporarily with his sister and her family at No.11 - her husband James was and old colleague of Charles and Jim.

2   *Aberdeen Journal* report, March 1866.

3   JMA, TBG/Nagasaki to WK/JM/Shanghai, 1 and 12 Feb. 1866.

4   JMA, TBG/Nagasaki to WK/JM/Hong Kong, 10 May, 2 July, 1866.

5   *Bocho Shidan-kai Zasshi,* Glover interview.

6   Ibid., In the interview, Glover goes into the comings and goings at this time in some detail.

7   From the obituary of Glover in *Japan Times,* Dec. 1911, 'The late Mr Glover: A Japanese appreciation'. A *koku* was a Japanese measurement of rice, used to denote levels of wealth; 300,000 koku would have made him very rich in Japanese eyes.

8   Ibid.

9   *Bocho Shidan-kai Zasshi,* Glover interview. This uncorroborated and undated account of Glover's efforts to bring Parkes and Satsuma together is taken from the above interview.

10  See *Sakamoto Ryoma and the Meiji Restoration* for a full account of the negotiations, especially p.220.

11  See the *Japan Times*, Yokohama, 16 March 1866.

12  *Britain and Japan*, p.179.

13  Ibid., p.175.

14  See the *Japan Times*, Yokohama, 19 May 1866.

15  *Western Barbarians,* p.255.

16  *Mitford's Japan,* p.22.

17  Ibid.

18  Sakamoto Ryoma, p.258, quoting Otsuka, *Fukkoku Koshi Leon Roches no seisaku kodo ni tsuite*, p.833.

19  Ibid., p.259.

20  Black, John R., *Young Japan Yokohama and Yedo 1858-79*, vol. II, Oxford University Press, Oxford, 1968; pp.2-7 contain an eye witness account of the visit by an officer on one of the British ships.

21  *Bocho Shidan-kai Zasshi,* Glover interview.

22  *Dr Willis in Japan*, p.76.

23  *Bocho Shidan-kai Zasshi*, Glover interview.

24  *Britain and Japan*, pp.187-8.

25  Brown, Sidney Devere, and Hirota Akiko (trans.), *The Diary of Kido Takayoshi, Volume I: 1868-1871,* University of Tokyo Press. In his entry for 30 June 1869 (p.235), Kido tells of the Glover/Gower controversy over the shogun in the mid-1860s. See also Dr John McMaster's penetratingly unique look at the diplomatic manoeuvrings of the British and Japanese during the 1860s in *Sabotaging the Shogun*, Vantage Press, New York, 1992.

26  Uesugi was also known as Chojiro Kondo. See *Sakamoto Ryoma*.

27  'Tea-house' is perhaps a misnomer. In *Mitford's Japan*, p.35, he describes a tea house as a wine shop or tavern ... Many of them are houses of the worst repute where these Japanese drink, whore and gamble themselves into a state of frenzy'.

28  *Bocho Shidan-kai Zasshi*, Glover interview.

29  *The Chronicle and Directory for China, Japan and* the Phillipines, 1866.

30  *Western Barbarians,* pp.264-5.

31  *Bocho Shidan-kai Zashi*, Glover interview.

## 13  ENTREPRENEUR

1   JMA, JM/Shanghai to TBG/Nagasaki, 12 Feb. 1867.

2   *Thomas B. Glover*, p.122.

3   The remains of this dock and its machinery have been retained as a National Historic Site in Nagasaki.

4   JMA, KR McK/Nagasaki to JW/JM/Hong Kong, 27 April 1867.

5   Ibid.

6   Pointed out to the author by the then owner, Colin Allan, in 1990.

7   It has been suggested that another reason for Glover's trip to Europe in 1867 was the Paris International Exhibition of that year where Satsuma began Japan's first export drive. But no evidence of a visit there by Glover has survived.

8   Thomas B. Glover, p.129, quoting Netherlands Trading Society archives *Memorandum of* Agreement between Messrs Alexander Hall & Co., The City of Glasgow Bank and Messrs Glover Brothers. JMA, TBG/Nagasaki to FBJ/JM/Shanghai, 30 June 1870, for Glover's debt to his father.

9   JMA, G & Co./Nagasaki to JM/Hong Kong, 19 July 1867.

10  Taylor, Ann, *Laurence Oliphant, 1829-1888*, Oxford University

Press, Oxford, 1982, p.143, quotes from a letter from Oliphant (in the USA) to William Cowper (in England), dated 1 Dec. 1867, in which he enquires about 'the Japanese in the care of the Glover family at Aberdeen'. Oliphant was 'especially anxious' about them, 'these merchants care for nothing but money'. The *Aberdeen Herald*, 5 Oct. 1867, has an article on Murata-san.

11  Checkland, O., *Britain's Encounter with Meiji Japan, 1868-1912*, Macmillan, London, 1989, p.141. Dr Checkland's book traces the lives and careers of many of the young Japanese who came to Britain at this time.

12  *Register of Deaths, Old Machar, 1867*. Held in Aberdeen Register of Births, Marriages and Deaths. 'Chronic Diarrhoea' most probably meant cholera.

13  Later the Glover parents would be buried in the plot. The plaque on the wall commemorating Jim has gone, but an old photograph in the Glover Nagasaki albums show it quite clearly.

## 14  ᴄhe shoguɴ's surreɴᴅer

1  JMA, JM/Shanghai to G & Co./Nagasaki, 11 May 1867. The Armstrong guns never reached the shogun.

2  JMA, TBG/Nagasaki to WK/JM/Hong Kong, 27 Jan. 1868. In this letter Glover says that he has arrived back from Europe 'a few days ago'.

3  *Britain and Japan*, pp.353-4, and JMA, JM/Shanghai to G. & Co./Nagasaki, 21 Feb. 1868.

4  *Aberdeen Journal*, 29 Jan. 1868, p.5, on the launch of the *Helen Black*.

5  *Britain and Japan*, p.259, quoting Ad.I/6068, James to Admiralty, 12 Oct. 1868. The 'corvette' referred to at the Admiralty enquiry was Glover's next warship for the Japanese, the *Jho Sho Maru*.

6  *Register of Marriages, Foveran, 1868*, Aberdeen Registrar's Office.

7  JMA, G. & Co./Osaka to JM/Shanghai, 10 May 1868 and TBG/Osaka to WK/JM/Hong Kong, 11 May 1868.

8  *The Diary of Kido Takayoshi*, 12 May 1868 entry, p.30.

9  See McMaster, J., 'The Takashima Mine: British Capitalism and Japanese Industrialisation', *Business History Review*, vol. XXXVII, 1963, pp. 217-39; and Checkland, Olive & Sydney, 'British and Japanese Economic Interaction under the Early Meiji: The Takashima Coal Mine 1868-88', *Business History*, for detailed accounts of the story of the Takashima mine.

10  Heco, J., *Narrative of a Japanese*, 2 vols., Yokohama, 1899.

11  *The Diary of Kido Takayoshi*, 1 June 1868 entry, pp.29,30.

12  *Aberdeen Journal*, 8 July 1868.

13  See Kido's *Diary*, entries for 5 and 10 July 1868. Also JMA, TBG/ Nagasaki to WK/JM/Hong Kong, 11 and 25 July 1868.

14  JMA, TBG/Nagasaki to WK/JM/Hong Kong, 11 July 1868. Glover quotes the weight of the copper in *piculs*, which equate at about 133.3 per lb.

15  Aberdeen Journal, 26 Aug. 1868, p.4, on the trial trip of the *Ho Sho Maru*.

16  The original log of the *Ho Sho Maru* for its maiden voyage to Nagasaki is held in Aberdeen Central Library.

17  Ibid., Log of the *Ho Sho Maru*.

18  *Japan Chronicle*, Jubilee Number, 1869-1918, pp.10,11.

19  Nagasaki British Consul's Report of Trade, 1868.

20  *Aberdeen Journal*, 31 March 1869, p.5, quoting *Nagasaki Times* of 23 Jan. 1869.

21  Nagasaki Prefectural Library, *British ConsulateDespatches*, 1868 (to the Governors of Nagasaki)26 Feb., 14 & 18 April, 30 Dec. 1868.

22  JMA, TBG/Osaka to FBJ/JM/Shanghai, 3 Dec. 1868. Also ibid., 16 Dec. 1868. See also *Britain and Japan*, pp.355-6.

23  JMA, Hong Kong Ledger, 1868/69; ibid., Shanghai Ledger 1868/69.

24  *North China Herald*, 5 Jan. 1869, Notices of Firms.

25  See *The Story of Holme Ringer & Co.*

26  *Thomas B. Glover*, p.127, for this information quotes Dutch sources at the time of Glover's bankruptcy.

27  Ibid.

28  *Guraba Tei Monogatari.*

## 15 BiRTh OF A NAVAL POWER

1  Letter in Aberdeen Maritime Museum's Glover file.

2  *Aberdeen Journal*, 31 March 1869. See also *Aberdeen Herald*, 3 April 1869.

3  See McMaster, J., and Checkland, O.& S., op.cit. This account of the Takashima mine uses these sources.

4  JMA, TBG/Nagasaki to JM/Hong Kong, 9 June 1869.

5  Kido, Diary, entry for 30 June 1869.

6  The *Wen Yu Maru* is found in Japanese records as the *Unyo Maru*.

7  JMA, TBG/Osaka to FBJ/JM/Shanghai, 10 Aug. 1869.

8   JMA, TBG/Nagasaki to FBJ/Kobe, 23 Jan. 1869.

9   JMA, TBG/Nagasaki to FBJ/JM/Shanghai, 21 Dec. 1869.

# 16  ᴄAKAShima ᴄROUBLES

1   *Nagasaki Express*, 15 Jan. 1870.

2   *Nagasaki Express*, 29 Jan. 1870, carries articles on Kosuge Dock's anniversary, William Blaikie's duties and the Takashima mine.

3   JMA, Captain James/Nagasaki to JM/Shanghai, 20 Feb. 1870.

4   JMA, TBG/Nagasaki to FBJ/JM/Shanghai, April 1870.

5   JMA, C. Maclean/JM/Nagasaki to JM/Shanghai, 15 March 1870.

6   *Nagasaki Express*, 16 July 1870.

7   *Nagasaki Express*, 30 July 1870.

8   JMA, TBG/Nagasaki to FBJ/JM/Shanghai, 12 May 1870.

9   JMA, TBG/Nagasaki to FBJ/JM/Shanghai, 30 June 1870.

10  *Nagasaki Shipping List*, 17 Sept. 1870, report on bankruptcy meeting.

# 17  ᴅuᴄCh maSᴄERS

1   In a letter from the British Consul to the governor of Nagasaki, held in Nagasaki Prefectural Library and dated 9 Dec. 1873, mention is made of seven debtors of Glover who had still not paid. The list includes H.H. the Prince of Tokuyama.

2   *Thomas B. Glover*, pp.129-30.

3   Nagasaki Prefectural Library, File of Correspondence between British Consul and Nagasaki governor, letter dated 28 July 1870.

4   Ibid., 29 July 1870.

5   Ringer House has also been restored by Nagasaki City Council and is part of the Glover Garden complex.

6   Burke-Gaffney, Brian, *Hana To Shimo Gurabake no Hitobito* (Blossoms and Frost - Members of the Glover Family), Nagasaki, 1989. This account of Thomas Glover's life (in Japanese) reveals the details of the birth of Glover's son Tomisaburo for the first time.

# 18  meiᵢi muSCLE

1   Cortazzi, Sir Hugh, *Victorians in Japan: In and Around the Treaty Ports*, Athlone Press, London, 1987, pp.26-9, has almost the full text of this letter.

2   Fred T. Jane's *The Imperial Japanese Navy*, Conway Maritime Press,

London, 1904, lists the 'Rio-jo' (formerly the *Jho Sho Maru*) as meaning in English 'powerful as a dragon'. This is a Chinese word. 'Ho Sho' is the name of a 'scare bird'.

3 Nagasaki Prefectural Library, British Consul/ Nagasaki governor correspondence, dated 12 Dec. 1871.

4 *Some remarks on the Island of Kiu-Shu and the port of Nagasaki,* by US Consul Alexander C. Jones, 5 Jan. 1881.

5 See *The Story of Holme Ringer & Co.,* pp.29,30.

6 See *Victorians in Japan,* p.29.

7 See 'The Foreign Colony in the Early Meiji Days'.

8 Ibid.

9 See *Britain and Japan.* p. 339.

10 See *The Story of Holme Ringer & Co.*

11 Aberdeen Maritime Museum, Glover File, letter from Professor Paul Kadota of Kagoshima University to a Mr McCombie of Aberdeen, dated 1 Aug. 1976.

12 Tamaki Miura, a famous soprano and the first Japanese to sing the *Butterfly* role, claimed in an article in the *Jiji Shimpo* magazine, 24 Dec. 1935, that the author of the short story *Madam Butterfly* had told her that his story ending was based on a true incident and that the real Butterfly had survived her suicide attempt; that the boy in his story was called Tom Glover, the mixed-blood son of a wealthy English [sic] merchant in Nagasaki. In Mosco Carner's *Puccini,* Gerald Duckworth, London, 1974, p.126, the 'director of the Nagasaki Museum' is quoted as saying that her [Butterfly's] real name was Tsuru Yamamura, born Osaka 1851, died Tokyo 1899. 'Her son was Tom Glover (or Tomisaburo Kuraba, the Dolore of the opera'). It goes on to say: 'On the other hand, K. Watanabe, a Nagasaki historian, maintains that ... the real Cio-Cio-san was the daughter of a samurai family named Date, whose head committed hara-kiri in Nagasaki'. Clearly, neither of these sources were aware of the existence of Maki Kaga. If Maki is substituted for Tsuru, the contradictions disappear.

## 19 ADVISER TO MITSUBISI

1 Much of this short account of Glover's years in Tokyo and Yokohama is taken from *The Story of Holme Ringer & Co.*, pp.20-3.

2 Letter in the Glover File, Aberdeen Maritime Museum, from Japanese historian Professor Paul Akira Kadota of Kagoshima University, dated 1 Aug. 1976.

3 See *Nagasaki Harbor Light* (ed.), Brian Burke-Gaffney, 15 Dec.

1987 (final edition of this English-language monthly), for a full account of the *Star Queen* disaster.

4    See Checkland, O. & S., op cit.

## 21  REÐ-FACEÐ ÐEVÌL

1    Article in (undated) Japanese magazine *Nagasaki Dangi*, titled *Chichi To Mister Glover No Koto Domo (My Father and Mr Glover's Business)* by Kazuhara Maekawa.

2    See Barr, P., *The Deer Cry Pavilion*, Macmillan, London, 1967.

## 22  FROM KEELS CO KÌRÌN

1    Kirin now accounts for about 60 per cent of the massive Japanese beer market. On a visit to Nagasaki in 1991 Glover's face could be seen on advertising hoardings for Kirin beer - 'the beer he loved'.

2    See 'The Foreign Colony in Early Meiji Days'.

## 23  ÐONOUREÐ BY EMPEROR MEÌJÌ

1    In March and April 1931 (she died in 1933) Sarah Jane Correll gave a series of talks and interviews in Japan and China. See *Japan Times*, 15 March 1931; *The China Press*, 2 May 1931; 'Madam Butterfly; Her Long Secret Revealed', *Japan Magazine*, 21, 1931.

2    *The Letters of Puccini* (ed.), Mosco Carner, Harrap, London, 1974.

## 24  CÐE FÌNAL YEARS

1    See *The Story of Holme Ringer & Co.*